Born in Cawnpore in the last years of the British Raj, Charles Allen shares with many of his subjects a long-established family association with India that dates back to the battle of Seringaputam in 1799. His great-grandfather brought the young Rudyard Kipling out to work on his newspaper, the *Civil and Military Gazette*. Mr. Allen is a traveller, writer and broadcaster, specialising in India and the Far East. While researching and interviewing for *Plain Tales from the Raj* he travelled the length and breadth of the United Kingdom, taping more than 250 hours of recorded interviews.

Edited by Charles Allen

Plain Tales from the Raj

Images of British India
in the Twentieth Century

Edited in association with Michael Mason
Introduction by Philip Mason

Macdonald Futura Publishers
A Futura Book

A Futura Book

First published in Great Britain 1975
by André Deutsch Limited
and the British Broadcasting Corporation

First Futura Publications edition 1976
Seventh printing 1980

ISBN 0 8600 7455 2

Printed in Great Britain by
Hazell Watson & Viney Ltd
Aylesbury, Bucks

Macdonald Futura Publishers Limited
Paulton House
8 Shepherdess Walk
London N1 7LW

To the men, women and children,
British, Anglo-Indian and Indian
who were the British Raj in India

CONTENTS

ILLUSTRATIONS

The editor and publishers are most grateful to all those listed below for permission to reproduce photographs from their collections.

ACKNOWLEDGEMENTS

The tape-recordings from which this anthology is composed were made for *Plain Tales from the Raj*, a series of programmes first broadcast on BBC Radio 4 in 1974. More than sixty men and women – all survivors of the British Raj – were good enough to allow me to interview them at length and my primary indebtedness is, of course, to them, without whose co-operation, candour and generosity neither the radio programmes nor this book could have existed. Among these Survivors I must thank especially Philip Mason, whose characteristic generosity extended far beyond the writing of the Introduction, and Raymond Vernede, whose many suggestions and corrections are to be found in the Glossary. Many others, both from among the original contributors and elsewhere, have been most generous in offering not only advice and suggestions but their own private material in the form of photographs and other illustrative material – of which only a tiny proportion can be included here. To these many friends of India may I couple my thanks with the hope that this book will to some extent justify their trouble.

Plain Tales from the Raj was the brainchild of Michael Mason, who also composed and produced the original radio programmes – and whose encouragement and advice in the preparation of this book has been quite invaluable. While I have taken advantage of many of his suggestions at the manuscript stage, the final responsibility for the choice and presentation of the texts remains my own. Widely known as one of the pioneers in what is now coming to be known as 'oral history', Michael Mason made a remarkable start in this field with his work on *The Long March of Everyman*, a 'vox-pop' history of the ordinary people of Britain broadcast in 1971 (published by André Deutsch and the BBC in 1974). A natural next step from that series was *Plain Tales from the Raj*, when Michael Mason's own long-standing fascination with British India happily coincided with the enlightened interest of the late Anthony Whitby, then Controller of BBC Radio 4, who was the godfather to these programmes, and who died at a tragically early age in 1975. It was in the most characteristic tradition of BBC patronage that he commissioned the gathering of fifty in-depth interviews with survivors of the British Raj, which were both to be used for programme-making and preserved in their entirety in the BBC Sound Archives. Additional interviews were collected in India by Prakash Mirchandani and Mark Tully of the BBC's New Delhi Office. However, I have limited myself in the present volume to those interviews recorded in the United Kingdom.

The presentation of oral history is a matter of some controversy. One kind of historical truth could have been served by simply printing the texts in full, with the traditional scholarly apparatus of notes and references. I have tried to present another kind: one man's impressionist mosaic of the general image which this material has left him with after long familiarity. As far as possible the excerpts have been given exactly as they stand in the original, but where necessary I have made minor amendments for ease of reading. I have also selected and compressed, so as to convey as rich a density of material as possible within the space at my disposal. The responsibility for all this, as for the way in which the texts are juxtaposed and related, is mine and necessarily represents my own assumptions and judgements. But I hope it also reflects a fair assessment of the material itself and faithfulness to the spirit of a group of people who are remarkable by any standards – and for whom I have a great respect. Widely separated by age, occupation, rank, geography and personal character, these Survivors all share the experience of British India in the twentieth century. In this sense they are representatives of their age. Accordingly, I have not always identified quotations where commonly expressed attitudes or experiences are given. Similarly, whether well known or relatively unknown, I have referred to my Survivors in the text as they were then. Brief details of their careers and distinctions may be found in the appended biographical notes.

In structure this anthology follows the general experience of the great majority of its contributors, most of whom were born at the turn of this century, many into the India of Curzon and Minto, with forebears whose service in India then already stretched back a hundred years and more. Exiled from India as children they returned as adults – together with the new-comers to India – after the Great War, which stands as a divide between the old Imperial India of the Edwardian age and the newly self-conscious India of the twenties. They grew to their maturity in the inter-war years and saw the Raj through to its decline and sudden end with their late middle age.

Not all these Survivors fit this pattern. Some were already in India as adults long before the First World War: Claude Auchinleck, whose father fought in the Indian Mutiny and who himself rose to preside over the bisection of the Indian Army, came out in 1903; H. T. Wickham joined the Indian police in the Punjab in 1904; Kenneth Warren followed family foot-steps into Assam as a tea planter in 1906. Outdating them all is Mrs Grace Norie – ninety-nine years old at the time of writing – who was born in Roorkee in 1876 and retired to England in 1919 – only one year before the youngest Survivor represented here was born. Young and old, in India they lived out their lives – as we all do – without self-conscious regard to their times and the great events that shaped them – and this is how I have presented them. It is not a romantically idealized picture; the speakers themselves have been remarkably frank and self-critical – and yet, when told about it 'warts and all', I for one find their Raj no less impressive.

INTRODUCTION

PHILIP MASON

It is now nearly thirty years since the partition and independence of India. That means that any Briton who was once accustomed to drinking the toast of the King-Emperor is likely to be over fifty. Two generations have grown up in Britain who have no first-hand knowledge of the life their countrymen lived in that strangely alien part of the Crown's dominions, not even that second-hand knowledge from brothers, sisters and cousins that was once widespread. It was therefore an admirable idea of the BBC's to record on tape the memories of as many as possible of the survivors.

There have, it is true, been quite a few books in the last fifteen years which attempt to reconstruct some aspect of British life in India. But most of those that have come my way have had their origin in a post-graduate thesis; they are usually heavily tied to written sources – and such sources tend to recount the breaks in routine, whereas it is the everyday detail that is so fascinating to a later generation. 'Strange encounter with a bandicoot' will go in the memoir-writer's chapter heading but what we really want to know is what he had for breakfast. Nor have the kind of books I am thinking of always been written with much concern for the general reader. A most distinguished member of my former service once remarked with dry realism: 'No one will ever read anything that I write unless he is paid to.' And some of the recent academic books have been rather like that.

Charles Allen's pot-pourri from the conversations he recorded with survivors of the Empire – I cannot bring myself to use the expression 'Raj' of which the BBC are so enamoured – has come down firmly on the side of being readable rather than pedantic. I am sure this is right. The purpose of his book is to give the general reader some feeling of the flavour of a

life that has gone for ever. A serious historian can go to the
tapes themselves where he will identify each remark in its
context. And in the same spirit I think he is right to use what
he calls 'basic' spelling of Indian words rather than be phone-
tically accurate. I was taught Urdu at Oxford by a most accomplished linguist who hated the use of English words in Indian
languages and prided himself on the accuracy of his pronuncia-
tion. He was an examiner in Urdu (and other languages) and it
was said that he once found himself sitting at lunch at the Naini
Tal Club next to a subaltern whom he had that morning failed
in Urdu. He wanted a tomato but there is no word for tomato of
Arabic, Persian or Sanscritic origin so he used an expression of
the purest linguistic respectability meaning 'a round red fruit
that grows on a small plant not a tree' and the *khidmatgar* was
puzzled. 'Can I help you, sir?' asked the subaltern politely.
'Want a tomato? Oh, yes, I see. Boy! Tamata *lao*.' And of
course it came at once.

This book would have been less readable if it had been
arranged by provinces or periods – although either method
would have been more helpful to a historian. Arranged, as it is,
by subjects, it has to blur the differences between different parts
of India and different periods. And the very fact that Charles
Allen was so successful at getting the confidence of the people
he talked to has encouraged them, talking at their unbuttoned
ease, to utter generalities that they would not have put in writing. We, who served in a particular district at a particular
moment, are bound to grumble at *something*; it wasn't, we are
bound to say at some point, like *that* in my time and in my
province. For example, I am astonished to find someone saying that many posts in the police were reserved for Anglo-
Indians. I don't think there was one Anglo-Indian in the police
in Bareilly, a fairly average UP district. It is asserted that it was
a rule of pig-sticking never to hunt alone – and I remember one
of my first commissioners who maintained that hunting a pig
alone when in camp was the cream of the sport. I am shocked
to hear of a memsahib who allowed a sweeper to handle bacon
which she meant to eat – but I suppose we were more infected
by Hindu prejudice than most.

None the less, I think this book, in which most of the talking is done by people who were actually there, gives a total effect much more like the India we knew than any of the more learned productions I have referred to. It is sometimes a trifle Turner-esque – but then *Rail, Steam and Speed* is alive, while a drawing of a locomotive in a shed by a mechanical engineer is likely to be dead.

Apart from details, the aspect in which this picture differs most from my own experience is in regard to the lives of women. No doubt there were many who did find life dull; perhaps it is inevitable that those I remember best should be those who always found plenty to do. I recall for instance one formidable old lady – she seemed old in those days – who after her morning ride and her inspection of the stables and the garden, the cook-house and the cook, would then be off to her maternity centre and child welfare clinic in the city and would fit in a purdah party for Indian ladies before her dinner party for the brigadier. *She* told the cook exactly what to do; she saw that his pans were properly scoured and the kitchen table scrubbed; she inspected the dishcloths. She told me that when the camping season began, the first thing to start was the cold weather stock-pot – a huge iron pot into which must go a hare, a duck, a quail, a snipe and a partridge; it travelled from camp to camp every other day in a bullock cart and it must be brought to a simmer every day – and she must see it simmer, just as she saw the water boiled and the cow milked. She had done twenty-five Hot Weathers in the plains – and I silently resolved that my still problematical wife should not! She really was the platonic idea of a memsahib. And another, who always comes to mind very elegant in camping or riding clothes, made herself a most accomplished water-colourist and experimented with coloured lino-cuts. And another, an army wife, took as a ruling passion her clinic for soldiers' wives. But it is odd that so few ladies since Fanny Parks – who was interested in everything – have left lively memoirs.

The life of the British in India, even in 1939, was still Victorian. Clothes had changed, some customs a little, but the framework of life had been settled in the last years of the old

Queen. And since it was a country ruled by an official hier-archy, it was socially conservative. Seniority played a big part in promotion and senior officials do not usually undervalue the wisdom that experience has brought them. In social matters they are likely to prefer the standards of their youth and long before the young men of their day have become old enough to change things they too have accepted the standards of their seniors. Of course this was not the same everywhere; Delhi was less behind the times than a provincial capital and broadly speaking the further you went from headquarters the more Victorian survivals you would find. Here and there in the UP in the thirties you might find a little old lady, altogether Indian in features and complexion, a descendant of the Hearseys, the Skinners or the Gardners, heroes of the early days of the Com-pany. She might be ruling two or three villages with feudal autocracy but in her front parlour she would sit among her sofas and antimacassars, modelling herself on the Great Queen. And again, the time-lag was greater with the ICS and the Indian Army than with officers of the British service, who were often more aware of modifications in the social climate in England – but then they seldom stayed in India long enough to have much influence.

The time has come, I think, to look at this fragment of the Victorian world – stranded in time, like a lost world – with some attempt at a more kindly understanding. The Victorians themselves were inclined to be contemptuous of other cultures and often took it for granted that any custom different from their own was wrong or barbarous or even wicked. Today anthropologists have taught us to look more enquiringly at the habits of other people and also of ourselves. What exactly is it that they do, we begin to ask, and why do they do it? What is the effect of this custom on their society and economy? And surely it is with no less sympathy that we should look at frag-ments of our own past too.

In the fifties, even in the thirties, it was enough to raise a guffaw to mention dressing for dinner in the jungle. But there were three good reasons for keeping up in India a custom which was obsolescent in Esher or Weybridge. For a great part of the year, it was a matter of elementary comfort and cleanliness to change clothes in the evening and, since the bearer, who put them out for you, had nothing like enough to do, it was no more trouble to put on one kind of clothes than another. But there was also the more complex feeling that it was necessary to 'keep up standards'. This of course did influence us a good deal and it is easy to make fun of it. But there was a good reason. Aldous Huxley, on a tourist's visit, noticed that many of the inhabitants of India might have sat as models for the old man of Thermopylae who never did anything properly. And in a sense it was by doing things properly – more often at least than most Indians – that the British had established themselves in India and that so few ruled so many with so slight a use of overt force. There was a subconscious awareness of this that involved us in continual effort and expressed itself in all kinds of ways – from insisting on absolute precision in military drill to the punctilious observance of outdated etiquette, or a meticulous insistence on a knife-edge crease to khaki shorts.

The effort was all-pervading and probably more exhausting than we realized at the time. My first responsible job was as sub-divisional magistrate in Bareilly. When I went in to the court room where I was to try cases I saw that the immensely lofty ceiling – perhaps thirty feet high – was draped and festooned with cobwebs – stalactites and stalagmites of cobweb, hanging curtains of cobweb six feet deep. I told the clerk of the court to see that they were removed and he said that of course it should be as I wished. Three days later it was just the same. The court clerk had passed my orders to the *nazir*, who was a kind of quartermaster to the headquarters of the district. I sent for the *nazir*; he, too, had passed on the order, to the head messenger. I told him to make sure it was carried out. Three days later, the cobwebs still stirred sluggishly in the increasing heat of March. I sent for the head messenger; he too had duly passed on my order to someone else. It took about a fortnight to reach the final link in the chain of command. This man, I resolved grimly, would *have* to be punished. But they led in an old, old man, hardly able to walk. He had been a messenger fifty years, on ten rupees a month, and since his pension was only two rupees a month he had been given the job of dusting the court for another two rupees. It would be only the walls of the court he was expected to dust and the furniture; no one but a sweeper could do the floor and messengers were often men of high caste. But even that was beyond him and probably a grandson actually did dust the court for eight annas. Of course, the old man couldn't be punished, so we found a contractor with ladders and strong young men and made a special occasion of it.

That was the kind of thing that made us a little fussy about doing things properly. But there was another side to it. Most of us – soldiers and civilians alike – had far more responsible jobs than we could have expected at our age anywhere else in the world and off duty – out of our own district, away from the regiment – we were sometimes a trifle irresponsible. Even the ICS played rugger in the ballroom after their annual dinner in Lucknow; two young officers from Delhi who had to wait at a wayside railway station on their way to my Christmas camp in Garhwal passed the time with rifle practice at the insulators on the telegraph posts – but it was outside my district and I conveniently forgot that they had told me. Youthful high spirits often merged subtly into middle-aged eccentricity – both perhaps as a reaction against too much insistence on doing things properly. Eccentricity indeed – as Ian Stephens says in this book – was one of the pillars of the Empire. It was the lubricant that enabled the machine to work. It sprang from confidence; you can afford to be eccentric if you know that you can get away with it and that is why it was common among English aristocrats and Indian bureaucrats. I have perhaps in other books told enough stories about eccentrics in India but I have so often been asked about something to which I merely alluded – the Gambit of the Second Reminder, said to have been an infallible recipe for disobeying the orders of higher authority – that perhaps it should now be released.

Huish Edye, who invented the device, was a determined district officer, well known for his witticisms at the expense of the secretariat. But when he received instructions of a general kind of which he did not approve, he would – he alleged – write an

18

effusive letter to the chief secretary congratulating him on this far-sighted measure but adding in a postscript: 'Of course I assume this is not meant to apply in this district.' Warmed by the unexpected tribute, the chief secretary would mildly ask the reason for the exemption. This letter should be left unanswered, and preferably concealed in some unlikely place. The secretariat clerks had precise instructions as to the interval before they should send a reminder; when it elapsed, off would go the first reminder. This Edye would ruthlessly destroy. After the prescribed interval, the secretariat clerks would send the second reminder. The head clerk in the district would be puzzled that he had no first reminder and would feel his professional efficiency aspersed. He would indignantly point out that there had been no first reminder – and he and his colleague in the secretariat office could be trusted – Edye maintained – to argue about that for a couple of years. He cannot really have used the ploy very often but it does illustrate that humorous, confident, essentially aristocratic aspect of British rule in India which sweetened the whole and might not – one suspects – have been so much in evidence if the officials had been French or German or Japanese.

No one who wasn't there will ever really understand what it was like – but this book may be a step on the way towards understanding.

THE SHRINE OF THE 'BABA-LOG'

*She will be zealous in guarding her children from promis-
cuous intimacy with the native servants, whose propensity
to worship at the shrine of the* Baba-log *is unhappily apt to
demoralize the small gods and goddesses they serve . . . The
sooner after the fifth year a child can leave India, the better
for its future welfare. One after one the babies grow into
companionable children. One after one England claims
them, till the mother's heart and house are left unto her
desolate.*

MAUD DIVER *The Englishwoman in India* 1909

'I grew up in bright sunshine, I grew up with tremendous
space, I grew up with animals, I grew up with excitement, I
grew up believing that white people were superior.' Every
chota sahib or missy *baba* whose first years were spent in India
would echo such sentiments – be they the sons and daughters
of state governors or, as in this instance, the son of a British
army corporal. The extra dimensions of India took immediate
effect. First memories are of mosquito nets, of ponies rather
than prams, of a father 'killing a snake in my bathroom,' of
'nanny getting smallpox'. The youngest in a distinguished line
of Napiers, Rosamund Napier, is admonished with, 'Soldiers'
daughters never cry!' and the infant John Rivett-Carnac,
whose family is mentioned by Kipling, is informed by servants
that 'without doubt the captain's little son will be an officer in
the army'. Their first common image is of ayah.

The figure of the native nurse dominates the 'Anglo-Indian'*

---

* The word 'Anglo-Indian' was applied originally to all the British
in India but was officially adopted in 1900 to describe persons of
mixed descent, then known as Eurasians. However, since 'Anglo-
Indian' continued to be used in both contexts for the next forty years,

nursery, usually in sari and blouse and 'covered in nose-rings with bangles on her wrists and ankles: when she was moving about you could hear her a mile off'. Archetypal ayahs are always 'very gentle, sweet-natured women with beautiful hands, very gentle and beautiful in their movements'. They had their own hierarchy, headed by the Madrassi ayah, the cream of ayahs, mission-educated and thus given 'a good many civilized ideas'. The virtues of the trained ayah were considerable. 'They had this capacity to completely identify with the children they looked after,' explains Vere Birdwood, 'and it seemed as if they could switch on love in an extraordinary way. They were so dedicated to their work, in a sense so possessive of their children that it was almost impossible for a good ayah to yield up her charge even for a few hours.' One such paragon was Lewis Le Marchand's ayah in South India:

She was very fat and Madrassi and very, very oily about the hair. Her toes were quite enormous and cracked like dry wickets that had had the sun on them for a few days. If the day *chokidar* didn't give me another biscuit with my early morning tea or if there was any sort of trouble, I used to go to her and she usually managed to solve it. I didn't know her name; I called her ayah. Sometimes, being a fairly naughty boy, I would anger her, but she'd never show it. She'd turn her back and go and sit down cross-legged on the floor of the verandah and take out her knitting, and the more I called her or the more I was naughty or rude, the more she ignored me, until finally I would come along and say, 'Ayah, I'm sorry,' and then all would be well.

Ayah ministered after me during the day and very often during the evening, but it was mother's privilege – heaven knows why – to bath me and put me to bed. Ayah used to wait and, if necessary, sleep outside the doors of her children's rooms, lying down outside on the mat until such time as my mother would come along and say, 'You can go, ayah, little master's asleep.'

I have used inverted commas to differentiate between 'Anglo-Indian' (British in India), and Anglo-Indian (person of mixed descent).

Ayah was the open door through which contact with India was made. 'One of the most charming things I've ever seen,' declares Reginald Savory, 'was the ayah squatting down on her haunches on the verandah with a little child, saying their rhymes together. Most of them they had translated into a kind of curious Anglo-Indian patois. There was "Pussy-cat, pussy-cat where have you been? I've come out from under the Ranee's chair". Another one was *"Humpti-tumpti gir giya phat"*. Then there was *"Mafti-mai"*: Muffety mother was eating her curds and whey on the grass . . .' There were also the Urdu songs and rhymes that ayahs sang to put their charges to sleep and which many never forgot: '*Roti, makan, chini, chota baba nini*' [Bread, butter, sugar, little baby sleep] and:

Talli, talli badja baba,	Clap, clap hands baby,
Ucha roti schat banaya.	They make good bread in the market.
Tora mummy *kido.*	Give some to your mummy.
Tora daddy *kido.*	Give some to your daddy.
Jo or baki hai.	What is left over
Burya ayah kido.	Give to your old ayah.

As well as nursery rhymes there were the stories that began '*Ecco burra bili da* . . .' [There was a large cat then] and, for older children, tales that took a more sinister turn. John Rivett-Carnac remembers a story about a leg-eater which lived under one's bed, and if a small boy got out of bed the leg-eater snapped off his leg. We were terrified of getting out of bed and once we'd been put to bed we stayed there. The other story was about an old man of the wood, black and hairy, who used to come from the jungle into small children's bedrooms and tickle them to death. This proved even more frightening than the leg-eaters and one evening we got so terrified that we leapt from our beds – jumping as far as possible away from the bed so as not to lose our legs – and dashed into the dining room where my parents were having a big dinner party. We took a great deal of persuading to go back to bed.'

More often it was the children who had the upper hand:

'Ayah would pat us gently until she thought we were asleep and then creep silently to the door, and just as she reached the door we would open our eyes and say, "Ayah!" and she had to come back and pat us again.'

If ayahs had a fault it was that they spoilt their charges, that they never said no. Nor was this lack of discipline confined to ayahs. 'This is the one thing over which the Indian fell out badly. Because he loved children he was quite incapable of exercising any sort of discipline over them, and therefore children brought up entirely by Indian servants were reputed to be extremely undisciplined.' There was also the largely unspoken fear – a hangover from Victorian 'curry and rice' days – that an ayah would give a child some opium on the tip of her finger to make it go to sleep.

England provided both temporary and final solutions; imported nannies or governesses . . . and exported children. But before this last drastic step there were the years of temporary reprieve. Outside the nursery a host of followers stood ready to serve and spoil: 'If nanny or mummy was busy, one of the Indian manservants was detailed to look after us, which meant that he would devote the whole of his time to entertaining us, to making sandpies or whatever it was that we were doing, and this of course was simply wonderful because boredom was completely eliminated from our lives.' Indian servants had the capacity 'to become children at the time they were playing with children', and to forget their own differences. Radclyffe Sidebottom recalls seeing his 'six foot four Pathan bearer and the sweeper, who was of a different religion, each carrying a child on his shoulders, with the sweeper chasing the Pathan round the drawing room'.

Outside the bungalow there was the compound and yet more followers. Nancy Foster, the youngest of three sisters, remembers that 'the *malis*, the gardeners, were always getting into difficulties with my parents for coming and helping us build houses in trees or set up a bazaar or to make wreaths from flowers that they would never normally think of picking – or perhaps for pulling up vegetables and bringing them to us to sell in mock bazaars'. There was also the man at the gate: 'The *dewan* was perhaps one of our greatest friends and he used to join us in our games whenever he possibly could. One of the games that we used to have again and again was collecting various flowers and making up a brew and dyeing things, and he joined in to such an extent that he let us have all his clothes and his white uniform, which was dyed yellow – and he got into great trouble for this.'

When the children ventured beyond the compound there were eager escorts, as Nancy Vernede remembers from her childhood in Allahabad: 'The *syce* was probably the servant I knew best, because I used to ride my pony every day. All I really did was either walk or trot or canter slowly up and down the road outside our house while the *syce* either walked or jogged along by my side. I think we carried on a non-stop conversation. I learnt nearly all my languages from him and he was one of my best friends.'

For the *baba-log* language was the least of barriers: 'We used to talk to our servants in Hindustani. In fact most children learnt Hindustani before they learnt English.' Adults had their reasons for wishing their children to speak to Indians in their own language: 'My parents always told the servants to speak to us in their own language,' explains Nancy Vernede, 'partly so that we could learn the language, and partly because they didn't want us to keep the *chee-chee* English accent, a sing-song accent rather like Welsh which I believe originated from the original missionaries in India who were Welsh and were the first people to teach English.'

For all the familiarity and affection there remained 'a friendly barrier between us and the servants', so that 'you were always treated with respect. You were called little master and you just took it for granted.' The *chota* sahib, in particular, enjoyed a special status: 'In talking to a small English boy the Indian servants used to use the same word that they themselves used when speaking to an old man, particularly a religious old man or a *saddhu*.' Not surprisingly, such respect led to abuse. The young George Carroll remembers ruefully how he kicked his *chaprassi*, an ex-soldier who had served with Lord Roberts at Kandahar, 'just to show that I was master'. Being born of the sahib-*log* had given him strange notions: 'I remember my utter disappointment when I learnt that the great Queen Victoria, who was known as the Great White Queen to all Indians, was not omnipotent and she could not, of her own will, order any person to be shot or killed or hanged.'

For John Rivett-Carnac this early deference 'made me have a great opinion of myself. There were many servants and orderlies who treated me as if I was an adult, with the same respect as they treated my father. The result was that I got a very great idea of my own importance, so much so that in later life it never crossed my mind that I could be killed or be in any danger from an Indian.' Even when playing the *chota* sahib could not forget his privileged status: 'Games were rigged so that we always won,' recalls Terence 'Spike' Milligan, whose first years were spent in the Poona military cantonments. If the games were not rigged the results were always the same: 'Even though I had a fine hockey stick from Timothy Whites, the English stores in Poona, they would win the game with a stick taken out of a tree. They beat me at everything – yet I never thought of anything else except the Indians being inferior. I was born to believe that we were the top people.'

But even subordinates had rights and chief among them was caste, as the young Joan Allen discovered when she attempted to water her garden: 'Outside the gardener's hut I saw a nice little earthenware bowl so I picked it up. The *mali* came rushing out of his hut and he was furious. He picked this bowl out of my hands and dashed it to the ground. This was his bowl, and by touching it I had made it untouchable for him, and so he broke it.'

Other restrictions had also to be observed. Neither parents nor children would think of entering the servants' quarters without warning or permission. The native bazaar was also out of bounds and was thus a constant source of fascination to all European children, as Deborah Dring asserts:

Our parents always thought we'd catch something if we went down to the bazaar. But my brothers and I always looked upon the bazaar as being too exciting. All those

26

lovely stalls covered with sticky sweets and silver paper and piles of fruit and those little flares they lit, the old boys sitting stitching clothes or boiling things in huge *dekshis*. I'll never forget the smell – partly a very strong spice, an incensy smell – and all the heat and the movement and the people and the colour. There was a little temple which had rows and rows of little brass bells all round. If you were a good Hindu you jingled all the bells as you passed, and I remember thinking, 'Now that's marvellous! If only I could go past and jangle a few bells.' But no, the bazaar was a forbidden land when I was a child.

Daily routines were always well established. The children woke early to the sound of crows, had their *chota hazri* – a banana, perhaps, or a glass of fruit juice – and took morning exercise. Prams were soon abandoned. Instead: 'You were placed in a saddle which had a ring round it so you couldn't fall out, and you were led by a *syce* and taken out for a walk.' After an hour's ride there was a bath and a change of clothes – a complicated process if you were a girl. 'White starchy petticoats, white starchy knickers, starchy cotton frock, all of which were pulled up on tapes round one's neck and were so hot. Hats made of cotton or muslin which were starched and then hauled up like a mob cap on a string to fit over your *topee*. When they got the slightest bit damp they flopped all over your face.'

Breakfast was taken with one's parents, often on the verandah or under a shady tree. The older children started lessons and the younger ones played in the garden until it got too hot. Out with the sun came – invariably – the topee: 'We were never allowed out in the sun without a topee on our heads, and we were very severely punished if we forgot our topees. They were very pretty, but very uncomfortable.'

A light lunch would be taken early and then, after a long siesta, more dressing up; 'It didn't matter how hot it was in the afternoons,' continues Nancy Foster, 'we were always changed into white, frilly dresses, usually starched with big sashes. Very pretty but intolerable in the heat. In the morning we were allowed to have our hair screwed up in a bun on the top of our heads for coolness, but for some reason in the afternoons we had to have our hair hanging down over our shoulders and very well brushed and this was very hot indeed. We were full of envy of the little Indian children running about with almost nothing on.'

At teatime one's father might be expected to put in an appearance, to 'collapse into a chair which had legs sticking out and a cane bottom and put his feet up and savour a cup of tea and anchovy on buttered toast, before changing and going off to the club to play his game of squash or tennis'. If the children went out to tea they took their own milk 'because nobody trusted any other mother to boil the milk properly. Everyone was very germ conscious because of typhoid and dysentery and all the various things you could catch. So all the children used to go out to tea with their bottles of milk wrapped in tissue paper.' The milk usually came from the nursery cow which, in Iris Portal's household, 'was brought round to the verandah every morning by the *gai-wallah*. He used to milk it in front of our Scottish nanny who was supposed to watch over the milking to make sure first, that his hands were clean and secondly, that he didn't put water in the milk.'

If the children lived up-country and the station was large enough, tea might be taken at its focal point. 'We generally used to meet other children at the club. Most English clubs in India had very good gardens so all our nannies used to like going there and chin-wagging to each other outside the club.' In smaller stations the children might well have only adult company. 'I think the nearest European child must have been twenty miles away,' remembers Joan Allen, the only daughter of an indigo planter, 'with another about thirty miles away. It was very, very seldom that we met. One was a little boy who was about four when I was about nine, and yet I used to be frightfully pleased when he came over and played with me.' Similarly, there were other children, the sons and daughters of forest officers, perhaps, or of those whose jobs took them deep into the *mofussil*, who grew up as close to nature as any latter-day Mowgli. John Rivett-Carnac grew up in the jungles of

28

Bengal, surrounded by wild animals: 'We ran completely wild, climbing trees, shooting small birds, looking for birds' nests and seeing how far into the forest we could go. We used to set traps for wild cats at night with a hill boy from a jungle tribe who helped to look after us and taught us jungle lore. He showed us what was dangerous and what was not. We used to get a lot of fun turning stones over for dangerous snakes, which we killed.'

Although snakes presented no major threat to Europeans in India, they had still to be avoided. A pet mongoose often helped. Another well-established manner of ridding oneself of snakes was snake-charming. Lewis Le Marchand remembers how a king cobra was once observed under his father's office and a snake-charmer sent for: 'I can remember the fellow playing this extraordinary flute instrument for hour after hour after hour. This went on for several days but nothing happened and the servants would say, "Oh, yes, it will happen, we'll get him out." Then finally this huge snake, a hamadryad probably about six feet long, was piped out, literally, from its lair underneath my father's office. It came out swaying to the music and by that time my father and his assistant were both there with 12-bore guns and despatched it.'

A much greater threat to European children was rabies. 'We were never allowed to stroke dogs; there was always the fear of rabies. For a long time we weren't allowed to have dogs because of this.' Sometimes the fear became a reality. F. C. Hart was five when he was bitten: 'This dog came into our house one morning while I was having breakfast and bit me on the shin under the table. Later in the afternoon it returned and attacked my younger brother, biting him rather severely. Eventually the dog was killed and found to have rabies. We were immediately ordered up to the only Pasteur Institute in India, at Kasauli in the Simla hills, and we left that night. This was a distance of about four hundred miles.' Treatment lasted three weeks and involved a course of very long hypodermic syringes driven into the stomach. Even then the Hart family's troubles were far from over. On the day before he was due to leave hospital the younger boy was asked to stay on another night: 'That night the nurses had some custard pudding for their dinner and, liking my brother, they asked him if he would have some. Being a child he said yes, so they gave him some pudding and some also to the little girl who was in the bed alongside his. That night fourteen nurses and these two children died of Asiatic cholera.'

Disease and death were a constant preoccupation: 'There were many, many sights that you never forgot. The armless and legless beggars and the lepers. You would see them and your servant would take you away.' Sometimes you could not be shielded, as in the year of the world influenza epidemic, when Vere Birdwood rode to school in Simla with the roadside ditches full of unburied corpses: 'I had a *syce* of about nineteen of whom I was very fond and we used to chat as we went along the Simla roads to school, and then one day I heard that he had been struck down and, two days later, he was dead. In a strange way the piled-up corpses meant much less to me than the death of my *syce*.'

Diversions came at regular intervals with the festivals, both Indian and British. 'We loved the Indian festivals,' says Nancy Foster. 'Some were very frightening, like the *Holi* festivals in which we were never allowed to join. We used to watch from the top of the house, rather fascinated but rather frightened. Some of the goddesses were beautiful, some were terrible. We used to ride out on our ponies and watch them being made in the villages from wire and straw and clay, very cleverly and beautifully modelled. I think the only one that put any terror into us was *Kali*. We never liked *Kali*, she was grotesque in our eyes, but the others were very beautiful.' As well as the spring festival of *Holi* there was the Mohammedan festival of *Mohurram*, originally a festival of mourning, but to Deborah Dring and her sisters more in the nature of a carnival: 'We looked forward to the *Mohurram* far more than Christmas or Easter. Men used to come gambolling into our garden dressed up as horses and do a most extraordinary dance in front of our house. They used to give us sweets – which was absolutely forbidden – which we used to eat. It seemed quite the most perfect festival.' After the Rains came *Diwali*, the festival of light, when the children copied the servants and 'lit lights in little clay dishes with oil in them and a twist of cotton, and placed these lights on the gateways, along the walls, along the sides of the houses, windows, steps, anywhere'.

Christmas was heralded with catalogues from the big Calcutta emporia, the Army and Navy Stores, Whiteaway's and Laidlaw's, Hall and Anderson's. Best of all, from the young Spike Milligan's point of view, was the big Army and Navy catalogue:

It used to arrive three months before Christmas which was just enough time for you to rush through it and order things for Christmas. A large part was devoted to the military services and I remember this complete page of how to go on a military picnic. There was the tent and there was a gentleman opposite with this picnic outfit on, which consisted of shorts, gaiters up to the knee, boots and a topee. There was a lady with a hat and a great net over her face to stop the mosquitoes, with two children likewise garbed. And then there was a series of stools, one made very large to take the bustle of the lady. And there was a servant's tent, much smaller and inferior, with a hole in the side through which you could shout, 'I want so and so!'

I found it more interesting to look through this book than the Boy's Own Annual. I used to mark with a red pencil all the toy soldiers I wanted and then on Christmas morning there would be a parcel from the Army and Navy Stores with the band of the Royal Marines in a red box, all with blue and white helmets, a box of Cameron Highlanders charging and Arab horsemen at the gallop.

Attempts to reproduce an English Christmas were rarely a success. In Western India Father Christmas arrived on a camel, elsewhere, on an elephant. In the railway communities he very often came on a loco engine. In the bigger stations there would be picnics and, of course, fancy dress parties, but the one local Christmas tradition that suited India perfectly was the Christmas Camp: 'The Christmas we liked best of all was when we used to go up into the jungle camping with my father. We used to go out on the elephants and watch the shooting, and we'd camp and fish. That was the best Christmas present.'

Camps were a feature of the cold weather, as were the tours undertaken by a great many fathers in their official duties. Touring in the days before the widespread use of motorcars had a leisurely pace of its own, as Iris Portal recalls from her own childhood:

I can remember the sun just rising, pink on the huge, great plain and being wrapped up in a quilted Rajput dressing-gown and put into the cart pulled by two ponies called Peter and Polly, while my parents rode. We proceeded slowly along because the camp kit had to be put on camels. We had a special nursery camel and the man who drove it had a red *puggaree*, and there was a terrible day when the nursery camel fell down and everything was broken.

An advance party would have struck a few tents for us at the next stopping place and we would get there in time for a late breakfast. Then my father would set up his table for petitions and we would be turned out with our toys to play among the tents, with nanny keeping an eye on us – although she and my mother also did a lot of first aid and medical work for villagers who came in. We were always told not to slide down the tents but, of course, it was a great temptation to scramble up part of the tent flap and come sliding down.

I can remember watching my father sitting under a tree with this crowd of petitioners around him and thinking what an important person he must be because he had all these people standing round the table. But it was the simplest thing, just a tree in the middle of an open plain and a wooden table underneath it, and that was how a district officer did his job in those days.

Towards the end of the day he and mother would go out with a gun to shoot something extra for our meals, because in those days game abounded. I can remember one camp on the edge of the jungle where father went out and shot a bear

32

and I was made to stand beside it holding the rifle. I was very frightened because I didn't feel quite sure that the bear was dead. I remember the smell of the bear and the cordite of the rifle, which made a great impression on me One had toy bears and it seemed so sad that the bear should be shot.

Another daughter of an ICS officer was Nancy Vernede: 'We seemed to travel mostly on elephants from camp to camp. We had a rough mattress thrown across the elephant's back and tied with a rope and we just sat on top. If we ever went into the real jungle the grass would be well above our heads and the elephant would move through slowly and very, very quietly and one could see many more wild animals.' At night, lying under a mosquito net, which 'gave you a great feeling of security', the children heard the sounds of the jungle and, in particular, the sounds of the jackals, which were said to howl, 'I smell the body of a dead Hindu! Where? Where? Here! Here! Here!'

The cold weather ended abruptly in mid-March. Then, as Nancy Foster describes, the annual migration of mothers and children to the Hills began: 'We usually left about the end of March and came back when the monsoon had broken, so we were usually away for the very hot months. But even then it got so hot sometimes that you got terrible prickly heat, and that was a thing you never forgot at night. You would wake up with sweat pouring down your face and you'd hang over the side of the bed trying to get cool.' To reach the nearest hill station could mean a journey of several days and nights in a train: 'Usually you had a whole carriage to yourself, a first class carriage with four bunks in it, two up, two down. You'd have a tin bath in the centre of the floor with a great big block of ice which used to be renewed at the stations, and there would be two small fans that used to blow down on the ice and keep you really very, very cool. We loved these journeys. At night when you stopped at the stations and you looked out you saw the vendors going up and down past all the forms asleep on the platforms and heard the various calls they used to make.'

For Spike Milligan, too, the train journey, which could be a tedious business for parents, was 'a golden experience. One time we were going along and we came across a whole British regiment bathing stark naked in a river. I remember my mother saying to my Aunty Eileen, "Don't look, Eileen, don't look, they're all males." Then one dark night I was lying looking up at this chain and I thought, "I wonder what it's for?" and I just pulled it. The train came to a grinding halt in the middle of some mountainous area of India and there was a slow walk of footsteps and the Goanese guard said, "Did somebody here pull the chain?" My mother was terrified.'

Each district had its hill station to which wives and children and senior officials retreated and sat out the hot weather and the rains; Ootacamund in the south and, in the Himalayas – 'which seemed to stretch for millions of miles' – Mussourie, Simla, Naini Tal and Darjeeling. Towards the end of the hot weather came the rains, tremendous downpours that would ease off for a while and then return as endless torrential rain, bringing only temporary relief from the heat. 'We used to rush out,' says Deborah Dring, 'and stand in it and let it pour over us, and we were soaked to the skin. If we could take our clothes off so much the better. We'd be soaked and probably come in to a jolly good spanking.'

For the first years of childhood there were few shadows. The more observant children of officials would have noticed their parents' preoccupation with saving and their fears of the family being left penniless in the event of the father's death; fears which undoubtedly left their mark. But the real threat to happiness was something that no English parent with children born in India could ever forget. 'When my first son arrived,' recalls Kathleen Griffiths, 'I looked at him and I thought, "Oh dear, you'll soon be five or six and then I will have to take you home and leave you there and be separated from you." This is always at the back of your mind, that separation has to come eventually.' Some saw this separation as 'a sacrifice made by children to fulfil the aims – and very worthy aims – of their parents.' But not so the children: 'We never thought of England as home,' recalls Nancy Foster. 'It never occurred to us that our home wasn't India.' England was a land of 'straw-

34

berries everywhere', or, as Spike Milligan imagined it, 'a land of milk and honey that used to send us Cadbury's military chocolates in a sealed tin once every four months. England was the land that sent us the *Daily Mirror* and *Tiger Tim* comics. England was a land where you could get chocolate and cream together for a penny, that's what my mother told me. But it never happened like that – England was a gloomy, dull, grey land.'

'When I brought my two children home,' remembers Kathleen Griffiths, 'we got into the train and the younger one, aged five, piped up in front of a carriage full of people, "Mummy, why hasn't the guard come along and asked your permission to start the train?" and I replied, "Darling, we are not in daddy's district now! They do not come along and ask me if they may start the train here. This is England, you must get used to English customs now!"' And now the children learnt that most dreaded and incomprehensible of 'Anglo-Indian' customs – separation from one's parents at an early age. If it was hard for the parents it was twice as hard on their children. Not only were they deprived of their parents, but they were deprived of all the life they had become used to. 'We had nothing in common with our new friends,' explains Nancy Vernede. 'They'd never heard of the brain fever bird or the sound of jackals, and they'd never ridden on an elephant. We just had nothing in common.'

The regular exchange of weekly mail provided a frail link between parents and children that weakened as every month and year of separation went by. 'When they came back on leave,' says Frances Smyth of her parents, 'they were like beings from another world – but it wasn't my world.' On the other hand, as Vere Birdwood observes, 'separation made us immensely independent, and to some extent independent of love. I think it probably hardened us. My brother, I remember, would pack his school trunk alone from about the age of eight. We got used very early on to making our own arrangements for travelling or doing whatever it was. Perhaps it also helped young men to go out to India at the age of nineteen and immediately take control of vast districts, take on enormous responsibilities, far and away beyond anything which their contemporaries were experiencing in England, because they had been conditioned earlier at a very vital age to managing on their own, coping with life.'

But India was never forgotten. 'All through the time I was at school and growing up,' recalls Iris Portal, 'India was a land of promise, something I would go back to. One was sustained throughout all those years by the thought that one would go back.'

2

THE TOMB OF HIS ANCESTORS

*If there were but a single loaf of bread in all India, it would
be divided equally between the Plowdens, the Trevors, the
Beadons and the Rivett-Carnacs.*
      RUDYARD KIPLING *The Tomb of His Ancestors*

At the close of the nineteenth century a powerful tradition of
service continued to dictate a choice of career. Few who went
into one or other of the Indian services could fail to claim an
'Anglo-Indian' ancestor. It was a fact of Empire: 'One's
brothers, one's friends' brothers and so on were all either in the
civil service in some part of India, or in the forces or the police
or in something else. The men of the family served the Empire
as a matter of course.'

In many families a connection with India had been established with Clive and reinforced many times over thereafter.
The Rivetts joined forces with the Carnacs to become one of
the best-known families of 'Anglo-India'. The Maynes 'flocked
into India' from 1761 onwards, leaving 'two graves in Darjeeling, two in Allahabad, one in Saharastra, one in Meerut,
one in Bangalore, one in Achola and another in Lucknow'. The
first Ogilvies landed four years later in 1765. When Vere
Ogilvie married Christopher Birdwood, the 'boy next door' –
and the son of the Commander-in-Chief – their offspring became in due course 'the sixth and seventh generation of children who had started their lives in India'. Some families
specialized. When Rosamund Napier married Henry Lawrence
in 1914 it was an alliance between two great families of soldiers
and administrators. When John Cotton entered the Political
Service in 1934 he was the sixth generation in an unbroken
male line to serve the East India Company prior to 1858 and
the Indian Civil Service thereafter.

The 'Anglo-Indian' family cherished its ancestors, whose achievements and eccentricities coloured and influenced the lives of its youngest members. The Maynes remembered Augustus Ottoway, killed at the Relief of Lucknow in 1857 and found dead on a *dooley* by Lord Roberts who 'took his dear friend Mayne out at early dawn and dug his grave and buried him in his frock-coat and top boots, and as they laid him there leant down and fixed his eye-glass into his eye as he always wore it in the heat of the fray'. His grave now lies on the seventh fairway of Lucknow Golf Course, 'a cause of great frustration to golfers'.

Vere Ogilvie heard stories of her grandmother, who went out as the young bride of Ogilvie *Dandi mar* or 'Ogilvie Beat-with-a-stick': 'The first thing that confronted her in this very lonely station in the Punjab was a compound full of native women with whom he had solaced his solitude, and several suspiciously pale-faced children running about. In keeping with the mores of the period, once my grandmother had arrived the native women were put aside. Nevertheless, it was not exactly a happy beginning for the bride and the story goes that my grandmother found a little comfort in the friendship of a very good-looking Pathan orderly who appears in many family photographs and is reputed to be the father of my eldest aunt, long since dead.'

Grandfathers and even fathers, exiled from home for many years on end, often seemed larger than life to their estranged children and grandchildren. Olivia Hamilton's grandfather, Resident in Kashmir during the Mutiny, was said to have drawn a line round a great deal of Kashmir and told the Rajahs that if they allowed their women to throw themselves on to funeral pyres the English would take that much of their country. Geoffrey Allen's grandfather had taken the young Kipling under his wing to work on his Lahore newspaper, the *Civil and Military Gazette*. Kenneth Warren's grandfather had pioneered tea growing in the tropical jungles of Assam, and was followed by a son who travelled alone for three months up the Brahmaputra river after being told that he would never come out alive. Kenneth Mason's uncle, who had taken part in the Great Game as an intelligence officer on the North-West Frontier, was said to be part of the make-up of Colonel Creighton in Kipling's *Kim*.

Few families were as packed with legends, both dead and living, as the Butlers. There was Uncle Charles, known as 'Smith of Asia', Uncle Willy who led a lonely life as an Assam tea planter and 'kept a tame bear which used to hurry people off the estate', and Uncle Harcourt, an outsize figure in every way, of whom Indian mothers in the *terai* sang to their babies, 'All is peace and quiet because the great Harcourt Butler Sahib is taking care of us, so my baby can rest in peace'.

If certain families made India their vocation so, too, did certain peoples: 'Anybody with a Celtic streak was immediately more at home in India. They seemed to integrate better than the very conventional English.' Ever since the late eighteenth century, when India proved 'a godsend for the younger sons of the Manse', Scots and, to a lesser extent, Ulstermen, had dominated the administration, continuing to provide nearly half the ICS well into the twentieth century. They also provided engineers and planters. According to Kenneth Warren, threequarters of the Europeans in Assam came from Aberdeen or elsewhere in Scotland.

The pattern of generation succeeding generation continued almost without diminution into the twenties and thirties. But there were other factors – romantic, practical, even involuntary – that caused this last generation of young men and women to strike out for India, knowing full well that Independence was going to come and that 'we were really there to guide it on its way'.

The romantics were those who were early 'victims of propaganda' and of the Empire's chief propagandist. 'The answer to why I went to India is Kipling,' explains Philip Mason, who went out as a member of the Indian Civil Service. 'When I was a small boy I had an absolute passion for Kipling and read everything I could get hold of. Something in those stories appealed to me enormously and gave me a romantic desire to go to this country.' This appeal reached far beyond the usual range of readership. The common soldier, whose enforced service in India Rudyard Kipling chronicled with such humour and sympathy, held him in rare esteem. Many of those who followed in the footsteps of Privates Ortheris, Learoyd and Mulvaney knew by heart 'Boots' or 'Gunga Din' or some other barrack room ballad. 'His soldier poetry and his Imperial stuff fired something in me and drew me to India,' remembers Stephen Bentley, a serving soldier in the Seaforths. Kenneth Mason who followed his uncle's footsteps and, in his turn, played the Great Game in the Karakoram, was a self-confessed disciple of Kipling: 'Kim was an atmosphere I lived in from about the time I was fourteen till I went out to India.' Others were fired by the writings of Flora Annie Steele or Maud Diver, or by the tales that old soldiers brought back of leaning out of barrack room windows and 'picking bananas and oranges off a tree', or 'shooting tigers from one's bed either before or after breakfast'.

Also to be numbered among the romantics were those thousands of young girls who went out to find love and marriage and willingly – sometimes blindly – followed fiancés and husbands into an unknown sub-continent beyond the splendidly marbled Gates of India that stood on Bombay's waterfront.

Realists chose India either because it promised them a life they could not lead elsewhere or because it came nearest to unattainable goals. For Arthur Hamilton, who went into the Indian Forest Service, India could satisfy his love of mountains and woods; for 'Jackie' Smyth, India offered campaigns on the Frontier and for John Morris, then with the Leicestershire Regiment in France, the very opposite – a chance to escape from the trenches of France. Others with military leanings had ambitions that could not be realized in England. 'I wanted to go into the cavalry,' states Reginald Savory, 'and my father, who was not a poor man by any means, nevertheless said he couldn't afford to put me through a good British cavalry regiment and if I wanted to join the Cavalry I'd have to go to the Indian Army and join the Bengal Lancers.' It was also a question of finance for Claude Auchinleck: 'In those days you couldn't live in an ordinary British Infantry regiment unless you had about a hundred a year, which today would be about six hundred a year. I had to either get into the Gunners or the Sappers – in which you could live on your means – or join the Indian Army.'

Money, and the lack of it, pushed many young men towards India. H. T. Wickham was told by his guardian to go and earn a living: 'He threw me a civil service book and said, "Take your choice." I saw the Indian Police and I saw the subjects for examination and I decided that I would go for it, although I had no leanings towards India or even the police for that matter.' Despite the legends that persisted, the prospect of making money and of shaking the pagoda trees of Calcutta and Bombay was no longer a realistic one. The days of quick fortunes made by men who risked much had gone with the John Company Nabobs and the importation of Victorian standards of rectitude and incorruptibility. Yet the established trading houses could still offer adventure and prospects to the right sort of public schoolboy, one who was ready to take on early responsibility and could survive the harsh baptism of a 'first tour' of four or even five years deep in the *mofussil* without a home leave.

The massive unemployment of the inter-war period meant good recruiting for the British Army, which provided India with a substantial if steadily decreasing garrison of British County and Cavalry regiments. 'The situation in '27 was very poor,' remembers Ed Davis, 'so one day my father said, "Would you like to join the army, because we can't afford to keep you in clothing." So I joined the Dorset Regiment and that was the start of my career in the army.' The recruits were not always given a choice: 'We were lined up on the square and they numbered us all. Numbers one to six went into one regiment, seven to twelve into another.' For these young Britons the Indian 'tour' was a rather bad legal joke: 'A soldier contracted to serve four years in India but there was a clause whereby the four years could be extended under certain circumstances, such as transport difficulty or what have you. As a matter of hard fact those circumstances invariably arose and so the soldier served what he bitterly called his *buckshee* year.' The British soldier's India was a very different one from that experienced by most 'Anglo-Indians'. Service in India would prove that caste applied as much to Britons as to Indians.

Nearly all the young men joining the Indian civil and military services – as well as those who went into business – shared the common background of the English public schools. When John Rivett-Carnac applied to join the Indian Police Service he observed that 'the mentality of the applicants was that of the public school prefect. We were very innocent of life in general. We were straight from public school, we had had no contact with adults but for the occasional schoolmaster. We had no idea at all about sex, we had no experience of English people who told lies and we never doubted the word of a fellow Englishman.' Yet it was precisely this innocence that made them ideal officers to govern a country like India, because they had the strictest ideas of truth, honesty, fair play and decency.

The better public schools – in particular Rugby, Marlborough and Wellington – supplied the Indian Army with its officer material. Since the Indian regiment had fewer British officers than the British regiment, vacancies were limited and the competition among those entering or passing out from Sandhurst was correspondingly fiercer: 'The stock of the Indian Army was so high that they could afford to give us an extra six months training and then only take the top twenty-five.'

The Indian Civil Service, which provided India with its administrators, magistrates and judges, sought out its recruits chiefly from Oxford and Cambridge. 'You couldn't read Kipling,' remembers Philip Mason, 'without knowing that the ICS was the premier service and that it ran the place.' It was an elite service, few in numbers, and could afford to pick and choose. Indeed, it was said with only slight exaggeration that nobody without a first class honours degree stood a chance. Successful applicants took a further year to learn both a vernacular and a classical language as well as 'something about the history of India and the law'. Some found this extra study 'an atrocious waste of time'. Penderel Moon had an 'efficient though eccentric teacher at Oxford who used to delight in counting backwards from one hundred in Urdu and seeing the shortest space of time he could do it in. We were never informed that the language of the Punjab was Punjabi and rather different from Urdu, with the result that when I got there I was most upset to find that I couldn't understand a word of what was being said. We went out totally unprepared.'

With fourteen provinces to choose from most recruits for the civil services put down the Punjab or the United Provinces. Penderel Moon chose the Punjab 'because that was the fashionable thing to do'. On the advice of a friend Philip Mason went for the United Provinces, because it had 'nicer people'. Less successful or bolder candidates got the 'undesirable' provinces like Bengal. A privileged few followed their fathers, so that 'a young man coming out before the First World War, being the son of a man who'd been in the ICS before him, was greeted in the station that he went to by people who'd known him as a baby, and they would give that man utter and complete loyalty, because he was the son of his father'.

Before final appointment there was a covenant or contract to be drawn up with the Secretary of State for India: 'A declaration that you would obey the Viceroy and behave as a decent chap and agree to the conditions laid down under the regulations of that present government.'

Having committed themselves, the young men had to kit themselves up and prepare for embarkation. Those who sought advice from old India hands were told to get 'one good pair of riding breeches and get them copied out there by a *derzi*, and to take a shotgun and a saddle'. The less well advised allowed themselves to be fitted up by Gieves of Old Bond Street with pith helmet and palm beach suits and duck clothes – half of which they discarded when they got there. Edwin Pratt, going out to join the Calcutta branch of the Army and Navy Stores, was persuaded to buy a tropical suit in the form of tussore: 'It was a bright yellow and I was told that that was what people wore out there. When I put it on people laughed at it and said, "Where the hell did you get that?" It was the bane of my life!'

None were put to more expense than the newly commissioned subalterns, who were required to buy their own uniforms, together with a sword and a revolver. Since British officers in Indian infantry regiments were mounted they were also expected to buy their own saddlery and, in due course, their own horses. 'The military tailors had a very expensive monopoly on providing kits for officers,' recalls Jackie Smyth. 'The fitting-out came to something like £150, which my mother couldn't possibly afford, but it was understood that every officer had to have all these things. If it hadn't been for my old headmaster who got together one or two people to pay the bill, I would never have gone. When I got out there I found that an Indian *derzi* would rig up all the things that you wanted for practically nothing. At least half the bill, if not threequarters, was quite unnecessary.'

The enlisted man in the British Army – the British Other Ranker – had no such problems, since everything was decided for him. Drafts were sent out at intervals and when names appeared on the notice board it was a great source of excitement. After a month's embarkation leave the men drew their new tropical kit: 'You were fitted with a cork helmet, a spine-pad which hung over the back of the helmet to protect the back of your neck from the sun, and the usual khaki shorts and jackets.' In the traditional army manner 'the kits you were issued with at home were never suitable for the regiment you were joining. The khaki was a different shade, your hose wasn't the right colour, the puttees weren't the right shape or size and everything had to be bought afresh, out of your own money, of course, from the *derzi* shop.' The men were also issued with pith helmets and topees. 'I saw the difference immediately,' says Ed Davies, 'the pith helmet was a clumsy looking contraption, very thick but very light, whereas the topee was very sophisticated and smart, with a *puggaree* wrapped round it bearing the green flash of our regiment. It was much heavier as it was solid cork.'

Others were also given topees – and parental advice 'The three most dangerous things that I had to watch out for in the East were wine, women and the sun,' remembers Rupert Mayne, 'and I had to keep my topee on after Port Said, the self-same topee which my father had brought back when he retired and which had resided in the attic in its tin topee case.

I also gave an oath to my father that I would never shoot East of Suez without cartridges of sufficient calibre to be able to defend myself against a dangerous animal. My father had been attacked by a panther near Meerut when he was partridge shooting; a fellow officer had shot at it with No. 5 12-bore cartridges and it had attacked my father and got him in the shoulder.'

The British troops were also given advice. Before final embarkation they were issued with a booklet which told them 'not to go down to the brothels, to wear a pith helmet or topee at all times during the day and not to drink water outside the cantonment, as it would be contaminated with typhoid, diphtheria and all the rest of the diseases prevalent in India.' At the dockside others were equally free with advice, as Stephen Bentley describes: 'You couldn't move but there was some do-gooder at your elbow. There was the Salvation Army, there were the Army welfare workers, there were Christian Union people, all handing you tracts and pamphlets not about India or anything connected with India, but about the way of life that you should lead – on a much greater spiritual plane than you were ever likely to encounter in any part of India. The troops were embarrassed but they didn't show it and they took all the literature as they always did and stuffed it in their pockets and never read it.'

Some were seen off in style: 'I had an uncle who was an admiral who happened at that time to be director of transport, and he, no less, came along to see me off. The result was that Second Lieutenant Savory, when he boarded Her Majesty's Transport *Dongola*, was seen off by this gold-braided gentleman who put the fear of God into the Captain and the Officer Commanding Troops and everybody else!' Others went with less ceremony: 'The last thing an old corporal said to me as he gave me my packet of biscuits and bar of chocolate was, "Now look after yourself and keep away from the women."'

3

POSH

It's so easy to love a little, flirt a little on a big ship, even if a husband or a bridegroom or duty with a big 'D' is waiting on the quay at the other end.

AMY J. BAKER *Six Merry Mummers* 1931

'There was the weekly P & O on which both officers and civilians were supposed to travel. You were thought rather badly of if you didn't support the British line.' Up to the early forties the standard mode of travel to India was on board the P & O 'travelling hotel' from Tilbury or Southampton to Bombay. Those going to South India or seeking to avoid a tedious train journey across India to Calcutta took a BI boat. Wealthy passengers and those prone to sea-sickness bypassed the Bay of Biscay by travelling through France on the 'Blue' train and catching the steamer at Marseilles.

Seasoned travellers had their passages booked on the port side of the ship going out and starboard home, travelling POSH and so avoiding the worst of the sun. The accepted time for 'coming out' was in the autumn. 'The ship was mainly full of people returning from leave,' recalls Kenneth Warren of his first voyage out, 'either civil servants or military or business people and quite a number of young girls going out for the Christmas holidays to stay for two or three months during the Cold Weather with their relations or friends. In those days they were known in India as the Fishing Fleet.' The Fishing Fleet was by long-established custom made up of the 'highly eligible, beautiful daughters of wealthy people living in India. This was the only way in which they could come out under the protection of their parents, to meet eligible young men and marry.' Those who failed returned to England in the spring and were known as the Returned Empties.

Besides members of the Fishing Fleet, there would be other women on board the outgoing liner. Norah Bowder was following another tradition by going out to be married in Bombay by special government dispensation. Her companion was the wife of a friend of her future husband who spent her nights weeping, because she had left her little girl behind in boarding school. Sometimes the mothers stayed behind and saw their children settled into school and then it was the fathers who returned alone from home leave. Some of the young men, too, were less than cheerful. 'Leaving England was really worse than going back to school,' recalls Penderel Moon. With him on board the *Viceroy of India* were a number of new ICS recruits, both Indian and English. 'Amongst many topics we discussed on the voyage out was how long the Raj was going to last. This was in 1929 and the general consensus was, "Well, at any rate it'll last about twenty-five years, which will entitle us to proportiate pensions." We were fully conscious that we were on a sinking ship, as it were.' Yet there was also the idealism of youth. 'We were all for conferring self-government on India,' declares David Symington, another ICS recruit, 'I visualized myself very rapidly achieving the ambition of becoming a viceroy and handing over the government of India to its elected representatives at some kind of big *durbar*.'

These young men who went out after the Great War regarded themselves as different from their predecessors, the 'funny old boys' who came back from India: 'We were quite clear we weren't going to be like that.' None the less, the codes of behaviour established by their predecessors continued to make themselves felt on board, as John Morris soon observed: 'The protocol which went on in most military cantonments was carried onto the P & O. If you saw a major or a colonel in front of you, you naturally stepped aside to let him pass, and if you were late coming back when we called at various ports you were sent for by the Captain of the ship and asked why you hadn't come back when you heard the ship's siren going.' The social divisions of 'Anglo-Indian' were also quick to establish themselves. Rosalie Roberts, going out as a missionary nurse, noticed immediately that there were different groups: 'The

47

military were separate, the ICS and government people were definitely on their own, and the planters, and then there were mothers with children going out to join their husbands. The purser arranged the tables very carefully for all the different groups.' Not always successfully, however, since her husband-to-be, the Reverend Arfon Roberts, found himself seated at a table of hard-drinking planters, one of whom, on hearing that a missionary's salary was £165 a year, informed him that he spent that amount in one month on drink alone.

Norman Watney, going out with one of the last groups of British recruits to the Indian State Railways, soon found himself observing another 'Anglo-Indian' convention: 'We had come to the signing of chits, which meant that everything was signed for and at the end of the week the cabin steward put on your table a nice bunch of notes, ringed by a rubber band which invited you to pay the total at the purser's office at the first opportunity. This signing of chits was a pleasant business because no money was needed and every time you signed you felt a feeling of affluence creeping over you. But as time went on and hotter weather came, drinking increased, the bills increased and it was difficult to restrict this signing, particularly if you were with others probably richer than yourself!'

As the voyage progressed it was also observed that 'evening dress was not now just plain black. Some were wearing black trousers and white dinner jackets, some were wearing the opposite. Enquiries soon revealed that the more important clubs in India had their own ideas of what should be worn. For instance, it seemed that the Punjab Club members must wear white jackets and black trousers, and Calcutta Club members black coats and white trousers, and so on. All this struck us as rather peculiar at the time because we had neither.'

Nevertheless, life on board the passenger liner was, as Rosamund Lawrence remembers, 'very pleasant and lazy – and I was very much intrigued by a young man who'd taken possession of a girl. These two simply couldn't be parted from one another; she'd go and knock on the door of the smoking room and he'd come out and then they would spend their time dancing together on a threepenny bit. I was only a young girl, about seventeen, and I was rather shocked with this – and very fascinated.'

Shipboard romance was a predictable feature of every voyage. But here, too, as Frederick Radclyffe Sidebottom observed, protocol had its place: 'I can remember one famous occasion when a governor's daughter happened to be a passenger aboard the ship. The first class was full of very stuffy people and she took a fancy to a very handsome young second class steward and when the fancy-dress ball was being held she danced with him all night, and the next morning – they having parted, perhaps, only half an hour beforehand – he approached her and she froze him absolutely stiff in his tracks and said, "In the circle in which I move, sleeping with a woman does not constitute an introduction." '

Some shipboard romances were rather happier. Kathleen Griffiths, going out to India as a governess, rose early one morning to see the sun rise: 'There by the side of me was a young man to whom I had not then spoken also admiring the sunrise. We had a few words, and after this we discovered that we'd been drawn in a deck game together. And from there on our acquaintance developed. In a few days under a full moon on the Red Sea we became engaged, much to the delight and interest of many people on board ship. In my cabin there was a rather senior lady who, rather looking down upon me as a governess, said, "Oh, I hear you've got engaged to young Griffiths. You've done well for yourself, haven't you. Don't you know? He's one of the heaven-born – the Indian Civil Service!" '

For one minor but significant section of the 'Anglo-Indian' community the voyage out was anything but a romance. The British troops went out on small, over-crowded 'vomit-buckets'. 'I don't think there will be one man who went to India on a troop-ship who won't remember it as one of the most sordid memories of his life,' declares Stephen Bentley. 'The officers got three-quarters of the ship with their lounges and smoke rooms and luxurious cabins, and the troops got only the troop-deck.' Troubles began with accommodation. Some men found that there simply wasn't any, so the unfortunate ones had to pick up their baggage and get up on deck, a favourite place being round the funnel, where it was warm, or under the boat deck. Then there was the problem of hammocks, as another soldier, E. S. Humphries, explains: 'On the very first night out from England two or three men lost their hammocks – and it grew like a snowball. Each night more and more people lost their hammocks and more and more people had to sit up and lie awake until they managed to pinch someone else's hammock because no one could face the indignity of being the sucker in the battalion who arrived in Bombay minus his hammock.'

But it was the Bay of Biscay that very often set the seal on the voyage:

When you see a thousand men in the throes of the most appalling sea-sickness and realize what it entails, then you have some idea of how awful it was. The whole administration just went to pieces. No one came round to see that the men were fed, no one came round to see if the men were really ill or just sea-sick. No one came to see that the latrines were working – and they weren't, so that the overflow from the latrines was swishing all over the middle deck. There was very little water. You couldn't get into a wash place, you couldn't get to your kit and worst of all, you couldn't get to your hammock. It looked like the carnage of a battlefield. I can honestly say that in the first five or six days I never saw an officer on the troop-deck. I don't think the troops resented it, because that was the sort of thing that you got in those days.

Once into the Mediterranean, however, prospects improved. There were concerts, with a wealth of talent available on every troop-ship, and there was housey-housey, the army version of bingo, run by members of the crew, who would make money out of it. There were also the unofficial gambling schools. 'The crown and anchor board boys who used to perform down in the bowels of the ship, with look-outs posted all the way up to watch out for the military police coming round.' Then there was PT every morning, and lectures from a medical officer on every danger to life in India from cholera and snake bites downwards, adding almost as an afterthought that 'On the other hand, you'll be much healthier than you were in England, because you won't catch colds.'

The East began at Port Said, where 'the bumboat men came alongside and tried to sell you things. They used to throw a rope up to the ship's side with a basket attached. You'd pull it up, put your money in the basket, lower it down to them and they'd put in oranges, apples, bananas or whatever it was.' Port Said was also where little boys dived for pennies and where the 'gully-gully' man came aboard. 'The gully-gully business was a family affair,' explains Kenneth Mason. 'Before finishing a trick he used to say "Gully, gully, gully, gully, gully." The people on board were gathered round and when he was going to produce a chicken from some lady he would say, "Now come on, Lillie Langtry, what are you doing with a chicken?" It was his patter. The last time I went out East Mrs Simpson had taken over from Lillie Langtry.'

The men who went ashore – always in parties since it was dangerous 'even for British people' – were introduced to the unsavoury aspects of the East: 'We went to a casino where we were duly robbed of our few odd shillings, we were taken to a brothel from which we had to drag one of our number and, of course, there were the smutty postcards.' For both sexes there was also the ritual of topee-buying at Simon Artz, since 'when one arrived at Port Said it was the accepted thing for every newcomer to buy a topee'. As Percival Griffiths recalls: 'No young civilian ever got out to India by sea without falling into the clutches of Simon Artz, where you were always inveigled into buying a Curzon topee which you probably never wore the rest of your life, because what you did wear was an old pig-sticking topee that you probably bought in Calcutta or when you first got to your station.'

Through the Suez Canal, too narrow for ships to pass unless one was tied up to the shore, and a halt for coal at Aden where 'coolies carried small buckets on their heads, up planks from the shore'. Then 'sharks, flying fish and no land for miles around for days on end', the routine only broken by an occasional passing ship. Ed Davies remembers the excitement on board at 'the sight of a troop-ship passing our own, going back to Blighty. We all rushed to the side shouting, "Troop-ship! Troop-ship!" and we felt our ship list. They could hear our cheers and we could hear theirs. So there were two ships nearly sinking, as we shouted hysterically at each other.' In the meantime it would be growing palpably hotter on board ship. The troops now wore tropical uniform on deck and a pair of shorts below deck. 'Even those travelling on P & O liners before the advent of the electric fan had to sleep on deck,' remembers Kenneth Warren. 'The cabin steward took your bedding up and put it on deck. The men all slept on one side and the women all slept on the other side. If possible you had your bedding put on one of the hatchways so that when they came to wash the decks down early the next morning you weren't disturbed.'

The voyage drew to a close: 'During the last few days a feeling of excitement did begin to build up. There was the hot, sunny weather, the flying fish dropping little droplets of water onto the smooth sea – everything seemed to be beautiful.' There came 'a difference in the air or in the atmosphere or in the heat or in the way the wind blew or possibly even in the smell,' and then the smell of India, 'difficult to pinpoint, partly the populace, partly the different vegetation, partly the very rapid fall of dusk and the cooling off which leads to a most lovely scent just after sundown.'

Then landfall: 'The *ghats* leading up to the Deccan mountains rising to three or four or five thousand feet, and all the foothills very green after the monsoon, the sea very blue, the buildings mostly white and looking rather gorgeous from the sea, and altogether a feeling of opulence and luxuriance.' Finally, disembarkation and first impressions. 'I felt happy,' recalls Ian Stephens, 'that somehow or other I belonged here, that this was the sort of place for me, and I've often wondered whether something like an ancestral memory wasn't ticking over, whether my great-grandfather and my grandfather and my uncle weren't in me in the reactions I had to the Indian scene.' Other reactions, like those of John Morris, were less favourable: 'I thought what a terrible place it was, with rather

"PUKKA" LUGGAGE.

The absolute reliability of which is guaranteed to each purchaser by a bond supplied with every article, undertaking to keep same in repair free of charge for 5 years, and replace gratis if beyond repair. No complicated conditions but a simple, straightforward guarantee

"PUKKA" SUIT CASE.

No. G.G.44.

Covered with brown flax-canvas, fitted with leather straps inside. Two good locks and clip in centre.

Registered design.

Size				£	s.	d.
Size 22	by 15	by 7½ in.		£3	15	0
,, 24	by 15½	by 8 in.		4	2	0
,, 26	by 16	by 8½ in.		4	9	0
,, 27	by 16½	by 9 in.		4	19	0
,, 30	by 17	by 9½ in.		5	10	0

"PUKKA" IMPERIAL.

No. G.G. 45.

Covered with brown flax canvas, fitted with tray 4½ in. deep, with 2 web straps in tray and body of trunk. Two good locks and clip in centre.

Registered design.

Supplied to order.

Size			£	s.	d.
Size 30	by 19	by 17 in.	£9	4	0
,, 33	by 20	by 18 in.	10	2	0
,, 36	by 21	by 19 in.	11	0	0
,, 39	by 22	by 20 in.	11	19	0
,, 42	by 22½	by 21 in.	12	19	0

"PUKKA" WARDROBE TRUNKS.

No. G.G. 46.

Covered with brown vulcanized fibre, fitted with drawers, garment hangers, soiled linen bag and shoe box. Strong clips, lock, brassed corners, locking bar to secure drawers.

Fitted with airtight waterproof and dustproof adjustment. Covered green Willesden canvas. To order.

"PUKKA" WARDROBE TRUNKS.

"PUKKA" HAT-BOX.
(Ladies'.)

No. G.G. 47.

Covered with brown flax canvas, fitted with removable wire fittings on which to fix hats or bonnets. One good lock and two clips.

Registered design.

Supplied to order.

Size			£	s.	d.
Size 20	by 16	by 16 in.	£5	19	0
,, 22	by 18	by 18 in.	6	9	0
,, 24	by 20	by 20 in.	7	2	0

"PUKKA" CABIN.

No. G.G. 48.

Covered with brown flax canvas, fitted with tray 4 in. deep, with 2 web straps in tray and body of trunk. Two good locks and clips in centre.

Registered design.

Size			£	s.	d.
Size 30	by 19	by 14 in.	£7	7	6
,, 33	by 20	by 14 in.	8	2	6
,, 36	by 21	by 14 in.	8	17	0
,, 39	by 22	by 14 in.	9	12	0
,, 42	by 23	by 14 in.	10	6	6

"PUKKA" WARDROBE TRUNKS.

Size		£	s.	d.
Size 37½ by 21 by 14 in. (6 hangers and 5 drawers) (supplied to order) ..		£13	14	6
,, 40 by 21 by 14 in. (6 hangers and 5 drawers)		13	18	6
,, 40 by 21 by 16 in. (6 hangers and 5 drawers) ..		14	5	6
42 by 21 by 21 in. (10 hangers and 6 drawers) ..		16	18	6

ALL PRICES ARE SUBJECT TO MARKET FLUCTUATIONS.

shabby Victorian buildings; architecture once described by Aldous Huxley as "a collection of architectural cads and bounders". It did seem like that.' Reginald Savory, expecting to find something full of magic, found instead 'a very ordinary, rather unpleasant, dusty country'. Even so, 'that was the first time in my life I saw an officer dressed up in khaki drill, which thrilled me to the marrow. I had visions of Piper Finlayson and Kipling and all those chaps'. Similarly, to drummer-boy Ed Brown, then just fourteen years old, 'it seemed as though the dream world I'd read about had come true; waving palms, coloured people, beautiful coasts, rock pools with mother-of-pearl flashing. I thought it was a dream land.' But not for long: 'An Indian woman holding a baby came up to me and said, "You're the father of my child, Sahib, give me some money, I want *baksheesh*."'

The native population – 'thousands of people moving, moving, moving' – could hardly be ignored. 'There were people in the streets and people working in the fields and your house was full of servants. Wherever you turned your head there were servants.' Nor could the sun be ignored: 'When you walk out of the customs shed into the sun of India it hits you like a blow, and it continues to do that all through the years you're in India. Every time you walk out of doors during the middle of the day you feel as if you've been hit by something. It's a mistake to think that people get used to heat – they don't. When they first meet it it doesn't worry them, but when they go on encountering it year in year out, then it begins to wear them down.' From the moment they set foot in India BORs were commanded 'never to move anywhere between sunrise and sunset without your topee. If you were ever found out in the sun without your topee you got fourteen days confined to barracks.' In the event, a topee was not enough: 'After a couple of hours the whole of our necks were red, all our arms were red and our knees were red and beginning to blister. That's how hot it was in Bombay, and if it hadn't been for a cool breeze blowing in from the sea we would surely have been roasted alive.'

Receptions varied according to status and connections. Those of high degree or with connections were garlanded and their

54

luggage seized by *chaprassis* in scarlet uniforms. Some were met by shipping agents and shepherded through customs. Others had less auspicious introductions. The troops' baggage was loaded on to supply and transport – or 'shit and treacle' – wagons and while they waited on the quayside they began to understand why India was known to seasoned veterans as 'the land of shit and shankers'. Stephen Bentley met his first beggar, whose head was a mass of running sores: 'I thought it was his hair at first, but it was black with flies, and it came to me very forcibly in that moment that this was the East and one of the things you are going to live with in the East is flies.'

E. S. Humphries, disembarking with the 1st Battalion, Royal Scots, met the 2nd Battalion about to embark: 'The 2nd Battalion were all spick and span, upright, soldierly-looking people, lithe and suntanned, many of them wearing moustaches. We poor souls, just off the ship after weeks of lolling about on deck and with no opportunity to shave, to wash properly or wash our clothes, looked a decrepit-looking lot by comparison. However, on further inspection it was seen that two out of three of these fine, stalwart-looking, lithe fellows were in fact sufferers from malaria. This could be seen by their yellowish skins, their sunken cheeks and their fleshless limbs.'

After inevitable delays at the docks – 'They gave us a couple of packets of cigarettes and a meal and said, "You're on your own for today"' – troops were often moved to Deolali transit camp, where mental patients on their way to Netley Mental Hospital had their papers stamped. Thus 'Doolally tap' came to mean 'someone a bit round the bend'.

At the transit camp the British soldier made his acquaintance with the kite-hawk, known familiarly as the 'shite-hawk'. 'There used to be thousands of them,' remembers Charles Wright. 'When one drew one's food from the cook-house and went to take it across to the dining room to eat at the tables underneath the sheds, these kite-hawks would swoop down and take the lot off your plate if you weren't careful. So you had to walk waving your arms above the plate until you got in under cover.'

For the great majority of travellers Bombay, Karachi or

Colombo was only a staging-post in their journey. But before proceeding up-country some further – more practical – kitting-up was often required, as Norman Watney describes:

We were recommended to go to an emporium called White-away and Laidlaw, known universally as 'Right away and paid for' because of the necessity of paying in ready cash. Whiteaway's had acquired the distinction of being solely for those with small purses and had a large clientele of junior officers such as ourselves. Others in a more senior position used to go down the road about a quarter of a mile away to the Army and Navy Stores.

We went along in a four-wheeled Victoria, a musty-smelling apparatus with a driver who must have been at least ninety, and eventually landed at this rather imposing building. The doors were thrown open by stalwart Pathans in grandiose uniforms and we were directed to a counter where we obtained all the necessities required by the junior officer during his first tour of duty. The assistant was able to tell us that it was not expected of people in our position to buy indigenous articles; it would not look good for us to be seen to have inferior equipment and for this reason only the best would do.

First we had to have a canvas hold-all fitted with two heavy straps with internal flaps. Into this were put sheets and pillows, together with a sort of mattress filled with kapok. This was the *bistra*, or bedding roll. In addition we had to have an enamel basin, together with a top cover made of leather with straps running underneath. With these two articles you could travel the length and breadth of India.

4

ALIENS UNDER ONE SKY

English men and women in India are, as it were, members of one great family, aliens under one sky.
MAUD DIVER *The Englishwoman in India* 1909

Frequent transfers and movements over great distances were recurrent themes in the 'Anglo-Indian' experience: 'As official people we were constantly on the move,' recalls Vere Birdwood. 'After I married we moved fourteen times in fourteen months, and a move was not just packing a couple of suitcases. It had to be planned like a major operation.' With the exception of the *pukka* Grand Trunk Roads that linked the larger stations of upper India – the road systems of India were best suited to the bullock cart. The natural life lines of India were its great rivers, familiar to Nancy Foster both as child and adult: 'The river was vast, almost a sea at certain places. It could be very cruel, very dangerous with sudden storms, or it could be very calm and beautiful. It had a great many moods. You could see for miles from the decks of the steamers. You'd see fishermen with their long, slim boats, shaped like the new moon. You'd see the much bigger dhow type of boat with huge patched sails, sometimes made of matting. Then there'd be the humans packed solid in small boats crossing from one side to the other. Then you'd see the river steamers with their big paddles, taking the jute down to Calcutta. At times the river was so narrow that the jungle almost brushed you as you went past, endless birds, endless animals. Then you'd come to great wastes of marshland and nothing much there, just sky and very beautiful.'

If the rivers were the old lifelines of India, the railways were the new. A criss-cross of broad-gauge railway lines united India with a tediously slow but efficient system of communication that blended most agreeably with both Indian and British life styles. Before the Indian train journey all other forms of travel paled into insignificance: 'To people who lived in backwaters, leading very quiet, humdrum lives and not really seeing an awful lot of the country it was like going to the cinema nowadays, the complete panorama of India.' The Indian railway station was part of the social fabric of India. At night 'every platform was a mass of sleeping forms wrapped in cloth, always heads covered with the feet sticking out', over which passengers changing trains had to pick their way. By day 'you'll find beggars curled up in the shade, you'll find the odd pi-dog wandering around looking for food, the stationmaster would be having his afternoon snooze and the whole place is dead. But the people are there just the same, all curled up, waiting. They've probably waited for their trains for a couple of days.' Trains drew in to a rising crescendo of excitement and sound, as the station came to life: 'A terrific gabble in either Hindustani or Tamil or Telegu, probably all of them. Men with *dhotis* running along with things on their heads, men with broken-down umbrellas trying to get onto the train. You'd see people clinging on the carriages, even on the roof, and the stationmaster trying to pull them off.' There were also the station vendors and sweetmeat sellers with their hawkers' cries that quickly became familiar to the traveller: '*Hindi pani, Mussulman pani,*' from the water carriers who sold water to Hindus and Moslems separately; '*tahsa char, garumi garum*', hot fresh tea from the tea vendors; '*pahn biri*', cigarettes and betel nut, even 'Beecham *Sahib ki gooli*', Beecham's pills for those who required them. Less attractive were the child beggars who hung on to carriage windows as the train pulled out, 'screeching and looking at us with great big spaniel's eyes until you had to tap their knuckles, so that they would drop off all along the platform like little flies'.

The railway carriages themselves were 'highly hierarchical', reflecting the social structure of British India. Yet if they were 'very luxurious in the upper classes, the distances were great and the fatigue great and, in summer, the heat great'. As a

58

newly appointed assistant superintendent on the Indian State Railways bound for Lahore, Norman Watney's first experience of Indian trains was made aboard the Frontier Mail: 'A four-berth carriage had been reserved for us with a self-contained toilet compartment with a shower. All Indian railway carriages had the doors fitted with a throw-over catch which effectively bars entry from the outside. Furthermore, the windows, which were in triplicate – glass, venetian blinds and gauze – were also latched, so you were in a pretty impregnable position. We asked what would happen if anybody else tried to come into our compartment and were assured that nobody would turn up. No Indian would dare to attempt to come into our compartment so long as he saw more than one European therein.

'To break the monotony of the journey it was possible to go and have a meal in the European dining cars, which were run only on the mail trains and only between certain junctions. If you wanted a meal you had to get down from your carriage, lock it up, go down the track, jump into the dining car and stay there till the next stop.'

Indian trains were not free from dirt or disease. Seasoned travellers brought their own bedding and ensured that the floors of their carriages were swabbed down with disinfectant. Some even went so far as to take a bottle of Evian water with which to clean their teeth, because the water on the trains was considered to be impure. If the travellers were of some rank they might well be approached by the stationmaster for permission to proceed.

There were also troop-trains and once again, as Stephen Bentley records, the contrast was extreme:

We were put in six to a compartment and told to settle down. Which is just about the last thing you can do in any compartment on an Indian military train. They were about ten feet by eight feet in area and in each compartment there were racks, slotted like park benches and about two feet apart. You had all your kit, you had all your equipment, you had your blankets, you even had your greatcoat rolled up – and it all had to be stowed away. Having no room it was absolute chaos.

Like everything else in the army, we had been taught to make the best of a bad job. We had our emergency rations and we ate them and, as night falls very quickly in India, it was dark by the time the train got on its way and we were only too anxious to get the racks down and go to sleep. The train had been left in a siding all day and the heat in the compartment was fearsome. So, of course, we pulled all the windows down and set the fan going at full speed and went to sleep. Within the space of minutes the temperature had gone from hot to almost zero and we were nearly freezing. I never heard such cursing up and down the carriage.

Meals had been arranged at predetermined stations along the line, so that the train couldn't get there before time and couldn't get there after time. It had to get there military fashion, dead on time. You got out and there would be a group of military cooks on the platform with all their pots and pans and stewpots. In all my years in India I don't think I ever ate a meal on a station that wasn't smoked. It was nearly always stew and rice pudding, of such poor quality that very few of the troops ever ate it, and most of it was given to the begging Indians, of which there were usually scores, or to the pariah dogs that always seemed to be waiting for troop trains.

Nothing so clearly demonstrated the depth of India as that first train journey. Its size was brought home to Christopher Masterman as he crossed the Madras presidency: 'It took us two days and nights to get up to Madras, and there's more of the presidency north of Madras than there is in the south.' Travelling across central India to Bengal, Percival Griffiths was struck by the enormous variety of the country: 'Long before one knew one type or one caste from another, the variety hit you in the eye. You felt you weren't going to a country, you were going to a continent.'

Frances Smyth saw this 'continent' with a painter's eye:

The country stretched to eternity. The sky was immense and the whole horizon was far away. And you were very small in this immensity and in some curious way this gave you a heightened awareness of everything about you. There was this visual pleasure of great dun flat landscapes, no colour practically, and then against this beige, the trees. You would see the sudden flaming patch of scarlet, which was a gold mohur tree. The tree is the most important thing in India – a green shade. There are great big trees, banyans, with roots that grow down from the branches so that you get a kind of forest of roots. The old men of the village sit there and everybody comes and life goes on under this tree.

First impressions of the terrain were not always encouraging. Penderel Moon, travelling northwards into the Punjab, thought it 'a terribly dry, unproductive, unattractive country. Endless rocky hills with a few brambles or prickly bushes, no nice green verdure or waving crops. And when I got to the Punjab I was aghast at the flat, featureless character of the countryside and the constant wastes of sand and cactus bushes.' By contrast others moved across landscapes rich with fields of blue linseed and yellow mustard and backed by acres of sugar-cane. Others, yet again, found themselves in tropical jungles, in marshy alluvial plains, in snow-capped mountain ranges.

Yet the land also had its common elements: 'the curious, perfectly horizontal lines of fire smoke near a village in the sunset and the cows coming back to the village in the evening, with pale, pale golden dust hanging over the slow movement of the cows.' The evening, rich in scents and sunsets, and turned by dust 'into a sort of bowl of rosy milk', brought with it a sense of affinity. Even if the day seemed to take out most of the charm, 'when you got to the evenings you could begin to feel, "Well now, this is a country which I could belong to – if I didn't belong to a nicer one."'

The Indian sub-continent contained two Indias. One third of the land – scarcely known to any but a few British 'politicals' – was fragmented into 562 nominally independent princely states. The other two thirds of India came under the direct administration of the British Raj and were divided into fourteen provinces, each subdivided into districts. Thus, the United Provinces were divided into forty-seven different districts and in each the key man was the district magistrate, the deputy commissioner or the collector.

Socially, British India was divided in a far simpler manner: 'There were two areas of life, one of which was life in the big cities – Bombay, Calcutta and, to a slightly lesser extent, places like Delhi and Lahore – and the other the vast *mofussil* – "up-country" – which really embraced all the other stations to which Europeans were sent. This could be some really remote part of the country where perhaps you and your family were the only Europeans, or it could be a small military or civil station with perhaps fifty or one hundred Europeans living outside.' Those who lived up-country generally had a low opinion of those who did not: 'We considered the Europeans in Bombay or Calcutta, who dwelled only on business matters and dealt with Indians who were equally interested only in commerce, to be ignorant of the real India, whereas we in upper India had a much more intimate connection in the form of administration through the police, roads, buildings, the ICS and so on.'

Although the political axis shifted from Calcutta to Delhi in 1912, the former remained pre-eminent as the business centre of India. The old East India Company had been replaced by a handful of managing agencies, which had built up small empires of their own and ran their companies from head offices in Calcutta. As 'the most revolting' or 'the most horrible' city in Asia, Calcutta had no serious rivals. To Percival Griffiths, one of the very few to move from administration into commerce, it was 'a city of gulfs' where 'nobody knew anybody outside their own particular sphere. The civil servant didn't hob-nob with the businessman. The Indian businessman didn't hob-nob with the British businessman. The Bengali businessman didn't mix in with the Marwari businessman. It was a city of four or five quite separate communities which hardly mixed at all.'

For newcomers like Edwin Pratt, joining the Calcutta branch of the Army and Navy Stores, the extremes of Calcutta began at Howrah Railway Station, which 'was smothered with human forms all in very primitive attire, sitting and standing and wandering about, some eating, some cooking and some just sleeping'. Outside there was Howrah Bridge, 'a mass of moving humanity and merchandise jolting over the humps where the pontoon sections were joined together, in bullock carts, buffalo carts, rickshaws, gharries, taxis, buses and private cars, quite apart from the hundreds of pedestrians on either side'.

On the other side of the Hoogly River 'British' Calcutta was almost a world apart; its splendid Maiden flanked by palatial government buildings – a racecourse, cathedral and an ostentatious memorial to Maharanee Victoria. To the south there was Chowringee with such European emporia as the Army and Navy Stores, Hall and Anderson's, and Newman's. There was also the Great Eastern Hotel, the first place in Calcutta to be air-conditioned, and the Grand Hotel, which was said to be 'over-run with rats but comfortable'. There was Spence's, a small planter's hotel mainly frequented by men and an 'absolute gem of India' where, as Radclyffe Sidebottom describes, 'you could get exceedingly good food and with a vast billiard room where you could play billiards and snooker. The decor was entirely early Victorian, the various rooms being divided by lattice-work teak and cherry wood and with *punkahs* pulled by *punkah-wallahs*.' There was also Firpos, a smart Italian restaurant where, if you ordered whisky – 'which you could any hour of the day or night – you were not measured a peg, you were given the bottle. You went on drinking that bottle and when the bill finally came along the servant stood in front of you with a thumb against the mark where the drink had gone down to and you were charged by that amount and it was never, ever questioned.' Another famous lunching place was Peliti's, in Old Court House Street, where on Fridays 'you could guzzle yourself to death on just one rupee'.

Calcutta also had its residential areas, which reflected its social divisions: 'There were the old parts of central Calcutta where the old palatial *burra* sahibs' houses had been built, left as a legacy to those who came on afterwards, and around them came the new buildings, blocks of flats where the young sahibs

63

lived when they first came out. But as you became more senior and you wanted tennis courts and more servants, you moved into what would be called the suburbs. Ballygunge was the second stage, and Alipore, built under the wing of Belvedere, which had been the old vice-regal lodge and which therefore contained that air of sanctity, was the final stage.'

Up-country the social – and racial – divisions were even more clearly marked. Each district had as its focal point the Station, consisting of 'the cantonment where the military personnel lived and worked, the civil lines where the civilians such as the ICS and canal people and the police and forest officer and so on lived, and then the city, which was just a mass of small shops and rather smelly drains and was very densely populated. In the civil lines one had the Club, which was the meeting place for both army and civilian personnel of officer status and was a wonderful forum for gossip and games of all kinds, dinner, dancing, swimming, golf, squash, polo and so on.'

Military cantonments on the larger stations contained barracks for both British and Indian regiments, with their own family lines near by. Such stations were classified as first, second or third class. Ed Davies' first station at Meerut was a first class station where 'everything was clean, white-washed and red-ochered, so that if you looked at it too long it sort of blinded you. The bungalows were all well separated with bits of green in the front, and were very spacious with big verandahs.' Meerut had special associations for the British for it was the 'Mutiny Station'. Iris Portal, married to a cavalry officer, lived for four years in the lines where the Sepoy Mutiny first began:

On the gates of the bungalows were plaques which said, 'Here Mrs So and So and her three children were killed and thrown down a well,' or 'Here Captain and Mrs So and So were found hiding and killed' and so on. There was one bungalow near by where they had to take their beds out into the garden, not only for the heat but because things happened, like doors blowing open when there was no wind. Dogs would never stay in the house, and it was emphatically haunted. They all felt it and they all hated it, and that was one of the Mutiny bungalows with a plaque on it. In the church, where both my children were christened, you could see the places at either side of the pews where the side-arms were stacked.

By contrast, Jhansi was a third-class station. 'I don't think there were many stations in India worse than Jhansi,' declares Stephen Bentley, whose detachment of Seaforth Highlanders found themselves in this 'punishment station' because they had celebrated Hogmanay back in Aldershot rather too enthusiastically:

The barracks were miles away from the town and what town there was was really only a small railway settlement. There was only a very poor bazaar of about ten or twenty shops. There was one corrugated-iron cinema. There were no cafes, no shops, no civilian population except the population of this railway settlement which was principally Anglo-Indian or half-caste. As soon as we got to Jhansi the first order that appeared was that you shan't go into an Indian village. Then they put the civilian lines – this settlement of Anglo-Indians, which would have provided some diversion or change – out of bounds. So anyone coming to Jhansi realized that henceforth for as many years as he had to serve in Jhansi – which in my case was four – his life was the barracks, the canteen, the regimental institute or a walk round the roads immediately surrounding the cantonment.

In addition to its quota of British civilians and military personnel, any station that was on the railway line had a 'railway colony' composed for the most part of Eurasians – officially termed Anglo-Indian – and domiciled Europeans. A specific number of subordinate posts in the central services – the police, customs, railways and telegraphs – had been set aside for this twilight community, which saw itself very much as the 'backbone of the British administration'.

Outside the main stations there were the lesser outposts of British society, such as Darbhanga – 'a complete backwater that had once been a thriving community of indigo planters' – where John Morris was marooned for a year:

The times had gone forward and left it behind. It was full of huge bungalows, mostly unoccupied, and nearly every one had a curious little outhouse attached to it which used to be known in the early days as the *bibi-khana*, the place where the lady was kept – the lady being the planter's Indian mistress – a practice that went out with the arrival of the memsahib. I could have lived like a white rajah in one of these huge, decaying bungalows, but I decided instead to live in a tent in the camp where the troops were quartered. The first result of this was that my bearer – an ancient who had been in the regiment for many years – resigned because he thought that my doing this was not behaving in the way that a sahib should. The curious thing about Darbhanga was that there was a huge club there with a polo ground, all beautifully kept up. And one day an ancient gentleman with a hennaed beard, apparently a servant of the club, asked me if I wished to join. And I said, 'Well, what goes on in the Club?' And he said, 'Oh, the sahibs from the plantations come in at Christmas every year.' I didn't really think that was sufficient reason for joining the Darbhanga Club so I never did. The whole place was a ghost club really. The cloth on the billiard tables had faded to a sort of bilious yellow. There were a lot of books, mostly Victorian novels, mouldering away and the whole place was really most depressing.

The architecture of 'Anglo-India' came in three basic forms and was rarely distinguished. Palaces, public buildings and the larger railway termini were frequently 'unsuccessful Victorian attempts to synthesize Gothic with Saracenic'. Rather more successful was the 'English Palladian style adapted to India in the latter part of the eighteenth century', such as the British Residency in the native principality of Hyderabad, which reminded Olaf Caroe – then a very junior army officer – of the London Athenaeum and made him wonder if there wasn't something to be said for the Indian Civil Service if its political members could live in such dignity. In Southern India and Calcutta senior officials still inhabited relics of the first British settlements. Christopher Masterman, living in the Collector's bungalow in Cuddalore, where Clive had lived, found it 'architecturally very fine but very unsuitable as a modern residence, with walls six feet thick or more and very small windows on the ground floor – and vast rooms on the first floor which were impossible to furnish'.

Equally historic, but of a far simpler architectural design, was the Deputy Commissioner's bungalow in Peshawar, where Olaf Caroe followed in the footsteps of Edwardes and Nicholson, two of the great nineteenth-century Bayards of British India: 'A very pleasant mud brick bungalow with high, cool rooms and a wide verandah standing in wide lawns with huge banyan trees that dropped branches down to the ground.' This was the archetypal up-country bungalow, to be found in Eastern and Upper India and in the smaller stations, built 'facing the north-east, the coolest aspect, the rooms very high and very large in order to remain cool during the hot weather. There was no sitting room, only the verandah. In the old days the walls were simply a skeleton of timber framework with reed rushes plastered over with earth mixed with cow dung, then painted with whitewash; very suitable from an earthquake point of view. With most bungalows you got a thatched roof and then the ceiling of each room was a hessian cloth painted with whitewash. Between the hessian cloth ceiling and the thatch roof was a space which was usually inhabited by bats and often by snakes – you could look up and sometimes see a snake wriggling along the other side of the cloth.'

In Assam and Bengal a local variation, known as the *chung* bungalow, put the bungalows on pillars to avoid floods, with a bathroom under each bedroom, entered through a trap door. Percival Griffiths recalls that, before taking a bath, 'it was advisable to take a tennis racket with you, because bats used to come in and always seemed to want to have a splash in the bath beside you'.

The third form of residence, the *pukka* bungalow, most often found on the larger stations, was an evolved version of the country bungalow; often a two-storeyed structure, flat-roofed and incorporating arcades with Tuscan columns and round Renaissance-style arches. Variations on these basic themes were limited, 'so that one knew exactly what sort of accommodation to expect when one moved on transfer'.

Backing up these three basic forms of housing were the government *dak* bungalows, situated at strategic points throughout the countryside and which themselves came in three forms: 'The plains inspection bungalow consisted mainly of a living room which was flanked by two bedroom suites complete with bathrooms. The hills bungalows were double-storeyed and basically consisted of the same accommodation but on two floors. And the old forts were very old buildings dating back to 1700 or 1800, commandeered and made into very comfortable inspection bungalows.'

Against this topography of set and identifiable structures the *chokra*, the young man fresh from home, set out to make a *burra nam* for himself.

5

LEARNING THE ROPES

No deep division severed then
The Powers that Be from other men;
But all was friendly to the core,
When Thompson ruled in Thompsonpore.
                SENEX *The Golden Age* 1933

Philip Mason's arrival at Saharanpur typified the introduction
to the civil station that many young men experienced:

I arrived in the middle of the night, which one almost always
did in India. I don't know how they managed to arrange this
on the railways, but it was very cunningly arrived at. I was
met by a man two years older than myself, who was killed
playing polo about a year later. He met me at the station and
drove me to the Collector's house, where I was put into a
tent, a great big marquee. Its floor was covered with straw,
with a *dhurri* laid over it and there was a bathroom at the
back. I was astonished at how comfortable it was and how
fresh and clean and pure the night was in December up in
that corner of the UP. In the morning I looked out and I saw
trees which looked so like English trees stretching in every
direction, the most delightful landscape. There was a feeling
of freshness and vigour which I have never forgotten.

I met my Collector for the first time at breakfast. He came
in from his morning ride and said, 'Hello, Mason, I've got
a pony for you that you can buy immediately after breakfast
if you like. There's a dealer here and you might like to buy it.
Work? . . . no, you don't need to do any work your first year.
Here's a book about polo, you can read that and I'll examine
you on it this evening.' Also that first morning, very early,
there came a long procession of officials who said, 'Sir, I am

the *nazir*, have you any orders for me?' and 'Sir, I am the *tahsildar*, have you any orders for me?' I simply couldn't think what to do with any of these people, and I only gradually found out who they all were and how they all fitted into the hierarchy.

Young subalterns joining the Indian Army spent their first year attached to a British regiment: 'The object was to see whether under service conditions you were really fit to be an officer of the Indian Army – which entailed a good deal more responsibility than in the British Army. It also gave you a year to get used to the country and the people.' Some British regiments made their attached officers feel at home, others made them feel that they were 'outcasts and a nuisance'. John Dring's introduction to life in a cavalry regiment was characteristic – if a little abrupt:

The little train puffed into Mardan before light. I was met by the adjutant in a *tonga* and we rattled off to the mess where I was accommodated in the guest quarters. I had a bath and some breakfast and then I was taken up to the lines by the adjutant and put on a horse. He said, 'Follow me over some jumps,' and put me down a jumping lane, then more or less said, 'That'll do. Come along with me and see the remounts.' So we went over and saw some horses and the adjutant said, 'Take on one of these and go through with the training.' I selected a chestnut mare which looked very nice. The next morning I went out to mount the animal for my first parade and I'd hardly got in the saddle before it was all over the place; I was on the ground, the horse was on the way to the lines and I arrived at my first parade on foot.

Rather less typical was Kenneth Warren's first taste of plantation life in Assam:

Having had lunch, Bertie Fraser – with whom I was to share the bungalow – went off to play polo and I was left sitting on the verandah with nothing to do. I couldn't speak the

The A.-D.-C. ON DUTY.

THE MANAGER HOTEL.

	horse	घोडा
Please order me a	carriage	बग्गी
	Motor	मोटर
	elephant	हाथी

at_____ o'clock_____to take me

to_____

One hour's notice should be given and for Elephant
one and a half hour's.

Signature_____

Place :—

Room No._____   We found this in
                             the Guest House
                             at GWALIOR.

Date_____192

Elephant order form; guest house, Gwalior, 1931

71

language so I couldn't talk to the servants and I got more and more hungry. It was not until about eight o'clock that night that Bertie Fraser returned, having played two or three chukkas of polo and having spent the rest of the evening at the bar. He came home full of good cheer and called for dinner and we sat down for a meal. He seemed to be rather a queer sort of fellow; he was telling me all about various matters of which I had no knowledge whatever when he suddenly leapt to his feet, seized the lamp from the middle of the table and rushed out of the room, leaving me in complete darkness. I thought, 'Well, he is mad after all!' Then he started shouting at me from the lawn in front of the bungalow saying, 'Come out, you fool!' Then I suddenly realized that the bungalow was swinging about. I got halfway down the steps when the bungalow gave an extra heave and I slid down the remaining steps. That was my first earthquake.

Geoffrey Allen's beginnings as an assistant manager working for the Maharajah of Darbhanga were equally inauspicious:

Almost my first job was to bury my manager. He had been a very famous, very skilful polo player, a very nice person indeed and very happily married. Unfortunately he had taken to drink and this culminated in him being off work for about a week, when the general manager sent me out to take charge. I was let in to see him and I saw at once that he was very drunk. He cursed me up and down and said, 'You can get out of my room. I know you've come out to do me down.' Eventually with very ill grace he handed over his office keys and I took over. One evening, about three weeks later a *chaprassi* arrived on a cycle with a note saying that he had died from the DTs. This was the hot weather and anyone who died had to be buried within twenty-four hours. The graveyard was just beyond my house in a little grove, so I went out that night with a couple of labourers and two lanterns and spent the whole of the night digging by the light of the hurricane lamps. The extraordinary thing was that in this particular graveyard there were also buried the last three managers before this one. He was the fourth, all of them had died from DTs and all had been buried in this same little graveyard.

Other newcomers up-country made their first acquaintance with the land and its people. In Western India David Symington encountered the characteristic smell of the Sind plain, the smell of the salt land cooling off at evening combined with the tamarisks, 'an ammoniac odour which more or less grips you by the throat'. Meeting with 'great respect from the great majority of the inhabitants', he found it 'absolutely right and not surprising'. Kenneth Mason, posted to Meerut, found such respect unnerving: 'An Indian passing me got off his pony and salaamed me. I said to him, "What on earth did you do that for?" and he said, "Sahib, you are a young man. You will realize that in India we salaam those we respect. We do it to our Brahmins, we do it to our rulers." My comment was, "Well, you needn't do it for me."'

Some were temporarily disillusioned. Conrad Corfield, faced with an outside temperature of 115 degrees upon his arrival in Lahore, was lying on his bed trying to keep cool when a sleepy hornet dropped through the ceiling and stung him furiously, making him wonder whether he would not do better as a schoolmaster in England. Others had suspicions that required to be dispelled. Ian Stephens, coming to the Delhi Secretariat as 'a Cambridge prig', expected to be 'enmeshed in the administrative machine' and instead found his companions 'liberal-minded and far-seeing'. Penderel Moon, assigned to a remote district of the Punjab where there was no European except himself and no Indian officer who spoke English, disliked India at first but found – like so many others – that it grew on him.

For bachelors in the larger stations the problems of accommodation were simplified by the *chummery*, a household shared by three or four persons, with a cook 'who had to be accustomed to all sorts of late hours and producing a meal for any number of friends who might come at a moment's notice'. Since furniture was usually rented, the younger bachelor tended to live in considerable discomfort with only basic furniture; a *charpoy* bed and its mosquito canopy and perhaps some Roorkee chairs, made of canvas stretched on wood – and for the verandah, planter's long-sleevers, with long leg-rests and drink stands attached to the sides. Philip Mason recalls how when some young ladies came to stay in his bachelor *chummery* in Bareilly they were somewhat put out to find no curtains: 'We'd never thought of having curtains on the windows.'

Where there was no memsahib the running of the household devolved upon the bearer. 'The first thing I had to do on arrival in Lahore,' recalls H. T. Wickham, 'was to engage a bearer. There was no end of choice because bearers wanting situations would present themselves in queues with their chits or certificates of recommendation, and one had to choose from that.' Others, like Ian Stephens' Abdul Aziz, 'polished, humorous and excellent with my many guests,' were inherited from predecessors. The bachelor's bearer did the lot. 'When I was a bachelor,' recalls Percival Griffiths, 'I left everything to my bearer. A nice hot chicken curry for lunch and a mulligatawny soup and roast chicken for the evening, and that was the menu every day. He'd bring up the cook book at the end of the week and I handed out the money.' Ghulam Rasul, 'slave of the prophet', would tell his sahib, Penderel Moon, to get his hair cut: 'He used to say, "Your hair's getting long, I'll call the barber." Then I'd sit on the verandah and the barber would cut my hair while he stood and supervised.' Jackie Smyth's bearer was 'a frightful worrier' who never had enough to eat because he wouldn't take enough time off for his meals and made a point of sleeping outside his master's door when in hostile country.

This combination of devotion and personal service culminated with the dressing and undressing of those sahibs who could tolerate it. Cuthbert Bowder put up with it because 'if I hadn't he would have considered it not quite the thing. So my bearer used to undress me before I went into my bath and dress me when I came out of it and this literally meant putting on my socks, holding out my vest and shirt and helping me to put on my trousers and jacket.' Some would not be dressed. 'I found this highly repulsive,' recalls Norman Watney, 'and after two days of being a tailor's dummy I told my bearer to desist.' With a few exceptions – Radclyffe Sidebottom's bearer once enraged him so much that he 'picked him up by the seat of his pants and the neck of his shirt and dropped him down the lift shaft' – most bearers and their bachelor employers built up a close personal relationship that lasted until their employers married. Few such relationships survived the transition, 'because deep down they didn't like to see a European memsahib ruling her husband'. Rupert Mayne's bearer, Abdul, was 'a quite magnificent man but, as so often happens, he was a bachelor's bearer and after I got married we had to start afresh'.

While some sections of the British community – notably officers in British regiments and city businessmen – neither required nor made the effort to learn a native language, elsewhere it was an essential and even a compulsory requirement, encouraged by financial rewards or threats. In the Indian Army, where no soldier was – in theory, at least – allowed to speak English to an officer and no officer was allowed to speak English to a soldier, financial inducements made language study a 'paying proposition'. When George Wood, an officer in the Dorset Regiment, passed the Urdu examination in 1931 he got 'the princely reward of seventy gold sovereigns, which was the price of a pony that I badly wanted'. For Rupert Mayne, in the jute trade, it was a case of having to learn both Hindi and Bengali, as 'in our business contracts we had the ominous words that failure to do so would be taken into consideration in renewing our contracts'. In fact, learning a native language was perhaps 'the best thing that ever happened' to people who went out to India and those who failed to do so remained for ever at a distance from the land and its people.

The man who taught languages was the *munshi*, sometimes a scholar of considerable learning. Olaf Caroe remembers 'a very sweet old man with long eye-lashes and a beard, rather saintly to look at', with whom he had great arguments about Emperor Aurangzeb. 'I used to say that he was a tyrant who had overborne his Hindu subjects and undone the good which his predecessor Akbar had done. The *munshi* wouldn't agree at all. Our argument was a precursor of the deep-rooted Hindu-Moslem differences which have torn the sub-continent apart.' David Symington's *munshi* was Mr Chiplunkar,

A very dear old boy who used to dress in a white coat, a long *dhoti* hanging low towards his ankles, which was a sign of his high social status, a tight little purple turban wound round the head and a pair of steel-rimmed spectacles. He would come in carrying my yesterday's exercise with him which he wouldn't hand to me, but dropped on my table because, in spite of being a sahib, I was untouchable. We often went for evening walks together so that we could talk Marathi, which we did for a bit, then both of us got tired of my Marathi and we would speak in English. I learnt a great deal from him about the Brahmin's view of life and about Indian habits of thought and their views of political and religious matters. In fact he taught me a very great deal of what I've learnt about India.

The *chokra* also learned from his *burra*-sahib. Christopher Masterman, newly arrived in his district, was immediately taken on tour by his Collector, Charles Todhunter:

We started off very early in the morning and rode through the land inspecting things on the way, and all the time I was being given instructions by the Collector as to what these crops were, when they grew, what their seasons were, how they were irrigated and so on. After these long rides we returned to our camp and had the main meal of the day, which was a combination of breakfast and lunch, generally called brunch. All during lunch Todhunter was still examining me as to what I had learnt during the course of the morning's ride. And then after lunch I was despatched to my small tent to study the Tamil language. Well, after a long ride in the morning and going into a very hot, small tent, I'm afraid that my Tamil studies didn't improve very much. In fact I generally fell asleep.

Conrad Corfield, another junior Indian civil servant, also

learned much from example, watching his superior officer on one occasion move into a crowd of Congress demonstrators and 'gaze thoughtfully from face to face as though to mark well the features of each individual and bear them in his memory. No word was spoken but one by one the crowd began to melt till only a few loyal citizens remained.' He also watched him charm the villagers: 'I noticed that each gathering ended in loud chuckles of delight and I soon learnt the reason. He had a fund of Punjabi wisecracks of which few could be translated, most were proverbial and nearly all rude.' Learning 'by being put on a job and requested to get on with it' was another strong feature of the Raj: 'One had an initiative at a young age which one could never have got in England.' As a newly appointed assistant chief of police, John Rivett-Carnac 'was immediately put in charge of up to half the district with every possible case, including murder, robbery with violence and riot cases on my hands. The responsibility was very great.' The responsibilities of the young sub-divisional district officer were even greater; within a year of arrival and with two departmental examinations behind him he could be dispensing justice as a magistrate, first class, to some three-quarters of a million people.

Although 'built on European lines, with the same kind of taboos and snobberies', British social life in India was different in one major respect: 'It was twenty years behind the times.' It had also developed customs of its own. For the newcomer the first and most important of these was dropping cards on the station. The protocol for this 'absolutely ridiculous custom' was rigidly laid down: George Carroll remembers 'going out in the afternoon and dropping cards on various *burra* memsahibs, all dressed in my full Indian Police regalia, travelling in a bullock cart with trotting bullocks, my legs sticking out at the back with the full sun on my dress Wellingtons'. It was not enough, as Norman Watney discovered, simply to drop a card at every bungalow: 'As a bachelor I was to put two of my visiting cards in a little black box that always appeared on the outsides of my senior officers' bungalows. If the senior officer had a daughter it was the procedure to put in a third card with the right hand corner tip turned down. The reason for this always baffled me. You never got an invitation to dinner unless you had dropped a card.' Rupert Mayne, sharing a *chummery* with four others, failed to drop cards on a married couple: 'It wasn't until they'd been to the house on several occasions that one evening the lady said to me, "Oh, I do wish that you'd drop cards on us so that we could ask you back."'

The officers of John Morris' Gurkha regiment, newly returned from the war, had no cards and as a result 'were more or less ostracized by the local people because we didn't call on them'. The practice of calling reached absurd proportions in the larger stations, where 'You dressed for the occasion even though you never expected to meet anybody – in fact, it was socially improper that they should notice that you were there.' John Morris recalls how, when his regiment moved to Delhi; 'we were expected to call on all the senior officers at army headquarters and there were hundreds of them, so we used to parcel areas out between ourselves and drop each other's cards'. Just as you left cards when you first arrived, so you left them when you departed, writing PPC in the corner – *pour prendre congé* – which made it clear that you were going away.

The next item on the social agenda was joining the Club. For Norman Watney 'this meant the local Gymkhana Club, as against the Sind Club which was for the higher-ups. Armed with an application for membership my boss took me to the bar and I signed here and I signed there. Then he rushed around and found two other members who put their names on the application. Having now become a member I found that the usual custom was for the *burra* sahib to offer you a drink and without asking me whether I wanted it he order two *chotapegs*.' The next move was to revisit the club 'to see whether your cards had been returned. This meant that the senior officers had taken their cards, written your name on the top left hand corner and slipped it into the notice board in the club annexe.' One more essential had still to be completed: 'The Divisional Superintendent announced that he expected all new officers to join the Auxiliary Force of India. Considering it to be part of the white man's burden I had to go. Thus I became a private in the Northwestern Railway Regiment of the AFL.' Local detachments of the AFI, often in the form of Light Horse Cavalry, were to be found in all the stations of India. The Mutiny was not entirely forgotten; only Europeans or part-Europeans were allowed to join this local equivalent of the Home Guard.

The newcomer was also expected to conform to certain social standards. 'The British reputation in India was extraordinarily high,' declares Kenneth Mason who joined the Survey of India Department in 1909, 'I would have been the first to have told a man off if I thought he was lowering our prestige. We had to rule by prestige; there's no question about it. It wasn't conceit. We were there to rule, and we did our best.'

Kenneth Warren, isolated on a tea garden in upper Assam some years before the Great War, always made a point of dressing for dinner: 'If you lost your self-respect you were not looked upon in a respectful and proper manner. So in order to maintain my self-respect I put on a dinner jacket and dressed for dinner and I said to my servants, who were quite likely to get a bit slack just looking after a man by himself in the middle of the jungle, "Now this is a dinner party and every night is a dinner party and you will serve my dinner as though there are other people at the dinner table."' While such staunch attitudes softened considerably in the next two decades 'the attempt to push one into a mould' really only ended with the emancipation that came with the Second World War. Then it was best symbolized by the abandonment of the topee, leaving this 'status symbol of the European community' to be adopted by the Anglo-Indians, 'who practically wore topees in their bedrooms, because of the need to show that they were of European descent'.

The concern with maintaining standards was also reflected in the degree of 'vetting' that went on: 'I was full aware that my background, my actions and my manners were under careful scrutiny,' recalls Conrad Corfield, 'but as my family had connections with India, the name of my public school was known and I'd been through the discipline of an officer's mess, no obvious gaffes occurred.' John Morris remembers that over the question of newcomers joining his regiment 'the most tremendous argument used to go on for days over whether or not the candidate was a sahib and a gentleman. If he was the most fearful cad that didn't matter – so long as he'd been to the right public school.' This social snobbery could be extremely cruel. Irene Edwards, an Anglo-Indian nursing sister, had to overcome the 'terrible handicap' of a *chee-chee* accent and 'country-bred' manners; 'I had to learn not to offer my hand. I had to learn not to say, "Pleased to meet you." I had to learn to just bow and say, "How do you do?" I had to learn to say "Goodbye" and not "Cheerio" or "chin-chin".' She also had to face the supposed test of mixed blood: 'I remember a young subaltern coming up to me and asking me to open my mouth. I didn't know what he was after, but he looked at my gums and then he inspected my fingernails. Later on I was told that this young man was looking for the tell-tale blue gums and blue marks in the fingernails found in people of mixed races.'

Lord Linlithgow, Viceroy of India from 1936 to 1943, once admitted to Gilbert Laithwaite, his private secretary, that he had never seen an Indian rupee. Yet even those on less exalted planes rarely carried money about: 'It was like royalty. Everything was done by chit. If you went into a shop to buy something you signed a chit. Practically the only time you ever gave anybody any money was when you gave it to the caddy on the golf course, or to the cook in the morning when he had to go and do the shopping.' The great danger of the chit system was that it was all too easy to be given credit: 'At the end of the month you got a bill. Even though it might frighten you, the fright didn't last for very long. You either paid part of it or none of it and carried on to the next month. You weren't bothered by these chaps; they liked to get you into debt. They knew that sooner or later you'd pay up, to your detriment, perhaps, but you would. And ninety-nine per cent of officers, British Army or Indian, would pay up.' But if you didn't, you were in trouble because the non-payment of bills was looked upon by commanding officers as a slight on their regiment and by employers as a slight on the employing company. The unfortunate defaulters could, on occasion, be asked to transfer or even to resign.

None the less, the young Englishman, required to live to a

certain standard and return hospitality on inadequate pay, was very often obliged to live beyond his means. Herein lay the basis of one more unwritten rule: 'In those days we all married very much later,' says John Cotton, who went out to India in 1929 and married eight years later. 'First of all, we couldn't afford the luxury of a wife and family because our pay wasn't sufficient. Secondly, there was always a scarcity of marriageable girls and, thirdly, it was actively discouraged in certain walks of life and particularly in my own service. In the Political Service we joined at the age of twenty-six or so and then there ensued three probationary years during which time one was not allowed to get married. If one did get married then one was returned either to one's regiment or, in the case of civil service officers, back to one's province.' Similarly in Assam, as Kenneth Warren recalls, 'it just wasn't done to get married until you were a manager. Then you had a bungalow to yourself and you were in a position to get married. So it was only managers – and senior ones at that – who ever got married in those days.' When a newly promoted assistant manager on Kenneth Warren's tea garden 'had the cheek' to go and get married, the other assistants objected in the strongest possible terms.

Who one married was quite as important as when one married: 'There was one club in Calcutta where you had to come up for re-election if you married, merely for the noble committee and the balloting committee to ensure that your wife was of the requisite material and would not let down the side.' In one of the British regiments in India 'an unfortunate senior sub-altern was greeted by every one of his friends about twenty times a day with, "Sam, you're not going to marry that girl" – and Sam didn't marry that girl. The regiment was just making it quite clear that *that* girl was not going to come into the circle.'

But the young sahib did eventually marry. Though he may have kept to the pattern and returned single from his first home leave, thereafter he was free from social restrictions. Before the end of his second furlough the sahib had – usually – found his memsahib.

6

HOUSEHOLD

*Save for arranging a wealth of cut flowers laid to her hand
by a faithful mali, an 'Anglo-Indian' girl's domestic duties
are practically nil. All things conspire to develop the emo-
tional, pleasure-loving side of her nature, to blur her girlish
visions of higher aims and sterner self-discipline.*
                 MAUD DIVER *The Englishwoman in India* 1909

There was a great shortage of potential wives in India. The
Fishing Fleet did something to redress the balance but England
remained the chief source of brides: 'Men went home on leave
and got engaged and either married during their leave or a year
or two later, when the brides would come out to meet their
husbands at Bombay and get married within a couple of hours
of setting foot on Indian soil. This was made possible by a
special act of Parliament which did away with the premarital
residential requirements.' Such arrangements did not always go
to plan. It sometimes happened that a man went to meet his
fiancée off the boat only to find that she had already left with
someone she had met on the voyage.

The English bride, as Vere Birdwood describes here, did not
always transplant well:

They never entirely integrated with India and this was terribly important as far as the whole ethos of the Raj was concerned. The men were very closely integrated but not their
wives. We were in India, we were looked after by Indian
servants and we met a great many Indians, and some of us
undoubtedly made a very close study of India and Indian
customs, but once you stepped inside the home you were
back in Cheltenham or Bath. We brought with us in our
home lives almost exact replicas of the sort of life that upper

middle class people lived in England at that time. It was very homogenous in the sense that nearly everyone in official India sprang from precisely the same educational and cultural background. You went from bungalow to bungalow and you found the same sort of furniture, the same sort of dinner table set, the same kind of conversation. We read the same books, mostly imported by post from England, and I can't really say that we took an awful lot from India.

It was a shock to be met after a calm and lengthy voyage by 'the mass of humanity, the shouting and the jabbering, the smells and the noise, the poverty and the squalor, the cries of "*Bunby, bunby*"'. Mary Carroll, returning to the land of her children, thought it 'perfectly normal' to find a human bone dropped by a vulture on her doorstep in Bombay. But others were frightened and also lonely. 'Take a girl from a background which has no connection with India at all, to whom it's a totally strange country, and it is a frightening country. India frightened people, especially women. They'd been told you caught awful diseases, things like smallpox and so on, and they were all told about snakes and tigers and things which you don't really need to be too worried about in India.'

Since most brides married fairly junior officers or civilians their first homes were often far up-country. Thus, after meeting up with her husband and his colleagues in the Forest Service in Lahore, Olivia Hamilton was required to follow him to his headquarters in the hills, first to the railhead by train and thereafter on horseback: 'My husband brought me a waler – one of those huge Australian things – and he had the funniest little pony I've ever seen, roughly twelve hands I suppose. It either walked or it cantered. We had seven days of riding, anything between ten and sixteen miles a day, so you can imagine me bumping like a sack of potatoes and arriving at the other end barely able to sit down for my supper. But we arrived at what was going to be our little home, a very simple bungalow with just the necessities of life – no cupboards, but tables and chairs and two *charpoys* – and a lovely garden full of fruit and beautiful mountain scenery.' Olivia Hamilton soon found that her husband 'lived on the country. Only *chapattis* and home-made porridge or wheat ground on stones – and therefore full of stones – chicken and rice and no biscuits except ship's biscuits, which he seemed very fond of. If I wanted a plain biscuit or a cup of cocoa I had to write all the way to Lahore, and it took a fortnight to get a parcel and cost the earth.'

Some brides arrived in greater style, as did Rosamund Lawrence when she married the newly appointed Commissioner of Belgaum in 1914:

When we got to the station there was a band playing and banners saying 'Welcome to our new Commissioner' and rows of police on arabs all drawn up in the brilliant sunshine, looking very spick and span in dark blue uniforms with red caps on their heads. They brought garlands of roses and put them round our necks. Then my husband said, 'You'd better do just what I do,' and I saw him shaking hands. There were a lot of messengers and servants in dazzling white starched clothes with scarlet and gold bands all looking much grander than the others, so I started shaking hands with them, which seemed to surprise them. Then we got into a four-wheeled bullock cart painted white outside, with tigers and leopards painted inside, and drawn by great big bullocks with garlands of roses round their necks. We just sat there and rattled along with rows of people lining the road any saying 'Salaam, salaam.' I felt like Queen Alexandra driving through Hyde Park, don't you know!

A decade later, Kathleen Griffiths' introduction to her husband's first sub-division in Bengal was rather less grand. After losing the bearer and all the luggage on the way they arrived at Kontai Road Station where the only transport was a lorry:

Halfway along the road, after being smothered in red dust which blew up from all quarters, we had a rainstorm and a puncture. We all had to get out on to the side of the road where I was drenched in rain over the red dust. Eventually we proceeded to Kontai. Our furniture was supposed to have arrived but unfortunately it had been loaned to someone who had not sent it on to us, so for several days we had to stay in a *dak*-bungalow. My husband went straight into court and got on with his business while I borrowed a sheet and sent all my clothes to the *dhobi* to be laundered. There wasn't another European in the place within sixty miles of me. I had a week of this; then we moved into our bungalow and the furniture arrived – and much to my horror it arrived in pieces. There wasn't a leg on a table or a chair, the dining table was split right across, the mirrors were broken, not a glass or a cup was unbroken; they were all smashed. I felt like sitting down and weeping, trying to make up my mind whether I was going to stay in Bengal or pack my trunk and go back to England. However, I made up my mind. I told myself, 'Well, I fell in love with this man and I've married him; I'd better make the best of it.' So I decided to learn the language.

It took time for English culture to re-establish itself. As soon as the sahib left the house in the morning the new memsahib was on her own. Servants came for instructions and could not be answered. Rosamund Lawrence found that she was not allowed to pick up her scissors when they fell to the floor. Kathleen Griffiths attempted to plant seeds with a little fork and trowel, causing a deputation of *chaprassis*, clerks and *babus* to call upon her husband to say that it was not allowed: 'We will bring you ten coolies tomorrow to do the digging.' Wherever Norah Bowder moved in the garden a *chaprassi* followed her with a deck-chair. She also found – 'to my horror' – that her husband was being dressed and undressed by his bearer, 'even to the point of having his bath water poured over him. I found this extraordinary because when I first met him in England he was doing everything himself quite competently.'

Some, of course, felt perfectly at home and, indeed, regarded themselves as being back at home. They were the girls of seventeen and eighteen, not yet memsahibs but with the probabilities very much in mind, for whom education in England was merely an interruption of their 'Anglo-Indian' lives. Having only just arrived at her father's bungalow, Mary Carroll was killing a centipede in the bath when she heard her father running round the bungalow downstairs: 'He shouted, "Lock yourself in your room!" so I did, and then I heard the most extraordinary noises and a shot every now and then. I asked what was the matter and he shouted out, "There's a mad dog. Stay where you are." Eventually he shot it and I came out and saw this awful, mangy yellow thing and I thought, "Good old India. This is really it!"'

Similarly, Iris Portal found her father's bungalow perfectly familiar: 'It was exactly the same sort of bungalow we'd had in Lahore, and the thing that was very much India to me were the pots of chrysanthemums. An Indian winter garden in the north of India always has rows and rows of pots of chrysanthemums. *Gokhal*, my father's bearer whom I'd known as a child was still there, and far from welcoming me with cries of delight – the little missy *baba* come back – he was completely impassive. But there he was, and that was continuity.' Yet there was a significant change of attitude: 'Whenever my father came in Gokhal always bent down and dusted his shoes with a duster on the steps before he entered the house, and there was something worrying to me – I suppose I was the beginning of the new age – about any human being bowing right down to the ground before another. But it was an Indian custom and not imposed by the British.'

The memsahib's domain was contained within the compound, generally enclosed by a wall or a raised *bund* and containing garden, bungalow and servants' quarters: 'There was no kitchen as such in the bungalow because the cooking was all done by the natives in the cookhouse, which was part of the servants' quarters. The food had to be brought in from there and kept in a hot-case in the pantry which was in the bungalow. The memsahib did not do her own cooking, it was always done by an Indian cook on an Indian type oven.' In Eastern India where rainfall was frequent a covered gangway often ran between bobajee-*khana* and bungalow. Elsewhere a hazardous gap remained: 'We were having wild duck for lunch,' recalls Rupert Mayne, 'but when it reached the table there was a mound of chips but no duck, because a kite had swooped down and gone away with it.'

The bathroom was equally un-English: 'Now see that hole in the corner there,' Rosamund Lawrence was told by her husband, 'that is to let the water out. Snakes will come in from there, so you must always keep your eyes skinned.' The two main features in the bathroom were the earth closet – 'In the ordinary household you sat on a thing called a "thunder box" for your daily task and the sweeper removed the remains' – and the hip bath – 'You soon got used to folding yourself up in a tub with your knees up to your chin.' Water for the bath was heated up over a wood fire and carried to the *gussal-khana* 'in kerosene tins slung two to each person, rather like an old milkmaid'.

By comparison with the English home, the simple up-country bungalow with its primitive bathroom, white-washed walls and muslin cloth ceilings was an unattractive living quarter. Not surprisingly, memsahibs 'took a great deal of trouble to have nice English rooms, the same as in England'. Their first difficulty lay with the furniture: 'Just cushions and bamboo furniture and very little else.' What there was might well be standing in saucers of water to prevent the ants climbing up. Many memsahibs had still to familiarize themselves with the *punkah*, 'a long pole which hung across the room with a deep frill of material on it. A rope attached to it ran through a window to a man on your verandah who pulled it and made the fan move the air in the room. As a rule he lay on his back on the verandah with the string attached to his big toe, pulling this string and going to sleep at intervals.' Despite the advent of electricity the *punkah* and the *punkah-wallah* persisted in many outlying districts well into the forties.

The great difficulty with household furnishing was that so many Europeans were constantly moving. Because of this there was 'a feeling of impermanence. For instance, flowers grew very beautifully in the north of India but you knew when you planted some daffodil bulbs that you'd never see them come up. One did plant, and you even occasionally brought some furniture and certainly hung a few curtains, but it was all very transient.' Movement or the lack of it underlined the differences between the various sections of the British community: 'Whereas we in the army were on a mobile basis and hired our furniture, the businessmen stayed in one place year after year and of course they furnished their houses on a much more lavish and solid scale, many bringing out their furniture from England.' Others found it less expensive to have furniture made for them locally. It was considered 'rather smart' to have your own furniture: 'it showed you were better off than your neighbours.' Those forced by occupation to move frequently from one rented bungalow to another had also to hire their furniture. To do so they went, as Deborah Dring describes, to the furniture-*wallahs*: 'marvellous men who had whole *godowns* full of English furniture. We used to say, "I'll have that table, I'll have those two chairs, I'll have that sofa and those beds." If you were lucky and came down from the hills very early in the winter you probably picked out some jolly nice bits of furniture. If your move was delayed until later in the winter, then everybody else would have got there first.'

Most memsahibs added something of their own to soften the effect: 'I used to own all our curtains and all the material that covered the chairs. I used to buy printed linens and things in England and bring it out. It was rather nice to see a nice bit of printed linen on your chairs.' Gardens posed the same problems; 'Great efforts were made to grow English flowers, which generally looked rather sickly in the Indian climate. We could have had the most marvellous gardens with orchids and all sorts of things, but no, they must be English flowers.' Yet, as Deborah Dring explains, English gardens were terribly important:

You wanted to be surrounded by something that wasn't just dust and dead leaves. You could only hope to get a winter garden really. We had all the annuals, things like phlox and nasturtiums, and all those grew most wonderfully. It was wonderful how they grew – just to be ruined by the first blast of really hot weather. The hot weather used to destroy any garden that you'd made, so when you came back again at the beginning of the winter you had to pull up your socks and begin again. Of course, the great thing was pots. We had pots and pots and pots all along the edges of our verandahs. And very often when you left and went somewhere else the person who took over from you took over all your pots.

An Indian attempt at the English lawn was assiduously cultivated. 'Our lawns were made of a special kind of creeping grass, which we used to call *doob* grass. It made the most lovely lawn, so close it smothered most of the weeds. Of course, very often the rest of the compound was bare and hard.' Most lawns required constant irrigation and attendance: 'A little party of three or four men would spread out with a yard or two between them and go up and down the lawn on their hunkers, each man picking out a weed, with another man behind him with a basket egging him on. It was a nice way of mowing one's lawn.'

The memsahib's strongest link with India was through her servants in a feudal relationship that was clear-cut and long-established. 'Be very fair to your servants,' Olivia Hamilton was told by her mother before she left England. 'Always be very firm. Unless you're firm at the beginning, and also fair, they won't respect you.' Attitudes towards servants varied greatly, depending very much on the occupation of the employer, but were always double-edged. On the one hand 'one's attitude was that they were menials. You shouted "*Koi-hai*! Is anybody there?" and somebody came at once.' It was also perfectly true that 'the memsahib shouted and screamed at her servants – but then everybody shouted at the servants. They were the most frustrating people. They always had some very good reasons for why something wasn't done, which you knew – and they knew you knew – to be an absolute lie.' Yet at the same time there was 'a great deal of respect between master and servant and you felt very responsible for them. You were the person who knew whether they were ill, whether they had to be sent to the doctor or whether a dose of castor oil would do the trick. If you found that one of your servants appeared worried or distressed you said to him, "What's the matter?"

And then he would perhaps tell you that his brother was in trouble with the moneylender and you would either have the brother up or perhaps lend him money to pay off his debt. They gave you the most wonderful service in the world and in return you felt that they were your people and that you jolly well had to look after them.' This same feudal attitude allowed one to ignore the presence of servants, even when changing, as Radclyffe Sidebottom recalls: 'My wife would have the bath first and the ayah would dress her. I would go in and have my bath and my personal servant would bring in a drink and give it to me in the bathroom and my wife and I would carry on a conversation as if the two servants in the room weren't there.'

The question of how to address the servants varied with status. 'It was a point of honour with us in the established civil services never to talk to the servants in anything but their own language,' states John Cotton, 'the result was that he who spoke the language had a much better type of servant.' In much the same way Iris Portal was taught that 'you must never have an English-speaking servant. My father's attitude was that if you, an educated woman, can't speak the language of a man who is illiterate you really aren't fit to employ him.' English-speaking servants were very often thought to be untrustworthy. In the Indian Army it was generally held that British Army wives got 'scallywags' for servants, because 'you couldn't expect British Army wives to know enough to treat them well'. Although the government gave a grant to army wives who passed a test in rudimentary Urdu 'it just wasn't done'. Wives who knew the customs and languages of India 'would never think of asking a servant to do a thing that was beneath him or was in any way contrary to his religion'. The *pukka* memsahib was never 'tactless enough to bring back bacon from the Club and hand it to a bearer who was a very strict Mohammedan. One put it upon a table and the sweeper would come and take it away, because he was a Hindu and didn't mind touching bacon.'

The extraordinary number of servants required for every European household was very largely due to caste restrictions. When Marjorie Cashmore – newly arrived in Ranchi – asked a *mali* to remove a dead bird from the compound she was informed that he was forbidden to touch dead birds: 'So I told the bearer to call the *masalchee*, but the *masalchee* wouldn't touch it. Then I called for the sweeper and he wouldn't touch it, so I asked the bearer who could move it and he told me to send to the bazaar for a *dome*, a man of very low caste. So we had to pay to get this lad to come and take the bird away.' Status – and a highly developed sense of demarcation – also contributed to the general superabundance of domestics, who were there 'not because you needed them but because they were very strict about their own little trade unions. The man who waited at table might not be prepared to bring your tea in the morning; the cook would perhaps cook but he wouldn't wash up; there would be a special man to dust the floor; another special man to sweep out the verandah and so on. If you had a man to look after the horses he would need to have an assistant who went and cut the grass. As you rose in your career so the number of servants increased, not because you wanted them but because they insisted on it.'

But if seniority required more servants – and Gilbert Laithwaite recalls that on one of the Viceroy's tours in the thirties it was officially noted that there were 'also about two hundred inferior servants' – the easing of caste barriers and the rise in wages had the opposite effect. The household that employed two dozen servants prior to the Great War would probably have cut back to half that number before the Second World War. Average salaries in the thirties ranged from some 25 rupees a month (worth about £2) for the bearer, to 15 rupees for the sweeper, which was sufficient 'because nothing cooked was ever used again. It went out to the sweeper and his family.'

All household servants wore uniforms, usually white with bands on their turbans and cummerbunds in the colours of their sahib's service. Inside the house they went barefoot, 'the question of them wearing their shoes in the house never arose'. In earlier days – up to the threshold of the Great War – it was 'not considered right to inspect the servants' quarters, because of the purdah system'. In time this became the exception rather than the rule, with wives making regular tours of inspection.

Nor was it customary for the memsahib to go into the *bobajee-khana*.

While a senior servant such as the head bearer or the *khit-magar* might be known and addressed by his name, the others were referred to by their occupations only. The servants had their own hierarchy dominated by the twin figures of the head bearer and the cook: 'The key to the whole thing was a good bearer who was a sort of majordomo, and who was generally a Mohammedan. He would follow you around wherever you went on your moves and he would be the man who engaged all the other servants. When you went on home leave you paid him a retaining fee, which was half pay. You kept in touch with him and eventually he met you at the quayside, smiling broadly.' Wives who inherited their husband's bearers were well advised to leave the running of the household alone. 'I always found that if I left things to him the whole camp went like clockwork,' says Norah Bowder. 'Friends of mine who used to take the reins into their own hands had continual trouble.' Some bearers – even if they stayed on when the sahib married – never really accepted the dominant role of the new memsahib. George Wood's bearer, Mohammed Ishak, 'fought an endless war' with his new memsahib: 'I decided that my husband's grey homburg hat was rather nice for going out in the midday sun in, so I used to take it and push up the crown and turn down the brim, put it on my head and go out. In the evening Mohammed would rescue it from my room, knock in the crown, turn up the brim and put it back in the Major-sahib's dressing room. And every day this went on. It was not my hat and he did not approve.'

The cook was the great 'I am' of the staff, 'capable of culinary wonders at short notice and usually aided by an un-paid apprentice known as a cook's matey'. The best cooks had learned 'from our grandfathers and grandmothers. Their fathers had been with our grandparents, and they had passed the recipes down. Hence you got some recipes that even you didn't know. They learnt them all by ear and remembered them.' Olivia Hamilton recalls how even in the wilds her cook, 'a most splendid, devoted servant, could produce meals at any time of the day or night. Whenever you got into camp, the first thing he did was to make his fireplace, build his fire, get his charcoal from the village and get our meal ready for us. It was always three courses, it was always beautifully served, and almost anything I ordered he would be able to produce.'

It was not customary for the memsahib to intrude into the bobajee-*khana*. Instead, cook appeared armed with his account book every morning, to be followed by other members of staff in strict order of seniority. 'This magnificent figure,' recalls Mary Wood, 'would come in and we would gravely do the accounts for the day before. We had had so many plates of soup at one anna, we had had chicken for four, fish for four and so much fruit – and I would pay for that. We'd then decide what we would eat that day; whether anyone was coming to dinner. He would then produce a pile of plates and on these plates he would say he wanted flour, sultanas, this, that or the other.' Cook also did the shopping and always took his perk: 'If you tried to go down to the shop to do your own purchasing you were just asking for another twenty-five per cent more to be added to your bill. If your cook brought things for you he just put a little more on the list than he had paid, but that was his *dastur*.' *Dastur*, as Kathleen Griffiths explains, was an immutable fact of Indian life: 'You could leave your jewellery, your money, your bungalow wide open and nothing would ever be taken from it. Their devotion and honesty to you personally was absolutely amazing, but as regards their little perquisites in the way of food or making a little bit on the bazaar, all this was taken as part of their daily life and you accepted it. If I thought the cook was adding on a little too much I would say to him, "Oh, cook, I think you've made a little mistake; you'd better go into the cook-house and reckon it up again and then come back to me and tell me." And he would come back and say, "Oh, yes, memsahib, I wrote five rupees instead of five annas."' June Norie, faced with a similar situation, observed that her cook cracked his toes under stress: 'I noticed that when there was a large number of eggs or something coming up he'd stop suddenly and I'd hear him crack his big toe and I'd know, "Aha, you've got a guilty conscience over that!"'

Apart from his *dastur* the Indian servant was scrupulously honest and, in turn, 'you trusted your servants implicitly. Once you'd got your servants round you they usually stayed until you went, and you left them with a pension after you'd gone.' Characteristic of the close relationship between master and servant was the behaviour of Dorothy Crichton's bearer when his first son was born: 'He came to tell us about it. He was very, very happy but he didn't say, "I've got a son!" He said, "The little sahib's bearer is born!", referring to *my* son.'

7

THE ORDER OF PRECEDENCE

FOURTH CLASS

74 *Members of the Indian Civil Service of 12 years' standing and Majors.*
   District Judges in Lower Burma and Judge of the Small Case Court, Rangoon, when without their respective charges.

75 *Lieutenants of over eight years' standing, and Chief Engineers of the Royal Indian Marine.*

76 *Government Solicitors.*

77 *Inspector-General of Registration.*
   Sanitary Commissioners.
   Directors of Land Records and Agriculture under Local Administrations.

78 *Officers in the 3rd Class Graded List of Civil Officers not reserved for members of the Indian Civil Service.*
   Agricultural Chemists.
   Assistant Directors of Dairy Farms.
   Assistant Inspector-General of Forests.

   Excerpt from *The Warrant of Precedence* 1921

'Precedence in India was most important.' The stress on protocol and hierarchy that characterized the British Raj had its roots as much in Hindu and Moslem culture as in the British. Conrad Corfield, who spent many years in the native states, saw its origins in Mogul times when 'precedence was your place in court. Where you sat in the row or where you were greeted on arrival was the most important thing. For instance, if you were greeting a prince of a certain standing you had to go down to the bottom of the steps outside to meet him. With one of less standing you would greet him at the top steps and one of no standing you would probably greet while you sat in your study – and that meant everything to the prince. Another way of expressing this protocol was through the gun salutes. In fact, very often before a prince arrived a special envoy would be sent in advance to count the number of booms.' Protocol was important on both sides. As official representative of the Viceroy in a native state, the Resident could not be kept waiting: 'I was shown into the drawing room where I sat down. No ruler. I waited for a quarter of an hour and still no ruler. I thought, well, this isn't good enough, he's trying it on. So I said, "Do you know, I've heard from His Highness that the garden is vastly improved recently, I'd just like to go and see it." The ADC said, "Oh, no, it's perfectly all right, Sir, he'll be here any minute." But I said, "No, I'd like to go." And I went and walked away from the house through the gardens as far as I could on a very hot morning. I'd gone at least half a mile before His Highness came running up behind pouring with perspiration. The next time I arrived there he was standing at the bottom of the steps to greet me.'

Ian Stephens, who as a journalist moved in all sections of British and Indian society, found a strong Hindu influence in the hierarchy of 'Anglo-India':

The Brahmins, the so-called heaven-born, were the members of the topmost British Government service, the Indian Civil Service. They were the *pukka* Brahmins and below them were the semi-Brahmins, the various other covenanted services – the provincial civil services and so on. Then you had the military caste, composed partly of members of the British Army and partly of members of the Indian Army. They all strikingly resembled the Hindu warrior caste, the *Kshatrias*. The British businessmen, very wealthy and powerful in places like Calcutta but fairly low caste, were analogous to the wealthy but also low caste mercantile and moneylending caste, the *Vaisyas*. These were the *box-wallahs*, a term of contempt applied quite freely by the two upper British castes to the British mercantile community. They might be merchant princes of the very highest quality but they were quite inferior to the covenanted services and the military caste. This mercantile class subdivided willingly – even strongly – into two. The upper people said that they were in commerce, the lower people said that they were in trade and there was a hard division between them. A member of the trade sub-caste, for example, would find it impossible to get elected to the best British clubs. They were inferior, they were people who actually traded and worked in shops, which was very demeaning. Then you went lower down to the menials, the so-called Eurasians or Anglo-Indians, people of mixed blood analogous to the despised Hindu lower castes. Another category here was the unfortunate domiciled community, people of pure British race whose parents, for one reason or another, had elected to settle in India.

Indeed there was no need to look to Hindu society for parallels. 'Most ICS people would have been the sons of moderately well-to-do people and would have come from the greater public schools,' asserts Percival Griffiths. 'That gradually changed and by the time that I went in possibly two-thirds came from the big public schools and the others came, as I myself came, from an ordinary grammar school and had then gone on to university with scholarships. The Forest Service had very much the same background as the Indian Civil Service and the Police Service would nearly always be boys who had not gone on to universities, probably the same social class as the ICS but recruited straight from school. There were from time to time what we used to call domiciled Europeans who came into some of these services. They were very, very few in number. I think we must be honest and say that there was a feeling that they were not quite out of the top drawer.'

The 'strong attitude' of the ICS towards *box-wallahs* was said to have had its origins in the old East India Company's hostility towards interlopers. 'It's true,' continues Percival Griffiths, 'we did regard ourselves as being a cut above the *box-wallahs*. When heads of big business houses came to my district, while I was polite to them, I was apt to regard them with a great deal of suspicion – with very much more suspicion than I regarded the ordinary Indians I was dealing with.' Accusations of excessive arrogance, of being 'the pedestal mob' and 'tin gods on wheels' were frequently levelled against the ICS. 'People did call us the heaven-born and I suspect that most of us felt heaven-born from time to time. If British rule in India was good for India, it wasn't always good for the British. No doubt we did tend to get aloof and perhaps a little bit conceited.' Nevertheless, this 'ruling class was never much more than a thousand strong the whole of the time we were in India – and it had great power, far more power than the civil services in Britain. The Indian civil servant, whether he was in district administration, in the secretariat of the provinces or the secretariat of the Government of India or working in one of the Indian states, had a much wider responsibility and a more testing one. He had to deal with people, with problems of famine and hunger and administration in a way which would not fall to the lot of the civil servant at home.' The result was 'probably the finest civil service that ever existed'. Even if 'they were sometimes pompous and stuffy, they were the heaven-born to many people, not in an offensive way but in an affectionate way. I think everybody realized that they were completely incorruptible and also that they really were the people who ran India.' The ICS was also 'one of the best paid services in the realm and the pension was always considered very remarkable: "a thousand pounds dead or alive" was how it was described'.

Standing between the army and the ICS and drawn from both pools was another even smaller elite, the Viceroy's corps diplomatique, known as the Indian Political Service. As agents or residents these politicals represented the British Raj in the more important native states and principalities scattered through India.

If a Resident became on occasion 'very pompous indeed' it was hardly surprising, since his power, exercised independently and depending much on his influence and personality, could be very great indeed. As a last resort he might even bring about the deposition of a prince or a rajah. As representative of the Viceroy he often moved in atmospheres thick with protocol and formality. Even exchanging calls with a maharajah was a com-

GOVERNOR'S CAMP,
UNITED PROVINCES.

November 6, 1933.

Dear *Mrs Kendall*

His Excellency will be very
pleased if you will reserve Dance No.1
for him on Thursday the 9th of November,
at Government House, Allahabad. If you
will please be near the dais at the
beginning of this dance, I will be there
to introduce you to His Excellency.

Yours sincerely,

D. A. Lambert

Mrs. Kendall,

7, Hastings Road,

Allahabad.

ADC's note, United Provinces, 1933

plex business that required a junior officer – in this instance
Conrad Corfield – to prepare the way:

> I journeyed solemnly through the city to the palace in a
> cocked hat and a one-horse Victoria which had lost most of
> its springs. The reception room was an octagonal chamber
> on the palace roof surrounded by a pillared arcade. There
> were two chairs, on one of which His Highness sat, and all
> round the room were senior ministers of state and palace
> officials seated on the marble floor. My spurs clinked as I
> walked across to pay my respects. There was silence until I
> was ensconced on my chair. His Highness then turned to his
> courtiers and said to them in a deep, commanding voice,
> 'You may go.' They all got up, bowed deeply and moved
> three yards behind the pillars of the arcade. I presented the
> Resident's compliments, which the Maharajah accepted with
> a gracious bow. We then sat in dignified silence, after which
> His Highness turned to the arcade and said, 'You may re-
> turn.' They all did and sat on the floor again, whereupon I
> took my leave. Protocol being thus completed, the Maharaja-
> jah set out to call on the Resident and he later returned the
> call.

If pomp and ceremony dominated the native court it was no
less in evidence in the higher circles of the British Raj. The
Prince of Wales was reported to have said that he had never
realized what royalty really was until he stayed at Government
House, Bombay, in 1921: 'If the Governor was entertaining,
all the guests would be arranged in a circle and he and his lady
would be led round the circle and each would be introduced.
The ladies would bob to him and the men would bow their
heads, and the Governor and his lady would then lead the way
into the meal.' Here, too, hierarchy was clearly displayed. 'At
any formal dinner at Government House the precedence was
of the utmost importance,' explains Christopher Masterman. 'I
once attended three dinners running at Government House and
got the same lady beside me each time, strictly according to
precedence. I was in the secretariat, he was a fellow secretary,

so his wife was always invited to the same dinner as myself and I always got her as a partner. I really got very knowledgeable about her family.'

To assist in the proper ordering of official society the Government published a warrant of precedence which was added to from time to time as new posts were created. This Civil List, variously known as the Blue, Green or even the Red Book, was to be found on every civil official's desk. 'The Warrant of Precedence,' declares David Symington, 'was a very humorous document if read in the right spirit. It occupied about ten closely printed pages and showed the relative precedence of various jobs. If you wanted to know whether an Inspector of Smoke Nuisances was a bit higher than a Junior Settlement Officer you had only to look it up and you'd find out what their relative position was.' Armed with his book the junior official or the ADC could plan the seating for a *burra khana* in full confidence. Only those outside the system created problems, as Christopher Masterman once discovered: 'A Mr Abrahams had written his name in the Governor's book and the police reported to me that he was a very important international financier who was making a tour of India. So Mr and Mrs Abrahams were invited to a state dinner. As Collector I was also invited and when I arrived I was greeted by a member of the staff who said, "You must go and see your Mr and Mrs Abrahams." So I went to see them and I found they were very black, and he was improperly dressed in a blue serge suit. So I had the rather difficult job of telling them we were very sorry but they couldn't come into dinner, but they would be invited to the garden party. They took it very well.'

If slip-ups did occur it was often the memsahib who objected. 'Women,' says Vere Birdwood, 'have a way of being more vocal about these matters. The husband might accept with a shrug of his shoulders that he had not been placed in quite the right position, but his wife would certainly be extremely put out.' In much the same way honours were extremely important. 'In the rather lonely life of the memsahib it became a very great thing for her to think that one day she would become Lady So and So. In those days it mattered terribly because there was not an awful lot else. They were the only critical record of a successful career. When the Birthday Honours or the New Year passed and there was nothing in the list there was quite a marked depression in the household for a few days.'

Although the ICS might not have agreed, the army certainly thought of itself as on a par with the ICS: 'British society in India was represented by the Army and the Indian Civil Service. Others were not admitted to this inner circle of good society.' From the army point of view there was a certain fellow-feeling between these two groups: 'We keep the law and they do the governing.' This was strengthened by the fact that whereas 'the business people concentrated in the great ports and cities, the army served up-country where the only British we came into contact with were members of the ICS and the Indian Services.' Although life in the Indian Army was 'a real gentleman's life', there were gentlemen and gentlemen, and while rank eliminated all problems of hierarchy there remained the hotly disputed question of regimental status. 'There was a curious snobbery about regiments,' recalls John Morris, himself a Gurkha officer. 'The Indian Cavalry considered themselves the cream of the Indian Army and so far as the infantry was concerned the Gurkhas were considered the *corps d'elite*. The Royal Ordnance Corps and the Royal Service Corps, upon which we all depended for the necessities of everyday life, were looked upon as tradesmen. The greatest punishment that could be handed out would be a transfer from a Gurkha regiment into the Royal Indian Service Corps.'

Nor was there much fellow feeling between officers of the British Army and the Indian Army. Claude Auchinleck recalls how before the Great War the Indian Army was looked upon as a 'Jim Crow' army by certain British army officers, although not among the 'good' regiments: 'It was ridiculous because very often the officer in the Indian Army came from the same school and had passed out higher at Sandhurst.' Indian army officers retaliated by looking down on British army officers as birds of passage: 'Few of them learnt the language or learnt to understand the native way of life, particularly the cavalry regiments which were more interested in their training and their polo.' The British cavalry were considered to be the 'real snobs'. Iris Portal, married to an Indian cavalry officer, observed them at close quarters at Meerut: 'They were, of course, richer than anybody else. They had the most beautiful houses all down the Mall at Meerut; lovely gardens and beautiful horses. But they did tend to keep among themselves because they were able to live a kind of life that the rest of us couldn't always keep up with. There was a bit of jealousy, I must admit, but we accepted it in the Indian Army because we enjoyed despising them for knowing so little about India. We got our own back that way. We used to say to each other in sniffy voices, "Tut, tut, they have English-speaking servants who, of course, cheat them very much, we're quite sure."'

The *box-wallah* was properly the Indian commercial traveller who came round on a bicycle with 'lots of silks and shawls in a tin trunk which he laid out on the verandah and said, "No need to buy, madam, just look."' The European connection was said to have begun with a certain Mrs Wood, living in Calcutta, who prepared boxes of babies' and women's clothes and sent them up-country. In time the term had been extended to include all European businessmen in India: 'The army, who were always jealous of the supposed prosperity of the man in commerce, got back at him by referring to him as the *box-wallah*.' It was said against the *box-wallahs* that they 'did not get to know the real India' and that they lived in the cities and rarely left them. This was certainly true of the average person who lived around his office: 'He played his regular games of tennis. He played his regular games of golf. He rode, played polo, went out paper-chasing. He was a member of the clubs and had a fairly routine existence – the same golf four on Sunday, so many pink gins, the inevitable curry lunch, the afternoon siesta and, often, the same seats booked in the cinema for the six o'clock performance throughout the year, followed by a buffet supper and more drinks.' Perhaps some of the feeling against the *box-wallah* had its roots in class prejudice, since the commercial sector of the business community was curiously divided. There were a great many Scots from the Lowlands who had made good, or whose families 'had made their own way up from the bottom' but whose companies were leavened by young men from a higher social background. These two very distinct types were also to be found among the planters. Curiously, while tea-planters and indigo-planters enjoyed considerable status, sugar-planters and jute-*wallahs* did not. The latter were classified as trade and not allowed to join the clubs of the *box-wallahs*. Rupert Mayne, with a foot in each community, recalls asking a *box-wallah* to come to dinner with three jute-*wallahs* and warning him in advance about his guests – 'that was how deeply engrained this feeling was'.

Edwin Pratt, whose association with the Army and Navy Stores placed him firmly in trade, was 'disturbed by the way one section of a small European community could treat another'. In his Auxiliary Forces Unit all sections of the business community were equals and got on well together 'but once one got outside, the barrier seemed to creep up'. In his opinion it was a division 'greatly accentuated and maintained by the wives, who insisted that the social groups remained apart. Men by themselves are inclined to accept each other for what they're worth. Women never will.'

The British soldier had very little status among his own kind. As far as the Indians were concerned he was 'a proud person and always walked about ten foot tall', but 'if you were a (European) civilian your status was far above that of a soldier. If people were seen talking to soldiers they'd be written down in the same way as a soldier would be written down for speaking to a native.' As a result 'there was absolutely no contact between the white element in India and the British soldier. We were less than the dust and it is well established that Lady Curzon thought so too, because she is reported to have said that the two ugliest things in India are a water buffalo and a British soldier dressed in his white uniform.'

At the bottom of the pyramid, caught between two strongly hierarchical cultures and looked down upon by both was the Eurasian, who was traditionally said 'to have acquired the worst characteristics of both races'. The attitude of the British towards the Anglo-Indian was in keeping with the age and, according to one view, was 'tempered by the fact that while the earlier generation of Anglo-Indians, going back over one hundred years, came from good stock – where it was a perfectly done thing for good quality Europeans to marry good quality Indians – in the last fifty years many Anglo-Indians were the result of sometimes pretty trashy Europeans and undoubtedly trashy Indians, prostitutes and women of the bazaar and so on. So that while there was a category of Anglo-Indian that was of high quality, there were a very large number who were pretty wishy-washy. They had no strength of personality, they were accustomed to being underdogs and they had that hangdog "chip on the shoulder" attitude to life. Some of them on the railways did first class jobs, and some of them as individuals were delightful. But not many companies were prepared to regard them as high management quality.'

When observed from a different point of view this attitude appeared in a much harsher light. 'There was a very strong colour bar,' declares Eugene Pierce. 'Conditions in those days strongly resembled present conditions in South Africa, with this difference: that while in South Africa it is imposed by government, in India it was accepted by a mutual arrangement and by tacit consensus.' This colour prejudice diminished as the years went on, but it remained one of the least attractive features of British India.

8

THE LAND OF THE OPEN DOOR

It is part of the immemorial order of things, in the land of the Open Door, where the wandering bachelor – sure of his welcome – drops into any meal of the four . . . India is the land of dinners, as England is the land of five o'clock teas.
MAUD DIVER *The Englishwoman in India* 1909

The memsahib's household duties were not onerous: 'Half the women in India left everything to their servants.' The morning consultation with cook, the refilling of the decanters and cigarette boxes brought by the bearer, the issuing of clean dusters; these and other similar routines did not take very long. 'One would go and do one's flowers which were always there, an enormous pile laid ready with the vases already filled with water. Where the flowers came from I don't know, never from my own garden. One didn't enquire. After that the day was yours. You could very easily get bored.' With her children in the hands of the ayah or the nanny or even packed off home for schooling, the memsahib's day was long and difficult to fill: 'After about eleven o'clock in the morning there was nothing to do except have people come to bridge or to coffee – and then the gossip started; scandal, gossip and conjecture. The husband came home to lunch and after lunch you went to your siesta. After that you went to play tennis at the Club. Then you sat at the Club drinking until you came home to dinner, and then you may have gone to a dance or a party. That was the life. That was how it went on every day.'

With few outside diversions and the same small circle of acquaintances, with whom 'one became too intimate', the average station or cantonment memsahib 'got into the habit of doing the same thing every day and never bothered to break it'. Unless she was a woman of considerable character or force of personality she could easily 'shut out the great world outside the station, the Indian world'. When India intruded it was often to conspire to make the memsahib's life more indolent still. 'One nice thing was handing out all the laundry in the morning and finding it all ironed and neatly folded on the bed in the afternoon.' The man responsible was the dhobi, who came with his donkey and 'took away the washing to a water point where the dirt was literally bashed out'. Rosalie Roberts recalls how he sometimes 'turned up in a most smart shirt and it was obvious it was the police sahib's shirt he was wearing'.

Even more important from the memsahib's point of view, and very often shared between several households, was the *derzi*: 'He'd come along and squat on your verandah on a little rug with his own sewing machine, and you'd give him a shirt or a coat or a pair of trousers to copy and there he would sit with half a dozen needles stuck in his turban, each one with a different size or different coloured thread, which he'd pull out when he wanted.' In a land where new or fashionable clothes were not readily obtainable the value of a personal tailor was immense. 'If you were dressing and you suddenly found you'd torn your frock all you did was throw it out of the window and say to the *derzi*, "*maramut karo!*" [mend it!] and you wouldn't see it again until it was all complete.' The *derzi* could also alter and copy: 'If you gave him a dress and said, "Now make me one like that," he was too clever for words. He altered things awfully well and made something out of nothing magnificently.' But he was not perfect: 'If you gave him an old thing that you'd worn before, he'd reproduce it exactly and if by any chance you'd patched it you had to be very careful or the *derzi* would copy the whole thing – including the patch.'

Where there were small children in the sahib's household a *ghai-wallah* and his cow were often in attendance. Memsahibs were well advised to watch while the cow was milked. 'I found all sorts of tricks,' remembers Marjorie Cashmore. 'You would make him turn the pail over so that you knew it was empty when he started, but then he squeezed water in using a goatskin up his arm.'

Less frequently there would be traders who came to call:

'the Chinaman, who made very good shoes to measure – you would stand on a piece of paper and he would draw round your foot – and the Kashmiri merchant who would arrive laden with bales of beautiful silken underclothes and Kashmiri shawls and rugs and delightfully embroidered cloth.' Chits would be sent round to friends and 'we would spend the morning trying on, holding up, examining and bargaining for the most delectable articles'. There would be other itinerants: The snake charmer with his cobras and his mongoose, the shaggy brown bear that 'used to come regularly every winter and dance pathetically in the compound'. Norah Bowder also recalls 'a nice old gentleman, well thought of in the neighbourhood' who used to share the well in her garden – 'a *sadhu*, naked except for a G-string and painted all over, who used to astonish my mother when she was staying with us'.

In many other respects the memsahibs tended to forgo the little luxuries of life. Outside the major cities there was no such thing as a hairdresser. Army wives could draw upon the services of the regimental barber but elsewhere 'either you didn't have your hair done or you did it yourself'. Dentists were also a problem: 'There was very often a doctor but never a dentist, although there were occasional itinerant dentists, mainly Americans or Australians who used to travel round the up-country places and set up a dispensary in a rest house for perhaps a couple of days.' Since telephones were rarely to be found outside the larger stations 'life went on with chits. If you wanted to communicate you sent one of your servants with a chit.' In the absence of telephones *dak* became a word of great significance. 'We relied a great deal on the post,' explains Vere Birdwood. 'Our books were posted, our newspapers were posted. Everything was sent for, everything had to be imported. We existed on the Army and Navy Stores catalogue from which we used to order a great deal to be sent up.' The mail order catalogue was a major institution: 'Everybody spent many hours browsing through it and one acquired all sorts of useless junk over the years.' Two means of payment were available. With VPP or Value Payable Post, you paid the postman the value of the goods in the parcel. Alternatively, you paid only for what you consumed during a particular month. Reginald Savory recalls, 'a well-known firm in Bombay called Phipson's who had an enormous stock of every imaginable English, Scottish or French drink, and ran what they called a Cellar Account. They would send us up so many dozen of each and we paid for it as we consumed it. Once a year one of Phipson's men would come round and say, "Six dozen bottles of whisky. You've only got half a dozen left so pay up for the rest." Then he'd make up the numbers to six dozen or so for the next year.' The most surprising feature of the mail order service was its range, which included perishable goods packed on ice and sent on special trains to arrive at destinations on specified dates and at specified times. Ice itself was a valuable commodity. It could be bought 'when the mail train came through' from Bombay, or, if the station was large enough, from the local ice factory: 'It used to arrive in large blocks which you threw into a thing called an ice box and it would last for a day. Ice was essential, particularly in the Hot Weather. A drink without ice was not in the least refreshing.'

Despite the lengthy time lag, links with home were strenuously maintained. Bundles of newspapers arrived weekly in specially bound editions, as well as the more popular magazines. *Blackwoods* and The *Tatler* enjoyed a special popularity. Local newspapers were read avidly. The *Statesman* – 'the *Manchester Guardian* of the East, liberal and outspoken in a high-minded Victorian way and respected as such by the Indian public' – was perhaps the most important, although equally influential in Upper India was the *Times* of India, published in Bombay. 'Circulation may not have been large,' recalls Ian Stephens, former editor of the *Statesman* of India, 'but copies were passed round from hand to hand and widely read. All the big cities had English-language newspapers.' As the only major source of communication and opinion the influence of these local papers was considerable.

With so many limitations and restrictions to equable living and with an 'alien' culture constantly lurking in the background it was not surprising that some turned – where they could – to a rather frivolous social life and others, prevented from doing so by seniority or isolation, to the preservation of English conventions: 'One always had to behave in a comparatively circumspect manner in the matter of drink or flirtations, because servants were constantly hovering around – and one felt that one must show the flag.' In fact, in terms of sexual behaviour the British in India were probably no more immoral than in any other place in the world but 'whereas in England you could be immoral and get away with it, you could be immoral in India and everybody knew exactly what was going on. Your bearer would pass the word to another bearer and soon it would be known that Mr So and So sahib was having an affair with such and such a memsahib.' In the small up-country station or cantonment 'the opportunities just were not there'. In the cities or in the hill stations standards were rather different and varied with the seasons.

English conventions were also preserved in the preference for expensive British goods rather than the cheaper 'country-made' versions. In the same way, food was often made 'as much like English food as possible' even if attempts to Anglicize the cuisine beyond a certain point were much frustrated by India. Meat had to be eaten on the day it was killed and so it was always tough. Since the slaughtering of cows gave great offence to Hindus there were many places where beef was unobtainable: 'The result was that we had to fall back on mutton, usually very tough, or the equally tough chicken which was the staple diet of many of us in India.' Chicken, usually not much bigger than a pigeon, was 'always dished up in restaurants, in *dak* bungalows or anywhere else where one happened to be on tour. One got sick to death of chicken, whether curried or done in some other way designed to make it attractive.' Preceding the chicken there would, in all probability, be mulligatawny soup and, following it, caramel custard, known as 'custel brun' among Indian servants. Currying – 'the men always liked it' – helped to make meat tastier, and many thought that 'you got the best curry in English households'. Eggs – 'the size of pigeon's eggs' – became 'rumble tumble' when scrambled and 'craggy toast' when taken with tomatoes. Bread was made with yeast that 'came by parcel post every month from somewhere near Bombay and was appalling'. Butter came in cases of thirty-six tins and was always oily, 'except around Christmas time when it just about set'. Where it was unobtainable, buffalo butter, with added colouring to make it pass for the real thing, was an adequate substitute. Vegetables, salads and fruit had always to be washed – preferably in the presence of the memsahib – in bowls of water mixed with potassium permanganate. Drinking water was always boiled and some memsahibs insisted that this, too, should be done in their presence – although it was unwise to be too watchful. One of the standard 'Anglo-Indian' jokes concerns the memsahib who visited the kitchen before every meal until one day she found the cook straining the soup through a sock: 'She was horrified and said, "Bobajee, what are you doing? That's one of the master's socks!" "It's all right, memsahib," he said, "it's not one of his clean ones."'

The memsahib of the twenties and thirties did her best to keep up with her English counterpart. Fashions were followed as far as the climate allowed. The inappropriate costumes of the previous decade – 'lots of underclothes and heavy skirts down to the ankles' – had been abandoned for practical informality. 'I look back,' recalls Mrs Lee of the Edwardian era, 'and marvel how we survived.' Now slacks, jodhpurs and breeches were worn, perhaps 'because we were perpetually jumping on and off horses', together with shirts, sweaters, and tweed coats in the cold weather. Such bold innovations did not always meet with approval. Vere Birdwood's cook deplored the fact that memsahibs now came in trousers to do the morning chores. 'He thought this was really quite indecent. As far as he was concerned some great dignity had gone out of English life.' Only headgear failed to move with the times. As long as the British remained 'very much afraid of the sun' the topee kept its place, although double-*terais*, 'two felt hats, one on top of the other,' provided a more casual alternative.

Old-fashioned convention made itself felt most obviously in company, and most often at dinner, for 'it was in the evenings that old traditions were maintained'. Thus 'it was absolutely *de rigueur* to change for dinner. It was only natural to change after the day's work and what was more easy to change into than a dinner jacket. If you did not want to do this then you could "dine dirty", but it was not looked upon with favour.' Even this represented a major social revolution, as Reginald Savory describes: 'If you dined out pre-1914 anywhere in India privately, it was a tail coat, a boiled shirt and a white waistcoat, with a stiff collar and a white tie. Long after they gave this up in England we continued to do it in India. I even remember up in the Himalayas where we had to ride about five miles to get from our camp to the station club where we danced, we would ride in on ponies in our tail coats. We'd put our tails into our trouser pockets and trot in and dance there. Then we'd stick our tails back into our trouser pockets and gallop home in tails, white waistcoats and boiled shirts, the lot!'

It was not done to wear gloves in the jungle. 'After the first time I did this,' remarks Iris Portal, 'my husband said to me, "If you wear gloves in the jungle again I will divorce you."' But on more formal occasions it was still thought correct to wear gloves, preferably kid gloves. Rosamund Lawrence thought this 'a perfect nonsense. To wear long, white wrinkled gloves for an ordinary dinner was simply absurd. It cost a frightful amount, it was very hot and uncomfortable and it was impossible to get them cleaned.' As the wife of the Collector of the district she could do something about it. 'The Lady Commissioner sahib is the head of the station and she can do what she likes – so white gloves disappeared and everybody was relieved.' Only a Senior Lady, a *sakt burra Mem*, could comfortably afford to flout convention. Mary Wood, going out to dine in Simla in borrowed white gloves with 'a very exalted old dear, the wife of a very senior army officer', arrived to find 'her very dignified bearer on his knees on the floor solemnly using a flit spray up the old darling's petticoats. She looked at me and said, "Quite all right, my dear, quite all right. I find this very efficacious for the mosquitoes."' By tradition the Senior Lady also 'dined the station' at least once a year, inviting in turn every senior official in her husband's district to dinner. 'As a bride and newcomer I found this very difficult to begin with,' recalls Kathleen Griffiths. 'When you were giving a big dinner party you always consulted what was called the Blue Book.

You had to do this most carefully as they all had a definite precedence. I've seen memsahibs extremely annoyed when they thought they were being put in the wrong place.' John Morris was once inadvertently placed on the wrong side of his hostess and next day received a note from her 'apologizing for not realizing that I was senior to the other man and for having put me on the wrong side'.

The *burra khana* brought out the best in the Indian servants. Unexpected guests were always catered for, even though 'the soup may have been a little thinner'. Extra places could always be laid. Cutlery and utensils passed along the servants' grapevine from bungalow to bungalow as the need arose and guests frequently found their own dishes – 'sometimes even your own vegetables' – laid out before them at the dinner table. 'You never had to worry about the meal. You came to the dinner table and it was always beautifully laid.' Table decorations proliferated. 'The *malis* were all perfect marvels. They would take all day arranging flowers and making beautiful arrangements on the table. In every finger bowl there would be a sprig of sweet-smelling lavender or scented verbena.' The cook also contributed: 'Cooks absolutely adored to decorate everything with lots of colour, especially in mashed potato. They'd make it into a motor-car with little lights or a bird of some kind – usually with an egg stuck on the back to make it more realistic.' The 'toffee-basket' was another great favourite: 'They used to make the most wonderful pudding out of transparent toffee in the shape of a basket which they used to fill with tinned fruit and cream.'

Nancy Vernede's father was High Court Judge in Allahabad and when she came out to join her parents in 1931 she found herself involved in frequent formal dinner parties for perhaps sixteen or eighteen people:

Guests would arrive at 'eight for half-past eight' with drinks beforehand in the drawing room. The bearer would bring in the drinks and the head *khitmagar*, who looked like Moses, would preside in the dining room and see that all the other *khitmagars* waiting on the table were ready at their places.

Then we would all proceed in at about half-past eight. The ICS were supposed to be the senior service and it could be rather difficult because if you were a young bride married to one you were officially senior to someone old enough to be your grandmother, simply because you were ICS and the so-called Senior Lady. She'd go in with the host and sit on his right-hand side while the hostess would have the senior man on her right. You had to arrange the dinner party just so. The table was very carefully arranged. Everyone had their names printed and you just looked for yours and sat down. A lot of the older memsahibs became very grand indeed – ships with full sail – and took themselves very seriously. They were very fussy about position, but not so much our own generation. Everyone knew it was just a little bit of play-acting.

I can remember being very nervous of the conversation when I first went out to India. My mother would say, 'You must make conversation. You must talk first to the man on your right and then to the one on your left – and you must talk. You must never close a conversation.'

We'd have about five or six courses and it always took a very long time. After the savory the bowli-glasses were brought out with the dessert plate, little bowls with water to wash your fingers in, and chocolates and little oranges in a sort of syrup, and all types of dessert and fruit and nuts. Port and Madeira would be passed round and then finally at the end of dinner the ladies would all go into the drawing room, leaving the men with their port. They would have their coffee in the next room and then about half an hour later they'd be joined by the men and one would carry on a fairly formal conversation, I suppose, until half-past ten, which was the magic hour. The Senior Lady had then to get up and say she had to go home now. Until she'd done that no one could move. The Senior Lady had to make the first move and sometimes she wouldn't realize it. She'd be new to India and just wouldn't know, and everyone would hang on and on and people would get sleepier and sleepier until someone had to pass her the hint. But half-past eight was the time of the dinner, and half-past ten was the official time of departure.

After the guests had departed everything could be left to the servants. The host and hostess could retire to their beds – but not to the silence of the night. There were always the night sounds of India, in season the cicadas and bullfrogs, and all the year round the nightly accompaniment of the jackals. 'Some people disliked this,' remarks Raymond Vernede. 'I can't understand why. I thought it was a most enchanting sound, very comforting and familiar. There was something homely about it.' The last sound of all would be the night *chowkidar* 'moving around at night, clearing his throat and spitting'.

9

THE CLUB

*In any town in India the European Club is the spiritual
citadel, the real seat of the British power, the Nirvana for
which native officials and millionaires pine in vain.*

GEORGE ORWELL *Burmese Days* 1935

Any member shooting a pig be expelled the Club.

Rule Eleven, Nuggur and Deccan Tent Club

The Club was a peculiarly 'Anglo-Indian' institution. 'A lot of
fun has been poked at club life in India, without those who
indulged in this sort of sport realizing how vital a part of the
life it was. Getting together for games and exercise and talk
was really a very important part of our life. It was the social
centre of the civil and military station.' A club was to be found
in all but the very smallest stations: 'The ordinary station had
a club of sorts, at least a meeting place, with a few old books
and some drinks. The bigger stations added tennis courts, a
golf course, even a squash court. It was of particular importance to the odd civilian who had not got the officers' mess
behind him.' It also provided 'a sort of get-together place for
the women-folk,' even though they had no official standing and
their names did not appear on its list of members. The Club
represented the 'hub of local society', principally of senior
officials. 'There would be the Collector, the headquarters Sub-
Collector, the Sessions Judge, the District Forest Officer, the
District Superintendent of Police, the Excise Assistant Commissioner and several other officials from the public works department and so on.' Not surprisingly, 'there were only a
limited number of places at which there were any Europeans
who weren't officials'. At such places army officers swelled the

list of members and the club provided 'a meeting place between the Civil and the Military'.

Many of the up-country clubs had their origins in sporting institutions. When Kenneth Warren first went to Assam all the clubs were polo clubs and it was only in later times that these clubs became more social clubs. This mixing of sport and social activities was a feature in all but the largest stations: 'You had to belong to the club before you could play any games.' Those who could join were not expected to do otherwise. 'It was considered obligatory to belong, even if one never went,' says John Morris. 'I certainly paid my subscription over a number of years but I shouldn't think I went to the club more than half a dozen times during the whole of my military service.' Others, like Philip Mason's first Collector, felt obliged to go to the club: '"I regard it as a duty to go to the club at least every other night," he used to say. He was a very light drinker and always used to drink what was called a *pau-peg* or a quarter of whisky when he got there.'

Some men, usually by virtue of their occupations, made poor 'club men'. 'My life was so different from theirs,' recalls Arthur Hamilton. 'When a forest officer returned from a tour and came to the club he was looked upon rather as a jungle-*wallah*. And, of course, he was a jungle-*wallah*. That was his job.' Olivia Hamilton, returning briefly to society after months in the jungle 'used to be absolutely petrified. One put on an evening dress every night but one felt rather like a sort of Cinderella. You'd never seen any of the theatres, you'd never been to a cinema, you didn't know any of the people they talked about, who was the "Belle of Lahore" and who was the most popular person, and I just felt that I couldn't fit in.' Nevertheless, you were unwise not to become a club member if you could. 'If you didn't belong to the Club you were an outcast,' says Reginald Savory. 'Some people refused to kowtow to all these social things and refused to belong to the Club, intellectuals very largely, who'd rather spend their evenings studying history or the Indian language or the classics and who thought the Club was a waste of time. Either you were a rebel, and a rather courageous rebel, who didn't belong to the Club, or else you were a social outcast who wanted to belong to the Club and couldn't get in.'

Club membership was dependent almost entirely upon occupation. Thus F. C. Hart who was 'country bred' and so prevented from joining the Indian Police at the same level as his public school contemporaries, was able to play hockey and cricket with them but could not join their clubs. Similarly, in a district dominated by cotton mills 'all the office people – nearly all Europeans but some Indians – were all allowed to be members of the club, but the technical people, the men who mended the looms, who were also Europeans and skilled workmen drawing much higher pay than most of the white-collar workers, were on no account admitted as members'. Christopher Masterman recalls an extended committee meeting to decide the status of 'a new man whom they called a coolie-catcher, whose job was to recruit Tamil coolies for the Ceylon tea estates. We eventually decided that he was eligible.' One section of the community whose status was indeterminate was the missionaries. In practice 'not many missionaries were members, partly because they couldn't afford to be members, and partly because they had moral scruples.'

In the cities discrimination over status was preserved but softened by a range of clubs: 'In Calcutta there were quite a large number of clubs solely confined to the European community and even confined to categories within that community.' These clubs were 'very carefully ruled', as Kenneth Mason observed. 'As an army officer I would not have been eligible for the Bengal Club, which was mainly commercial, nor would a man in commerce have been eligible for the United Service Club. On one occasion two brothers came out. One was in commerce and eligible for the Bengal Club but the other was not, being in trade and a distributor of imported wines. He joined the Calcutta Light Horse and so became eligible for the United Service Club.' Europeans in trade in Calcutta found themselves in an invidious position, as Ridgeby Foster explains:

People who worked in shops were known as 'counter-jumpers' and even the general manager of one of the biggest stores in Calcutta could not get into the more select clubs. If he was in commerce and therefore acceptable the first club which the young man joined was the Saturday Club, which was a social club for dancing and squash and swimming and a generally active social life. Next there was the Tollygunge Club on the outskirts of Calcutta, a very select club with a six-year waiting list, which had a golf course, a racecourse and a swimming pool. Many people used to ride from it out into the countryside and come back and have their breakfast in the club. Then, when a young man got more senior there was the Bengal Club, which was famous for its cuisine and was quite a landmark.

The subject of Indian membership of clubs 'almost split the Empire'. Reginald Savory maintains that 'one of the greatest mistakes we ever made was to frown upon Indians becoming members of the Club. Certain clubs would not allow Indians to be members. They had it written down in their constitution. When one considers that it was not every Englishman who came to India who came out of the top drawer, and that there were in India some of the most highly bred and cultivated and educated men in the world, to keep them out and allow the Englishman in was nonsense.' Yet there was a case to be made for segregation in clubs: 'We spent our time watching our step and watching what we said – and there was a certain relief to go amongst people of our own race and let our hair down.' At the time 'it didn't appear to us to be anything particularly reprehensible and nor, I think, did the Indians feel badly about it'. Indian objections were equally understandable: 'It was unfortunate and unpleasant that the rulers should gather together and spend their leisure time together, presumably hatching up further methods of enforcing their rule and things of that kind.'

The controversy over Indian membership, usually presented in terms of a colour-bar, began with the ending of the First World War and was still going strong in the big cities well into the Second World War. H. T. Wickham remembers how the question of allowing Indians to join the club came up when he was a Superintendent of Police at Bishraw in 1921: 'The club

ALLAHABAD CLUB

List of Members present in Allahabad—October, 1934

Telephone No. 221

Name	M for Married Member	Address	Remarks
A			
Allsop, Hon. Mr. Justice J. J. W. ...	M	16, Hastings Road.	
Alston, Sir Charles Ross	M	5, Edmonstone Road.	
Anketell-Jones, Major S. W. (I.A.O.C.)	M	4, Napier Lines.	
Apps, Capt. E. H. (B.A.O.C.)	M	No. 11 Quarters, The Fort.	

B

Bennet, Hon. Mr. Justice E. }	M	7, Thornhill Road.	
Miss M. Collett White }	...		
Biggane, P. (I.P.)	...	No. 6, The Club.	
Bishop, T. B. W.	M	Collector's House	... Tel. 214.
Bomford, H.	M	Commissioner's House	... Tel. 203.
Botley, T. M. (P.W.V.)	...	Officers' Mess, 2nd P. W. Vols.	
Bowden, F. H.	...	Mirzapur.	
Bradley, T. A.	...	15, Thornhill Road.	
Braide, Major R. W. (P.W.V.)	...	49, Napier Road.	
Bretherton, Capt. W. (P.W.V.)	...	Officers' Mess, 2nd P. W. Vols.	
Brooke-Edwards, L.	M	Dufferin Hospital	... Tel. 335.
Burmester, Capt. A. C. (I.A.O.C.)	...	5, Club Road.	

Will members kindly notify the Secretary of any alterations or corrections to the above list?

Club list, Allahabad, 1934; few Indians and fewer women

was a purely private club supported by subscriptions from members who had to be elected and when the question of permitting Indians to join arose a large number of the members didn't like it. Their chief objection was the fact that the Indians, if they joined the club, would consort with the female members of the club, while their own female members were prohibited from coming, because they would be in purdah and could not therefore mix with people while unveiled.'

The 'Indianization' of both the civil and military services made it difficult for all but the largest station clubs to preserve their exclusiveness. Up-country, where Indian membership of the civil services made itself most felt, the racial barriers fell easily and with only an occasional upset. In Deradoon Kenneth Mason was asked by an Indian IMS doctor if he would put him up for the Club:

There were Indian members of the club, but a restricted number, many of them descendants of Indians who had been loyal in the Mutiny days. I went to the ICS Superintendent of the 'Doon and asked if he would second this Indian officer. The members of the club then voted. They had to write their names in a book and then put a white ball or a black ball into the ballot box. A certain number of names were already in the book and the balls in the boxes when I invited the officer to dine with me in the club. He was quite nice to everybody but halfway through he cleared his throat, turned round and spat on the floor. He had only forgotten his manners for a fraction of a second, but I knew that he would not be elected to the club so afterwards I deliberately made the ballot void by shovelling a handful of balls into both boxes, far more than the number of names likely to appear in the book. The officer was then politely informed that the ballot was void, but that he would be at liberty to come up again for election in six months. Unfortunately he got someone else to put him up again. He got two white balls and all the rest were black. There was a frightful outcry and we got a raspberry from Simla saying that this was not the way to behave. Fortunately, we had a list of people who had voted and every

Indian who was a member of the club had blackballed that man.

In the cities mixed clubs – such as the Willingdon Club in Bombay and the Calcutta Club in Calcutta – attempted to by-pass the problem. Elsewhere a head-on clash became inevitable, reaching crisis point during the Second World War. President of the Madras Club at that time was Christopher Masterman: 'We had admitted all European officers as temporary members of the Madras Club, but the General commanding the Madras district said that he would not allow European officers to be-come members unless we also agreed to allow Indian officers to be members. The commercial element out-voted the officials and by a very small majority it was decided to still refuse to admit Indians as members. The result was that the European officers were also not admitted under the orders of the General.' Other attempts to break the bar were more successful: 'I had an officer in my regiment who had been a cadet at the Indian Military Academy under me,' recalls Reginald Savory. 'I put him up for the club and they turned him down. I put the club out of bounds to all my officers from that minute. Eventually the penny dropped and this man was allowed to become a member of the club.'

The Anglo-Indians had their own clubs – and their own restrictions. Wherever there was a sizeable railway colony there were two separate institutions – one for the Anglo-Indians and another for the Indians. Anglo-Indians, in their turn, were 'allowed into corporals' messes, even some sergeants' messes, but the Officers' Club was absolutely out of the question. We were not bitter about this because not only the colour bar but the class bar cut right across India and we as Anglo-Indians did not allow the Indians into our institutes.' Nevertheless, it was with regard to the Anglo-Indian that colour prejudice showed itself in its rawest form, as Irene Edwards describes: 'I knew an Anglo-Indian girl in Peshawar, white with blue eyes, who was known to be Anglo-Indian because her parents lived in Peshawar. She knew I used to go to the club because I used to talk about the parties there and she wanted to join. I asked a lady doctor who had influence to try and get Celia in and she told me it was no use trying "because everybody round here knows Celia is an Anglo-Indian". I told this lady doctor, "Well, so am I." "Yes, but people don't know it here. You have passed in the crowd, but Celia won't." The club was taboo.'

Despite the external controversies the club itself remained 'a very friendly place where you danced or talked or looked at the papers or played cards'. Most were old buildings of no architectural merit, and were hung with pictures of 'dead and gone cricket teams'. The Madras Club was exceptional both in its fine architecture and for what was said to be the longest bar in India. In other respects it was true to the norm: 'Up above the bar was the dining room and the reading room; really one huge long room. On one side were rows and rows of single chambers of residence and some married quarters. On the other side was a very good library and another small dining room. It had a large verandah where people met and talked. Then the men generally drifted off to the billiard room or to the bridge room.' A number of minor conventions had to be observed, for instance it was not considered at all the right thing to go to the club wearing a topee in the evening, and the bar was a male preserve. 'No women were allowed near the bar. They had a special area reserved for them called the *moorghi-khana*, which interpreted means the hen house.'

As a social spot the club verandah on a large station had few rivals. 'On almost any evening you would see the club verandah, usually a long deep area which was cool and in the shade and fitted out with cane chairs and tables, occupied by literally hundreds of people in groups of two, four and upwards. They would be busily chatting among themselves, drinks would be flowing freely and you would repeatedly hear the exclamation "*Koi-Hai!*" which was the call for one of the servants to come and attend.' Within these 'basket chair circles' the conversation was said to be 'trivial in the extreme'. A small community continually re-meeting could not be very original: 'People talked shop a great deal and women talked about servants and children.' Gossip of the 'most personal kind' was kept for the 'intimate little dinner party among a group of your friends'. In mixed clubs 'politics was not discussed with Indians' and it was considered 'injudicious to talk too freely about women' – except in the hot weather when, with the womenfolk safely up in the Hills, 'the conversation was uninhibited'. Tales of *shikar* were frequently exchanged and 'a great deal of the conversation consisted in talking about So and So, somebody whom everybody knew in the UP and of stories of his eccentricities'.

While the expression *Koi-Hai* was used principally to call for servants, it had another meaning; the '*Koi-Hai*' was the old India hand, the 'character' to be found on every station, like the man who 'kept a tame cobra on his office table to discourage thieves and whose wife left him because he used to go to bed in his boots', or the Chief Medical Officer who 'fired all six rounds of his revolver into the bonnet of his car when it broke down on a lonely road', or even the sugar planter who 'used to turn out every morning with a hunting horn, immaculately dressed in a well-cut riding coat and a cravat and a riding whip, and go off to inspect the cane on his horse blowing his hunting horn and shouting "Yoiks, Tally Ho!"'

If British India abounded in – and made much of – its characters there were good reasons for it. Eccentricity frequently grew out of isolation, from loneliness of the kind that forced a colourful character of Percival Griffiths' acquaintance – later shot by Bengali terrorists – 'to play bridge with his cook'. Similarly, John Morris recalls touring in Gilgit and being asked to dinner by a local political officer who added at the end of his note: ''P.S. Black tie.' Fortunately I had been warned about this man and told that he was a terrific stickler for the correct costume and so had carried my dinner jacket for miles and miles on porters' backs all the way up through Hunza and Kashmir and on to the Pamirs.' For many officials there was the added strain of having 'to be very careful not to mix too freely or make individual friends'. It was also true that eccentricity appealed to the Indians. The night before he reached Bombay Ian Stephens was told by an Indian acquaintance that he would probably do well in India 'for a reason which may sound rude to express. You are a little eccentric and eccentric Englishmen in India – provided they don't get all walled up in

the system within their first five years – tend to do very well.'
Undoubtedly those officials who got on best – and were longest
remembered – were those 'queer Englishmen who usually
arrived at the truth', like a Collector under whom Christopher
Masterman served in Madras who 'impounded a village headman in the village cattle pound and wouldn't release him until
he'd paid the ordinary fee for release, on the grounds that he
was no better than a buffalo'. This same Collector scandalized
the local European population by 'driving from his residence
to the Club in the evening in a horse-drawn barouche while his
wife was made to bicycle behind him'.

Perhaps because it was such a conventional society 'Anglo-
India' both fostered and made much of its characters. Among
Indians too legends were assiduously fostered in life and preserved after death. Thus the *dacoit*-catching exploits of Fred-
die Young sahib of the UP police, remembered by George
Caroll as 'an enormous man of nineteen or twenty stone who
wore an eyeglass which didn't suit him at all and whose compound was always full of Indians', were embroidered into
plays put on by wandering Indian actors. Olaf Caroe recalls
how, on one of his tours on the North-West Frontier in 1927,
an old man was brought out to recount how Abbott, a famous
deputy commissioner, had told his people to stand firm against
the Sikhs in 1845.

In a land where 'sociability was gauged in very large measure
by drinking habits' and where whisky came at less than three
rupees a bottle, it was nevertheless a severe crime 'to drink too
much or to be seen to drink too much before your Indian servants'. Some saw this as 'a reaction against the heavy drinking
of earlier generations'. If there was to be any hard drinking
the club was certainly not the place for it, and 'if a chap
showed any signs of being half-intoxicated he was hustled out
by his friends. Every club had a secretary, usually an ex-army
man who knew how to cope with that sort of thing.' Those who
indulged to excess did so in the privacy of their own bungalows.
A plantation manager dismissed by Kenneth Warren was found
to have 'replaced one of the panels in his dining room with
hessian cloth painted to look like the rest of the dining room.

Through a hole in this hessian cloth went a tube which led from a cask of beer in the dining room to the bedroom.' Public drunkenness was exceedingly rare, although Kenneth Mason recalls 'a lady in the club at Dehra Dun who was so intoxicated that she walked off the end of the verandah and landed among some ferns and screamed for help from an officer who wasn't her husband'.

Even if the cities may have had the conventional habit of 'short drinks before lunch', up-country 'the custom was that at six o'clock sundown you had your first drink. We were very often quite punctual – but never before. You'd say "No, no, another ten minutes," and that was that. There was no drinking at all during the day. The normal life was to go down in the afternoon, play three or four chukkas of polo, come in and change – because you were soaking wet – and then have a good, long drink.' Right up to the Second World War it was still generally accepted that 'the way to avoid heatstroke was to replace the moisture content of our bodies'. A great deal of drinking was done in consequence – but not in the manner commonly supposed: 'Whisky was the great drink, but drunk very diluted with soda water and ice.' Wines were 'not readily available', although popular in messes. There was also 'the gimlet, really a gin and lime, a long drink very much liked by both the men and the women. But mostly in the evening it was Scotch which was drunk – *chotapegs* or *burrapegs*, as we used to call them. The *chotapeg* being two fingers of whisky and the *burrapeg* three.'

At the larger stations dinner on Saturday night would be followed by a dance at the club. 'In Allahabad we had one every Saturday,' recalls Nancy Vernede, 'and on Thursdays dances which were held just between tea and supper.' The Thursday tea dance was less formal than the Saturday dance, although 'there was always a band playing, either a military band or a police band and sometimes Anglo-Indian bands'. But on most nights at the club the 'evening get-together' ended at eight o'clock or nine o'clock, when everybody returned home for 'a thumping big dinner'. Those who lived near at hand might be escorted, as Rosamund Lawrence was, by *hath-butti-*

wallahs 'who met us with lamps and sticks which they banged on the ground to keep away snakes as we walked through the darkness'.

10

HAZARD AND SPORT

Horsemanship and physical fitness were the only gods he knew.

GEORGE ORWELL *Burmese Days* 1935

'Sport was the great thing in the old India', an obsession that had its roots in the dread that unless one kept fit one would catch 'some dreadful disease or other'. It thus became a credo of British India that to indulge in some sort of physical exercise was essential – particularly in the hot weather – and the result was 'a generation or two of enormously fit people' who went in for every sort of game and every sort of sport, all of it cheap and very procurable: 'This played an enormously important part in our lives. To have missed taking exercise in the afternoon you would have had to have been really quite ill.' Sport was something that both sahib and memsahib could indulge in equally. In fact, in Iris Portal's opinion 'women took far too much exercise in India. One was always told that one ought to take a lot of exercise. One was told that a jolly good sweat was a tremendously good thing to do in India, but I think it was very much overdone for women. They used to play violent tennis, or even squash in later days, or gallop about in the hot sun and get exhausted, and probably have to have a fairly strong whisky and soda at the end of the day to pull them round. I don't think that that sort of thing is very good for a woman's constitution in a hot climate.'

Sport not only brought the sexes together. It could also bring British and Indian together. 'Playing games was of great importance in your relationship with educated Hindus,' declares Christopher Masterman. 'I got to know Hindus of the educated classes by playing tennis with them.' In the Indian Army and the police, where there was always some sort of exercise between five and dinner in the evening, games provided valuable opportunities for British officers to exercise and mix informally with their men. In mixed cantonments casual games also provided a link between British and Indian other ranks: 'In the evening we used to go along and have a chat with the Gurkha boys,' recalls E. S. Humphries. 'We would invariably find them playing football and they would immediately split up and demand that we should join them. From then on it was everyone for himself, with about forty Gurkhas on each side, each having two or three British ranks playing with them and with the ball being passed to the British ranks by every Gurkha on their side.' In the hill country British and Gurkha also competed in *khud*-racing, 'starting at the top of a small mountain and making your way to the bottom and then running up another one'. It was a sport in which 'the little, tiny Gurkha men could lick the best of our British boys to a frazzle'.

Very few individuals totally evaded the usual patterns of sporting orthodoxy. Ian Stephens was probably unique in his time in taking up yoga and cycling to his office in khaki shorts, singlet and *chapplis*, followed by his bodyguard-orderly on another cycle with a change of clothing: 'When one got to the traffic blocks there were one's friends, the more conventionally minded *burra*-sahibs. They'd have no ventilation to speak of in their cars and the armpits of their suits would be drenched with sweat.'

Many clubs had golf courses of varying quality laid out, complete with local hazards: 'Crows would come down and pick your ball up and fly away with it.' Squash and 'club tennis' was a feature of sporting life in all but the smallest stations. But the 'man's country' demanded more practical and more aggressive sports, involving either the horse or the gun. 'I went riding every morning of my life as far as I can remember,' declares John Dring. 'I always kept a couple of horses. I used them for touring as a district officer or just for exercise out in the early morning. When polo was available I used them to play polo or to hunt if there was a hunt available.' There were many areas where the horse was of great practical value. In the earlier days on tea gardens it was often the only means of communication. 'A married senior manager or superintendent had a buggy, and could drive about, but anybody else – an ordinary assistant tea planter or a junior manager – was expected to ride rather than drive. Your company always gave you an advance to buy the pony because you had to be able to get around on a thousand-acre garden.'

Rather better financial arrangements were available for army officers: 'Every officer in the Indian Army was supposed to have his private charger. It didn't cost him very much and it was fed free by the Government, and was used by him for his military purposes. In addition to that, you could always get from the local cavalry regiment a thing they called a seven-eighter. You paid the princely sum of seven-and-a-half rupees to hire one of His Majesty's chargers for one month.' Not surprisingly, the Indian Army was the most horse-oriented section of the British community. This 'tyranny of the horse, which was regarded as a sort of object of worship', reached its peak in cavalry regiments, where 'one lived and talked horses. Although a rule existed that shop could not be talked in the mess, it was accepted that horses did not constitute shop.'

The horse was also a great liberating influence for the memsahib. 'It took you where you'd never get in any other way,' says Nancy Foster. 'You always rode early before breakfast, riding for miles across country, riding out into the paddy-fields. You went through miles of mustard fields or beans with the most wonderful scent. You'd meet peacocks strutting about, you'd go through the villages and all the people were very friendly; they'd offer you a glass of milk or some fruit and they'd chat. I usually rode completely alone and never at any time, even at the difficult times, did I meet any unpleasantness or rudeness.' The ride was a rare opportunity for the memsahib to explore and make contact with the real India, as Iris Portal describes:

I used to ride out in the morning, very often alone, out into the blue, straight out into the plain and across the rivers. I took any little path I could find. It was the most beautiful country, not at all as people imagine India, but all up and down like downland with big fields and little villages dotted about. If you rode through a village the dogs would all rush out and bark and scream round your pony's legs and you'd crack your whip at them and they'd run away. You'd meet the villagers out in the blue coming home from the fields, or as you came near the villages. I must have looked very peculiar, a white woman with a pith helmet on a big, black pony, but they'd come out and put their hands together and say 'Ram, ram,' and you'd say 'Ram, ram.' As you went along the edges of the fields you would see a little tiny shrine, or perhaps a little tiny stone, a sort of lingam with red paint on it. I used to ride past these and I always touched my hat to the gods of the country as I went by – because they're there.

The early morning often saw other sporting activities get under way, some transplanted direct from the English sporting scene: 'In Lahore and Peshawar we had a hunt. We didn't hunt foxes but jackals. The jackals gave you as good a run as the fox – in fact rather better. We had fox-hounds imported from England, and we had marvellous days, just as good as a hunt in England except that there weren't many hedges to jump. You jumped over ditches mostly, irrigation ditches, and it was more like hunting in Ireland.' A certain degree of informality was allowed: 'Only the hunt staff wore a pink coat and white breeches. Some of the field wore a black tailcoat, but hardly anyone wore a pink coat and most wore an ordinary jacket. Everyone in the cantonment joined in; elements from the judicial side and the army, from the public works department, and some of the locals – the landlords used to come out mounted. The Viceroy invariably hunted when he came to Peshawar.' Girls from the Fishing Fleet were always enthusiastic followers of the hunt: 'They rode anything with four legs and fell into every river and had to be pulled out and generally speaking added an enormous amount of sparkle to our lives.' The big cities were by no means excluded from the early morning meets. In Delhi the Viceroy and his staff rode regularly to hounds and in Calcutta, paper-chasing provided a popular alternative. Specially designed courses and jumps were prepared, a paper trail was laid and 'you went out at half-past five or six in the cool of the morning. The Calcutta Light Horse and various different clubs would have their teams and you would go paper-chasing through the jungle.' Ridgely Foster recalls how Calcutta in the early morning 'was just teeming with high-quality horse flesh. The sight of the Calcutta Race Course on a December morning was quite tremendous. All the main princely houses, Kashmir, Jaipur, Bhopal, would have their strings of polo ponies and they would be ridden round, each one with his syce on, each one with the distinctive *puggaree* of the prince concerned. People would be doing 'stick and ball' in the middle of the race course and horses would be having practice gallops.'

'Stick and Ball' – 'cantering around, tapping the ball, practising shots, getting your pony accustomed to shots on either side, under the neck and under the quarters and so on' – was in preparation for the one local sport which the British took up with enthusiasm. 'The obvious thing was to play polo,' explains Kenneth Warren. 'Everybody else played polo and you were expected to, and if you didn't like it, well you'd jolly well got to lump it. I once had an assistant who came and said he didn't want to play, he wasn't keen on playing polo, so I told him, "Well, if you can't play polo you're not much use to me. I'll have to find somebody who can." And that was the sort of attitude in those days.' Polo was played all year round, but with its high season in the cold weather, when the tournaments and the polo weeks were held. In the hot weather 'station polo would be a pretty low standard affair. One played to get exercise and one played only slow chukkas because it was too hot for the horses to play fast polo. There might be a number of the ICS, a couple of military officers, a policeman and perhaps an Indian superintendent policeman if one couldn't make up the numbers. We bought our ponies from Afghan dealers in the local fairs or we might buy one – and sometimes regret it – from a senior officer in our own service who wanted to get rid of one.'

A remarkable feature of the sport was that the more senior

the sahib the better his game. Younger men lacked the means to support more than one pony: 'You had to ride it down to polo, you played it in a couple of chukkas, and that was about all it could do because you'd had it out all day and then you'd have to ride it home again. But as you got older and had a little more money you'd buy a second or perhaps even a third pony. Later on you could perhaps have one in a buggy and drive down and send your polo ponies down to the club ahead of you.' Here again the army enjoyed a great advantage. Whereas in other services it often proved that 'matrimony and polo were incompatible', this was rarely so in the army – and never in the Indian cavalry where horses for the Indian troopers were smaller than the troop horses used by the British cavalry and thus suitable for training as polo ponies. As John Dring recalls, 'When the remounts had arrived at my regiment we British officers all paraded under the Colonel to see which of the newly arrived remounts might make suitable polo ponies for our own use. Our argument was that if a troop horse developed into a good polo pony he was, by the nature of the thing, a good troop horse.' The game itself was 'rather similar to bob-sleighing, in the sense that you move at very great speed on something else, with the added excitement that you're very often riding somebody off or hitting the ball with someone trying to stop you. You got so excited that you shouted things like "Damn you, get out of the light!" or "Stop sticking your elbows into my ribs, you bastard!" – without knowing that you were doing it.'

It was only a small step from polo to pig-sticking, which some rated as 'the most dangerous sport of all. You can't see the country you're riding over because the long grass hides where you are going, and you have to go at a gallop to keep up with the boar. The horse may put its foot in a hole or a hollow and turn a somersault, and the spear itself is also a danger because of the heavy lead weight at its base.' John Rivett-Carnac recalls an instance of a rider who dropped his spear: 'The lead butt went forward, the point entered the horse's chest and came out behind his saddle, just missing the rider.' The boar itself was a formidable quarry: 'I had several horses cut and on one occasion a big boar charged me on and got right through my riding-boot. The tusk broke off in the bones of my instep and made quite a nasty wound. I had my boot cut off, disinfected the wound, then tied the boot on again and went on pig-sticking – which shows how keen we were in those days.'

The first rule of pig-sticking was never to do it alone. John Rivett-Carnac had a friend who broke the rule: 'The boar got him and stood over him and went on cutting his back as he lay with his arms along his sides. He was cut to bits and had to have over a hundred stitches in his back.' In more orthodox situations 'hog hunters' armed with 'hog-spears' rode in groups of four. 'It was a cruel sport,' admits Raymond Vernede, 'but the boar is a very valiant animal and he very often got away. When he died he died gamely, charging you, and this was why it was so important to have a really sharp spear to finish him off quickly. I can remember being charged by a pig head-on and getting my spear stuck in the front of his head, and as we passed each other I was carried clean out of the saddle and ended up sitting on the ground still holding the butt of the spear with the pig in front of me stone dead.'

Pig-sticking meets were held in the cold weather 'when the crops had all been cut and the land was fairly bare'. The largest of these meets was on the flat alluvial plain of the Ganges near Meerut, when teams and individuals competed for the Kadir Cup: 'One of the sights of dawn, just before starting the first beat, was that regular sight of all the chaps standing round holding their spears up and sharpening the blades to razor sharp with a small stone. Immediately a pig broke the horse-man nearest the pig was traditionally the first on and would normally have the first chance of spearing it. The first spear got alongside the pig and tried to make it charge him. This was the moment you waited for. You held the spear under your arm in the traditional tent-pegging manner and you depended on the pig charging to drive your spear into the shoulder of the pig. If you didn't get the pig on to the point of your spear and it grazed off, of course the pig could cut your horse terribly.' Not everybody took to pig-sticking. 'I was persuaded to go out pig-sticking one Sunday morning,' recalls John Morris, 'on a horse which was lent to me by someone I'd never met in my

"Whoof whoof"
A clever old horse taking care of a novice

'Whoof whoof' by 'Snaffles',
a popular illustrator of India sporting scenes in the twenties

life. While we were waiting in a sort of thicket for the pigs to break out the Master saw me on this rather restive white horse and shouted at me in a rather offensive way; "Take that bloody horse under cover!" When the pig finally appeared the horse I was on simply shot away like a streak of lightning. It had a mouth like iron and I was totally unable to control it, but I managed to stick on to it somehow or other until we arrived at its stable, by which time I'd lost all interest in pig-sticking and never indulged in it again!'

Riding after sows or leopards was frowned upon, the latter for reasons which soon became apparent to John Rivett-Carnac when he and three others went after one: 'I was going full gallop when the leopard leapt at me with his mouth open and his claws out. He just missed my thigh and landed on the back of my horse, made claw marks all down the rump of the horse and fell off. Somebody else charged it and speared it and finally it laid down and died.'

Both hunting and pig-sticking were never more than minority interests and not strictly a part of the great pursuit known as *shikar*. Up to the early twenties the Indian countryside was still 'teeming with game. Along the road you could shoot peafowl, deer, partridge, anything. Of course, it later on got shot out.' The opportunities for *shikar* seemed almost unlimited. 'More than once we got bags of more than a thousand duck in a day with eight guns,' recalls Kenneth Mason. 'One's gun got so hot that you had to have a second gun because you could no longer hold the first.' The general attitude to this overshooting was that 'there was so much game that there was no harm in it'. In time a new attitude began to take over. 'Having spent a year in the trenches in France I had no desire to kill or be killed,' declares John Morris. 'I paid lip service to *shikar* to the extent that I owned a shotgun and a rifle, but I don't think I ever fired off either of them.' Conrad Corfield was similarly affected by the Great War and never found any pleasure in shooting: 'I shall never forget seeing a German wounded and apparently blinded by a shell. He ran straight for us and of course was shot before he reached our trenches.' Others tried it and found that they did not always enjoy it, like the man who shot a brown bear and 'thought of all the little teddy bears that I'd ever seen before and hated myself'.

Despite the example set by viceregal and princely shoots, where game was 'slain literally by the hundreds and scores were kept to show how one viceroy had fared compared with a viceroy on an earlier occasion', trophy hunting and killing to excess was gradually being replaced by a more natural philosophy: 'It was in stalking and in hunting that you had your fun. The actual shooting meant nothing really. The only thing was to kill outright.' Chief among its rules was the unwritten law – 'never leave a wounded animal.' Equally important was 'the surrounding of the *shikar*, the camp and the camp fire mentality, which was more important to us than the actual killing of the animal'. Part of that surrounding was the 'complete quiet and absolute stillness' of the jungles and the hills. Here *shikar* assumed a very practical role, as Olivia Hamilton recalls: 'When I first went to the mountains I'd never used either a shotgun or a rifle but my husband said I must learn to shoot. The first thing he taught me to shoot with was a rifle, then he introduced me to a shotgun. This was very necessary because often we couldn't get either a sheep or a goat to kill so I'd go out into the jungle and shoot some green pigeon or a pheasant for supper, something to fill the pot.' *Shikar* was not a sport from which women were excluded: 'It was commonplace and usual for the women, the wives and the grown-up daughters, to shoot and some of them were very good.' Geoffrey Allen's mother was an All-India Rifle Champion, adept at shooting crocodiles on the Ganges – 'In those days full of crocodiles'. A far more common experience was sitting up at night for a tiger or leopard over a kill, as June Norie recounts: 'I had no idea that the forest could be so absolutely quiet, not a sound except for the wind and the dead leaves on the ground. I felt my face swelling every minute from all the mosquito bites. And then suddenly I heard a rustle and then this noise, a kind of woof, and I remember my heart beating as I thought, "Ooh, he's there." He came right up against the tree we were sitting on and I could almost feel his warmth as he walked round and round the trunk of the tree.' Olivia Hamilton, in much the same position, had no such warning: 'Suddenly I felt the tree dip. I couldn't believe it. Something shook the tree. So I cast my eyes down and there was the panther sitting right under my knees. I couldn't do a thing, I couldn't move, I couldn't get to my rifle. All I could see was those whiskers twitching, the eyes glaring, looking to and fro to see what was around. I just froze. I prayed that my husband would shoot the beast. Suddenly he jumped down and went very slowly to his kill. So then I got my hands out of my mackintosh and I raised my sights and I thought, "I must kill

138

and not wound." I took a neck shot and fired – and with two or three bounds he was away. I heard my husband's voice say, "You've missed him, you've missed him." But as I stood up I saw him fall back, stone dead.'

The tiger, the very symbol of India, suffered greatly at the hands of the amateur *shikari*, its skin becoming too common-place even to be put on display in the bungalow. Yet it was every young sportsman's dream to bag a tiger as soon as means or opportunity allowed. Geoffrey Allen shot his first tiger at the age of seventeen: 'It was Christmas Day, I remember. They'd all started dinner and I walked in and said, "I've shot the tiger," and nobody believed me.' Yet 'shooting from a *machan*, once you knew all about it, was not very sporting'. Very often it was simply a matter of holding the rifle straight and there was no danger to anybody – 'except the beaters of course'. By the early thirties shooting tiger 'for the hell of it' had largely disappeared: 'you shot a tiger because he was being a nuisance or because he was a man-eater.' Only in the princely states did the custom of laying on tiger on a lavish and totally unsporting scale persist, with an often docile prey being shot from elephants' backs or 'absolutely surrounded by *shikaris*' by vice-roys, governors or visiting VIPs. Viceregal tigers were usually bigger than other tigers 'because when they measured tigers shot by eminent people they pressed the tape down every four inches as they went along instead of taking the measurements, as true sportsmen did, from nose to tail'.

Where tigers or leopards were cattle-lifters or man-eaters villagers continued to turn to the nearest European for help: 'They had tremendous faith in the European, to such an extent that they looked upon him as utterly fearless and a dead shot.' Sometimes this faith was misplaced. The Reverend Thomas Cashmore was once 'shaken by his toe at four in the morning and told, "*Sahibji*, in my house there is a very big tiger."' He sent for a friend of his, a policeman, who had one shot and missed completely, 'which upset the tiger quite a lot. The second shot just seared the tiger's temple, cutting its fur and sending it into a rage. I said, "You're a mug, you know, you really are. What are we going to do, leave it?" "You can't leave it," he said, "it's a wounded tiger. You borrow one of the villager's axes and crawl in, and I'll shoot the tiger over your shoulder." I thought this was a very bad show altogether, but I crawled in and he came in after me. It was one of the most magnificent sights I've ever seen; the eyes of the tiger glaring viciously and the muscles all rippling as he got ready for the spring. Then Alfie shot and fortunately for us hit him and dropped him like that. I went outside and said, "The tiger is dead." '

11

THE HOT WEATHER

If Fate cast her lot in the North she is called upon year after year to face that pitiless destroyer of youth and beauty — the Punjab hot weather.

MAUD DIVER *The Englishwoman in India* 1909

The new year always began with a burst of military splendour, the King-Emperor's Parade on New Year's Day, when on every parade ground in India cavalry and infantry were to be observed 'marching past, trotting past or even galloping past in lines of squadrons'. This was 'the Army in India seen in all its glory,' a sight that few watched unmoved, as Vere Birdwood describes in recalling the scene as her husband's cavalry regiment passed the saluting base: 'There was a great deal of jingling harness, the cavalry regiments with pennants flying from their lances and their horses tossing their heads, all beautifully groomed. I doubt if there was a man in the regiment who was under six foot. They were all physically perfectly made and handsome to the nth degree, with a tremendous martial sense, a tremendous way of wearing their uniforms, a tremendous pride in what they were doing.' From a child's viewpoint the parade was 'a continuous conveyor belt of different music and colours – and all the time the dust rising up from the *maidan* and settling – like a dream picture seen through a gauze curtain!' In fact, this dream picture was the Armistice Day Parade on the polo grounds at Poona and the child in question, Spike Milligan, the youngest Survivor represented here, witnessing what was perhaps the last blaze of Imperial pomp before the slow eclipse:

The most exciting sound for me was the sound of the Irregular Punjabi Regiment playing the *dhol* and *surmai* – one beat was dum-da-da-dum, dum-da-da-dum, dum-da-da-dum! They wore these great long pantaloons, a gold dome to their turbans, khaki shirts with banded waistcoats, double-cross bandoliers, leather sandals, and they used to march very fast, I remember, bursting in through the dust on the heels of an English regiment. They used to come in with trailed arms and they'd throw their rifles up into the air, catch it with their left hand – always to this dum-da-da-dum, dum-da-da-dum – and then stamp their feet and fire one round, synchronizing with the drums. They'd go left, right, left, right, *shabash*! *Hai*! Bang! Dum-da-da-dum – It was sensational!

Also in the parade were the elephant gun-batteries, which came on 'in a phalanx of six in line, all polished up, all their little toes whitened up. They had leather harness and the regimental banner was hung on the forehead of the one in the middle. The *mahouts* wore a striped turban, dark blue with a narrow red stripe, and they came in to the drum beat – ba *dum* . . . ba *dum* . . . ba *dum* . . . ba *dum* – and when they got in line with the Governor-General's box the *mahouts* would put their knees behind their ears and they'd all raise their trunks and go "Uuerghhh!"'

The New Year's Day Parade did not always proceed without incident. Charles Wright remembers 'one particular occasion in Quetta when we fell in and the right hand man was a corporal and a pretty wild boy. Now when they give the command "Fix bayonets" the right hand man takes three paces forward to give the timing for the other people to fix their bayonets. When the company commander called "Fix" this corporal took not three paces forward, but ran right through the bungalows into a carriage that was waiting there and drove off to the city and that was the last we saw of him.'

During the early months of the year the major social activities of the cold weather, which had reached their peak over Christmas week, gradually diminished in scale and frequency. In early March 'the Fishing Fleet left, complete with the Returned Empties who had tried their best and failed'. An early blossoming of summer flowers ensured that most stations had a flower show at least once a year, and just before the end of the cold weather the 'outstanding social event of the year' took place in Delhi, with garden parties, polo and tennis tournaments and horse shows, played out against the background of the Red Fort – 'a superabundance of gaiety and pleasure' that culminated in the Viceroy's Ball, 'like something out of the Prisoner of Zenda'.

India's climate followed an annual cycle of three distinct seasons: Cold Weather, Hot Weather and Rains. In South India the climate was said to be 'hot part of the year and hotter the rest of the year. It was never pleasantly cool in the so-called Cold Weather, but the temperature never rose as high in the Hot Weather as it does in Central or North India.' In Upper India the extremes and the effect on life styles were more dramatic. There was no spring to speak of: 'You go straight from a quite tolerable climate into an intolerable one.' In mid-April, 'something happens' as Reginald Savory describes:

The wind drops, the sun gets sharper, the shadows go black and you know you're in for five months of utter physical discomfort. Mentally you have to battle against this heat. Physically you try and shut it out. When I first went out there was no electric light, there were no fridges and no electric fans – and to live in those conditions is pretty foul. We talked about 'shutting out' the heat. Hurdles of dried straw called *khas-khas tatties* were put across the open doors and the verandah, and a man would be kept outside to fling water on them now and again, so that such air as did come into the bungalow was mildly cooled. I can smell to this day the nasty, mildew smell of the water on these *khas-khas tatties*.

We never slept indoors in the hot weather. We always slept outside on the lawn under a mosquito net, with a little table by our sides with a thermos flask or something with cold water in it – and with our shoes always on a chair because if you left them on the ground they might be occupied by a snake or a scorpion. One used to lie and look through the top of one's mosquito net at the stars. It was peaceful, but very hot. Then in the early morning it would start cooling down. At about four o'clock you'd drop off to sleep. And then up the sun came over the horizon and hit you a crack with its heat. The result was you took up your bed and walked into a bungalow which was still over-heated from the night before and which was oozing heat.

The glare was one of the things that I found most trying. It used to strike right through your eyes into the back of your head. The first rays of sun that came through the windows struck the floor almost like a searchlight. One would wander round outside when one had to with half-shut eyes. Heat, light, headaches – right up to September. You think it's never going to finish. Then one day you hear, miles up in the skies, the honk honk of geese or wild cranes, and you know that they are the advance guard of the cool weather coming down from wherever it may be – Siberia or somewhere. It's the most wonderful sound in the world. And you say to yourself. 'Thank God the *kulang* know it's cooling down. It'll be all right in another fortnight or three weeks' time.'

Until the advent of air-conditioning the hot weather had to be suffered 'like toothache'. Penderel Moon recalls how 'as the year came round and you got to April you began to think, "Hell, another six months!" About the first week of May when you thought, "Now we're in it" my bearer would suddenly produce a mango, and that was the one redeeming feature. Then you knew you'd got this fearful grind of work throughout the hot weather with no relief, no let up.' It was a time when 'you longed for a grey English day', with 'the heat coming off the ground and up your shorts and hitting you in an unbelievable manner'. Unbelievable temperatures by day – the heat registering over a hundred and thirty degrees under a banyan tree – torrid afternoons with 'the air so still that if you ran a razor blade down it you could almost part it and walk through', and sleeping by night in the garden 'in a foretaste of Hades'.

The hot weather had its own characteristic accompaniments. There were the *koels* and brain-fever birds whose calls went

ayah with missy baba, c. 1900; in many European households the figure of the native nurse dominated the nursery, to be gradually superseded by that of the British nanny or governess.

Going up to the hills, children in doolies, Naini Tal, 1919; it was customary f[or]
women and children to pass the hot weather in a hill-station.

Interior, Forest Officer's bungalow. The jungle wallah often lived in far simpler
and less European style than his counterparts on larger stations.

he memsahib; Collector's wife, Belgaum, c. 1916. Often a victim of her own
inventions, the memsahib found it hard to acquire a positive role in a male-
oriented society.

Arrival in India; unloading at the quayside, Karachi, 1909

Up-country bungalow, Bombay Presidency, c. 1910; with flower-pots rather tha
flowerbeds, due to frequent transfers.

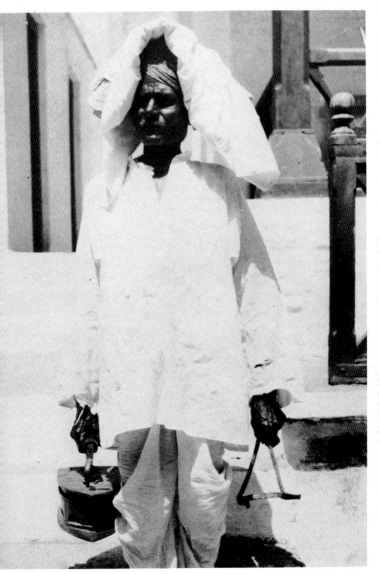

obi, with hot iron and laundry.

The boxwallahs; although looked down upon by both civil and military officers those in commerce generally lived in greater style. Cawnpore, 1921.

The missionaries; medical missionary in the field, 1931. Like the Eurasians, the missionaries had no place in British society — but by their own choice.

e sport of rajahs and viceroys; Lord Willingdon and tiger, 1933. By the thirties
r-shooting for sport was largely left to the VIPs.

-sticking; a cruel but risky sport, demanding nerve and a high degree of
rsemanship. Participants and wives at the annual Kadir Cup meet near Meerut,
1910.

The warrior caste; officers and their wives, Sam Browne's Cavalry (Frontier Force), Rawalpindi, 1930.

Route March; British troops on the Grand Trunk Road, scenes almost unchang since the days of Kipling.

right up the scale 'rather like a man describing a race, though it was never regular. You waited for those last few notes and they would always come a few half-beats off.' Another 'very monotonous and very trying sound' was that of the tin-pot bird, 'a hammer sound all the time like a small cotton-ginning factory'. A night sound which disturbed those trying to sleep outside on their lawns was the sound of jackals howling 'like babies being torn limb from limb' and in townships there was the incessant barking of pariahs. It was a time of year when 'mad dogs often came around' and stray dogs were destroyed on sight.

'I lost four dogs from rabies,' states Jackie Smyth. 'It was a very dangerous affair because if you had a dog that died of rabies you had to make up your mind whether you'd been licked by the dog.' The vital need for treatment at an early stage and the impossibility of knowing for certain whether rabies had been transmitted could turn a brush with the disease into a frightening gamble with death. In Delhi Jackie Smyth's dog, named Kim, was frequently taken for walks by one of the daughters of the Adjutant-General: 'Kim contracted rabies and died and I couldn't think of anyone who'd been in contact with him the week before he died. Shortly after the time limit for treatment had passed I was round at the Adjutant-General's house when the girl said, "Oh, Jackie, I forgot to tell you. I took Kim out last week and he was so glad to see me he licked me all over my face." My heart stood still – because at that stage nothing could be done about it. I had to make up my mind whether I was going to tell her father or anyone at all, and I came to the conclusion that it was quite useless and I'd got to bear it myself. I started to come round to call at their house almost every other day and they began to think that I had intentions with regard to the daughter, because I was always asking how she was. I knew it was all right if the rabies didn't come out within another week – and thank goodness, it was all right.'

The hot weather saw the employment of *punkah-wallahs*, for the hand-pulled fans in those bungalows without electricity and at evening time there appeared the *bheesti* with his goatskin bag, going round the bungalow sprinkling water into the dust and, with it, the unforgettable smell of evening: 'the smell of the grass when the heat has gone off it, dry heat and a quick cooling'. There were other ways of making the best of the hot weather. The first of these was to work and take exercise in the cool of the morning. Fitness was all-important and 'the only way to keep yourself fit is constant and regular exercise, being careful in your diet and your drink'. When the nights became intolerable 'we used to wrap ourselves in a wet sheet and lie down in it, so as to get the evaporation to cool us off a bit'. In the days before refrigerators there were simpler devices for keeping food and drinks cool. There was the ice box, which required replenishing every day and, where there was no ice, earthenware pots hung from trees in wetted straw-matting bags. Wherever possible movement and travel were avoided. 'I knew it was going to be a hot day,' recalls Norman Watney, 'because for the last thirty miles in the train I had stood up with my topee on, quite unable to sit on the hot seats.' Those forced to travel by train did well to secure a large block of ice so that 'you could sit with your feet on it until it melted away'.

The only sure way of beating the hot weather entirely was to avoid it. The time-honoured custom of taking refuge in the Hills persisted till the Second World War. Central and state secretariats retired annually to the nearest hill stations and wives and children followed suit, with a number of husbands taking local leave to join them for a month or two. 'Bachelors helped out by taking their leave in the cold weather so that they could be present in the hot weather to allow married officers to get away up to the Hills. It was done quite willingly, with great camaraderie.' Not all the womenfolk retired to the Hills. In the twenties and thirties an increasing number took to staying behind with their husbands. 'I always stayed behind if I could,' Frances Smyth recounts. 'The great thing was not to take any notice of the hot weather. I loved the hot weather because it was a challenge. I remember I used to say, "A wife's place is with her husband," but it was really because I wanted to stay in the plains myself. When all the women and children left, India heaved a deep sigh of relief and became herself. You really felt that you were getting to know the real India and not just the superficial British cantonment type of India.'

For those who stayed behind life continued, but in a more subdued manner. 'In the small district you had no companionship, you had no women, no club life. You did your work, you had your meals, if there was any shooting you would go out and do some shooting, you then had dinner and went to bed.' For John Rivett-Carnac 'the hot weather was quite the worst period of my life. Whenever I feel bored or lonely now I cast my mind back to what I went through and realize that I'm in heaven by comparison.' Where there was a club its role became doubly important. 'One lived in one's house – which was darkened to keep out the heat – in the gloom rather like a prison, and you just felt in the evening that you must escape.' In darkened offices and courts work went on throughout the summer: 'We had fans but even a fan couldn't cope with the climate after midday. It was really a struggle to keep awake, your papers were flying all over the place and your arms were covered with sweat. If you inadvertently put your arm down on something which had been written in ink, the ink was blurred and your arm was dirtied. It was not until we got air-conditioning that one realized just what a difference it made.' In the cities a certain social life also continued, as Radclyffe Sidebottom recounts of Calcutta: 'When the Fishing Fleet left you became freer. The weather was hot and passions were high and you behaved in quite a different way. The girls that you couldn't be seen with during the cold weather, the Eurasians and the "poor whites" who were absolutely riddled with sex and very beautiful, were comparatively fair game. You hadn't got to marry them and they courted you. Moonlight picnics were a very common event. You drove your cars or you rode your horses out until you came to a peepul tree. There you took out your cold chicken and your champagne or whatever it was and you had your party.'

Of those forced to endure the hot weather, few were worse off than the ordinary British soldier. 'You longed to go to the Hills,' states Ed Brown, 'but it was only the married people or boys who went to the Hills. The ordinary soldier was left on the plains. In the really hot weather he used to finish at nine a.m. and for the rest of the day had to occupy himself as best he could. You weren't allowed to go out, except to the latrine, and from then on you were incarcerated in your bungalow. It became dreadfully monotonous. The soldier sweated it out in one long torment of heat.' Spike Milligan remembers the soldiers on their *charpoys* in the barrack-rooms: 'They'd lie there, many of them naked, under a mosquito net to keep the flies off, and the only thing moving was the *punkah* above them going backwards and forwards, backwards and forwards. Many a man just sat there and watched the *punkahs*. I suppose there was little else one could do but just watch.' The army attitude to the hot weather was simple: 'It was just not recognized.' The daily routines continued barely modified: 'I remember seeing regiments go by starting a route march and I thought they were wearing a different colour uniform at the back because they were just soaked with sweat. There was a spine-pad parade first thing in the morning and these spine-pads used to get soaked through with sweat and transfer it on to their uniforms. But you never saw them slacking. They were very fit indeed and there was no surplus of fat on any soldier I ever saw.' It was a time when tempers frayed, when 'many arguments used to go on and sometimes blows were struck'. Charles Wright recalls how in Multan it was 'so hot and so dusty and so boring that it got on people's nerves. I remember one sergeant, he may have had bad news from home, I don't know, but he got his rifle and put a bullet through his head in his bunk.' Mental illness had no place in the army vocabulary. 'It was all just bad discipline,' says Stephen Bentley. 'Where a weak-minded chap's mind snapped in the heat then, of course, they said, "This is a breakdown of discipline. Court martial him and put him in detention for three months, four months, six months." This was commonplace.'

Towards the end of the hot weather there was always a great sense of expectancy. Living by the Arabian Sea at Ratnagiri, Anne Symington recalls how 'we used to go out every evening for a walk from Thibaw's Palace. It was right on the sea and you could see the monsoon coming, you could see it miles away coming over the sea.'

The coming of the rains was always dramatic: 'Hot wind blew through our bungalow day and night from this huge open plain, and then the clouds began to bank up and bank up and there was an unbearable feeling of pressure. Then the rains came down with a terrific force such as you hardly ever see in Europe, and probably for two or three days this would go on, and within those two or three days the whole area round the house turned green. We used to plant seeds of cosmea and zinneas and in no time at all they were up and flowering, and an extraordinary life burst out, with frogs and toads hopping about the paths. At first it was absolutely wonderful.'

Nowhere was the monsoon more eagerly anticipated than in military barracks up and down the plains. 'When it did start men used to rush out absolutely naked, dancing about in the rain after being confined in the heat for such a long time. There was so little to do that even the rain was an event, something to be welcomed, looked forward to and enjoyed.'

Those living in the old country bungalows had special problems, as Rosamund Lawrence recalls: 'Everything gets dried up with the intense heat and the bamboo poles shrink, so there are gaps. When the monsoon comes the rain simply crashes in. It's like living under a waterfall. During the first days of the monsoon my husband and I went to bed holding up umbrellas.'

Relief from the heat was always short-lived. If the hot weather was bad it was far worse in the rains, when a hot, dry climate was simply replaced by a humid one and 'the air got very, very sticky, with more or less constant rain for six weeks or a couple of months'. Stephen Bentley asserts that it was even possible to *see* the humidity: 'When it stopped raining the vapour used to rise out of the ground up to a height of about a foot and remain static. I saw a chap get a shovel and stick it into one of these banks of vapour, and it stayed on the shovel as he picked it up and took it right through the bungalow to the other side, where he just shook the shovel to release it.'

This humidity was at its worst in Eastern India: 'Because of its humidity the Calcutta hot weather was a horror,' says Ian

Stephens. 'I look back upon it with loathing and astonishment.' It was a time of universal sickness, 'a period when one's children invariably got ill,' when even the healthiest people suffered. 'It made me feel tired and slack,' remembers Raymond Vernede, 'as if my blood had been diluted. I nearly always got boils. I wasn't half the man that I had been in the hot weather.' Skin infections – eczema, impetigo and prickly-heat – became commonplace. In the army there was dhobi-*itch*, which was said to result from bad laundering: 'The dhobis would bring back your shirts ironed with knife-edge creases. Probably the seams inside were stiff with starch, and this resulted in the itch.' Prickly heat was a dreaded complaint: 'Little pimples rising over every inch of the body so that you couldn't put a pin between a pimple.' According to Ed Davies 'most soldiers had it. A chap would be playing cards and begin to scratch lightly. By the time the evening was out he'd be rushing round like a madman, tearing himself to pieces trying to quieten the irritation. I've seen one or two people tear themselves to ribbons, tearing their chests down till all the skin was hanging down in layers. We had to restrain people, otherwise they'd have done themselves further injury.'

The rains also brought out snakes, cockroaches, mosquitoes and a multitude of insects. In Bengal there was a month when 'you had nothing but large, repulsive greenfly over everything. They went just as suddenly as they came, and then you had a small black beetle, commonly known as the stink bug. It was in your soup at a meal, it was in your ink when you tried to write a letter. It was everywhere and was quite innocuous unless you squashed it and then it deserved its name. That again suddenly vanished, and then you had the small, white jute-moth which – again – was quite innocuous unless you knocked it and then you got a weal of eczema down your hand.' It was the rains above all other things that made India 'the land of sudden death'. Rosamund Lawrence recalls how, during the monsoon, 'we were giving a dinner party and I suddenly noticed a most awful smell. I thought, "Good heavens, whatever is this?" I was sitting next to a colonel of the IMS and he said, "For God's sake don't touch the fish, it's stinking." So I said, "Yes, but how embarrassing, what am I to do?" and I went on shovelling these bits of fish about and he said, "Oh, you can't possibly touch it; it's death." In India you could be ill one day and dead the next.'

12

THE HILLS

*Up in the hills young men are rare; down in the plains
young women are rare. Young men are spoiled in the hills
and lost in the plains.*

AMY BAKER *Six Merry Mummers* 1931

The great refuges of India were the Hills and in Northern
India, as Olaf Caroe describes, the proximity of the Himalayas:

You get these burning plains right across India, fifteen hundred miles of them, absolutely flat with rivers wandering
through them fed by the snows, and behind them the greatest
range of mountains in the world. You gradually go up from
tropical and sub-tropical climbs, through European and
Alpine flora until you get right up into the snows. I don't
think there is anything in life which is such a relief and such
a physical delight as going from the heat of the plains in the
hot weather up into the mountains, gradually feeling it getting cooler. I remember the first time one gets to a base in
the hills and the water is cold; what a delicious feeling to
have cold water on your hands!

The same sense of relief and delight was to be found among
the lucky ones among the British troops as they marched up
into the Hills: 'We'd halt at these wayside camps; there'd be
a rushing stream close by the camp, and you'd wake up in the
morning in the darkness before daylight to hear the bullock-
cart drivers getting their beasts on to the carts. You'd smell the
smoke from the fires, you know, with the stream rushing by and
then the piper would play reveille and it was rather wonderful.'

Even for the privileged the hill stations that the British built were often unapproachable except on foot or on ponies. 'Where the cars stopped,' remembers Nancy Vernede, 'we would get into our *dandys* or on to our ponies. A *dandy* for an adult would be carried by four men, and a child's *dandy* would be carried by two.' Earlier still, as Mrs Lee remembers, 'the wives and children went up to the hills in *doolies*, long box-like arrangements with a door that you draw back and crawl into. You take your bed-roll with you and you can barely sit up in it. All you can do is lie down.' On arrival visitors found 'a jumble of houses of every imaginable semi-suburban British kind perched on the top of a ridge,' houses with 'a sort of English feeling about them. The smell was English, the houses were furnished in a much more English kind of way and there were fires in the evening.'

The Hills provided a brief escape from the extremes of India's climate and culture – and something more: 'No Englishman of sensitivity who's been to India and loved the hills can deny the Hindu inspiration that the Gods live in the hills somehow.' The Hills had an atmosphere that 'stirred the imagination, something almost verging on the religious'. Part of the magic lay in the sounds; the doves, the barbets and the cuckoo, sounding 'even more beautiful than it does in England'. There were the sounds of water, 'a sort of pulsating coming up from the valleys below, the sound of the river rising as pulsating waves of air,' and the human sounds: 'A passerby singing at the top of his voice, or those little penny pipe whistles they made which would come right across the valley from where they were being played.' There was also the majesty of the Himalayan snowscapes, often veiled in summer but occasionally revealing tantalizing glimpses of themselves through the clouds, as in Darjeeling where 'you could look across miles and miles of tea gardens in the valley and then suddenly see this enormous great mass of ice and snow almost hanging in the sky, rather like a Chinese print.'

The retreat to the Hills in summer was part of an old tradition: 'The headquarters of government used to move up to the hill stations, taking with them all their files, an annual migration which cost thousands of rupees. And this of course set the standard. If government moved up a lot of officers had to move up, and so there was a social life. Wives moved up mainly because of the heat down below, and of course other wives weren't going to stay, so they all went. There was a considerable attraction in this annual exodus and they managed to have a pretty gay time.' At places like Simla, Mussourie, Naini Tal and Darjeeling the European womenfolk would 'take a house and share it with another wife or live in a flat or in a hostel and their husbands would take their short leave and join them for a week or a fortnight.' Of all the hill stations of India Simla was by far the most glamorous, so much so that some critics considered it 'not really part of India'. Simla provided a summer residence for the Viceroy and the Commander-in-Chief as well as for the Delhi and Punjab secretariats: 'It was plastered against the side of one of the lower ranges of the Himalayas. You came up and found yourself on these ledges, one ledge above the other, nothing but narrow paths everywhere and these appalling drops. You were constantly looking over an edge of some kind or up at a great towering hill. If you take a community and jam it on to this series of ledges at 8,000 feet you will get a claustrophobic and enclosed society.' Within this society that was 'unlike any place in India', the images of Kipling lingered on. 'I found it so like Kipling as not to be quite true,' recalls Mary Wood. 'It was what you expected Simla to be. One felt one might meet Mrs Hauksbee around any corner, especially when you walked down the Mall. I don't think it had changed very much.'

Sheltered though it was, Simla was one of those places in India where there was 'a tremendous feeling of the supernatural'. In Simla and elsewhere 'many people felt they had experiences at houses reputed to be haunted and there were many stories about hauntings. All around us there was death and that led on naturally to a feeling for ghosts.' In Mount Abu Vere Birdwood had a room in which both she and her mother's ayah felt 'something evil'. An old *chokidar* had the answer: 'In 1913 a young memsahib had died in that room and ever since her ghost had walked there. In the winter months when the house was empty he had seen this memsahib walking about this room. Many years later when I went back to Mount Abu I found out from the church register who the woman who had died there was, and sure enough she was the young wife of a British officer. And I went to her grave in the churchyard and I stood by this grave and I said to her, "You gave me a very bad summer."'

Ann Symington's encounter with the supernatural was even more sinister. Shortly after her marriage she took up residence in an enormous palace built for the exiled King Thibaw of Burma and his ill-reputed Queen Supalayat, known to the British soldiers as 'soup plate'. 'One night I was fast asleep under my mosquito net when something made me wake up,' she relates. 'I looked at the foot of my bed and there was a grey, misty figure indented into the mosquito net with a knife in his mouth leering at me. I couldn't scream but I went, "Ohhhh . . . ohhhh . . ." My mother heard me and came running along and I said, "Oh, I've just seen the most awful man and he's just disappeared!" And he did, he actually faded away! Some months afterwards when I went to another station someone said to me, "By the way, did you ever see the ghost in Thibaw's Palace?" And I said, "Yes I did!"'

Part of the nineteenth-century atmosphere of Simla was due to the absence of the motorcar. 'The annual move to Simla was romantic but rather horrifying,' remembers Ian Stephens. 'The memory that sticks in my mind is of these coolies pulling and humping terribly heavy loads on their backs up hill slopes. I felt the same repugnance to travelling around Simla in a rickshaw. Eventually one got accustomed to it, but never quite used to it. I always made a point of paying my rickshaw men very well which somehow satisfied my conscience – and thereby had the pleasure of a very fast rickshaw team to get me quickly to dances.' In summer, as in all the more popular hill stations, 'the sex ratio was reversed. There were a lot of married women and there were very few men – and most of the men were in the secretariat or some sort of office job and were, as a rule, rather sober sorts of characters. On the other hand, the young men who came up for brief periods were on holiday and on the loose.' This was the 'rather different kind of atmosphere' in which the Simla Season took place: 'Depending on their rank, they either came to dinner, lunch or a tennis party. You could get rid of an awful lot by a garden party. We used to reckon on three to four dinner parties per week, and the same with luncheon parties. It was a whirl of entertainment, interspersed with some quite gorgeous ceremonial and pomp, particularly in the Viceroy's house.'

As assistant private secretary to the Viceroy, Conrad Corfield observed court etiquette at first hand: 'One of the first things I learnt was that the court bow was only made from the neck, it was much easier than the curtsey, which everyone knows is a terror for the ladies, especially the elderly. Dinner every night at Viceregal Lodge was an occasion for full evening dress. At its close His Excellency would rise from his place at the dinner table and all the men would follow suit. The ladies then departed, led by Her Excellency, and one by one as they reached the door were required to turn and curtsey; an awkward manœuvre which was watched in fascinated silence by the men. At one time we used to have bets on the number of cracks which could be heard – the maximum was four, one by each knee at the dip and the same for the recoil.' A more active participant in this ritual was Sylvia Hadow, later Lady Corfield: 'There was a step just in the doorway and you had to be very careful when you did your curtsey to put your heel either below the step, which was the safest place, or the other side of it. Jordan, the butler, knew all about this and he stood behind the curtain waiting to catch any lady who made a mistake. We had a little rhyme about this: "A lovely party, dinner ended, Jordan passed."'

It was on one such occasion that the most famous faux pas of the inter-war years was made. Like the stock *babu* jokes and the one about the well-dined brigadier who tried to light his cigar with a geranium, it became one of the fixtures of the period, to be repeated almost ad nauseam throughout 'Anglo-India': 'The Viceroy had his own orchestra which used to play most evenings during dinner, and on one occasion Her Excellency enquired the title of the tune that was being played. No one could remember so an ADC was sent to enquire from the bandmaster. The conversation at the table changed to another subject during his absence. He slipped into his seat on return and waited for an opportunity to impart his information. At the next silence he leapt forward and in a penetrating voice said, "I Will Remember Your Kisses, Your Excellency, When You Have Forgotten My Name." '

Iris Portal, who was born in Simla and lived there as a child, returned as a teenager:

In the two summers I spent at Simla I never thought about doing anything but amusing myself. It was excessively gay. My record was twenty-six nights dancing running, at the end of which I could hardly keep awake, but I had to attend an official dinner that my mother was giving and was severely reprimanded for falling asleep in the middle when talking to a very woolly old judge.

You had to ride everywhere in Simla, or go in a rickshaw, which was expensive. So one used to ride out to lunch and to race meetings in one's best dress hitched round one's waist with a blanket tied round you, and a big floppy hat. You used a horse as you would a vehicle and the *syce* ran on ahead and waited for you and held your pony while you attended your function. Then you rode home again. During the summer this was all very well, but as soon as the rains began these poor men were drenched.

We were always meeting the same people. Everyone knew rather too much about everyone else's affairs, and it was a staple topic of conversation – what was going on, who was going out with so-and-so. If there was a very big party you always knew about it and if you hadn't been invited you took that very seriously.

There was the most marvellous Black Hearts fancy dress ball one year. They even went so far as to send for some of the prizes from Paris, which we thought was very exciting indeed. They always took the real tennis court of the United Services Club for their ballroom and did it all up with special Black Hearts decorations and coloured lights and so on. The British in India had a curious convention at all dances where sitting places known as *kala juggas* were constructed. These were coy little sheltered-off places where you were allowed to disappear with your partner. You were not allowed to go to the party unless you were chaperoned but it was understood that once you disappeared into the *kala jugga* you were left alone. Of course, you were never there very long because the next dance started. You did your dances in blocks. There were certain people you always had the same dance with, but if you had a blank space in your programme you hung about at the door for a bit hoping for the best. If nobody came to ask you to dance you went off to the Ladies and had a wait until the next item on your programme. At every one of the Black Hearts parties they had two sets of Lancers and the top set of Lancers, which the Viceroy danced in, was always girls, with the married women in the second set.

The Black Hearts were 'very rich bachelors', who in time became White Hearts – 'Black Hearts who had got married and whose wives were at home.' There was also the Gloom Club, made up of 'bachelors who wished to return hospitality'. Their invitations were all black-lined and couched something like: 'Chief Mourner and attendants of the Gloom Club request the pleasure of So-and-So to their wake which is to be held at the club on some-such day.' The dance programmes were shaped in the form of a coffin with a skull and crossbones and, of course, a black border. The Gloom Club members decorated the club in the most funereal drapings and everybody had to be in a costume dictated by the Chief Mourner.

Another popular source of entertainment and a major feature in Simla social life was amateur theatricals. The Simla Amateur Dramatic Company, composed of 'officers and their wives and sweethearts and anybody who aspired to act,' put on five or six productions every summer: 'We didn't do Shakespeare or anything like that. We did Frederick Lonsdale and Barrie and Pinero and so on.' The plays were put on at the Gaiety, 'an enchanting little theatre, beautifully built, like a little tiny jewel of a theatre in some small German principality. Everybody came, including the Viceroy, the Commander-in-Chief and the Governor who all had their special boxes. Everybody came in full evening dress, usually after dinner parties which they'd got up before the show. The rickshaws all roared up and down outside the theatre and it was very gay indeed. At the end of the run there was a great assemblage on the stage and then all the bouquets came pouring in and you looked enviously to see if anybody else had got more bouquets than you, and then you had a riotous party on the stage, which was awful fun.'

Within this marked holiday atmosphere and absence of officialdom, where 'wives very often got bored without their husbands', flirtations were inevitable: 'There were certain hill stations to which colonels of Indian Army regiments would not allow their subalterns to go on leave. Poodle-faking stations, they were called.' Those who went after the ladies were known as 'poodle-fakers' and were said to come down from the Hills 'fighting rearguard actions against the husbands coming up'. The husbands, in their turn, were 'fairly broad-minded and wouldn't really expect their wives to go up and live in monastic seclusion'. Both circumstances and surroundings were highly conducive to romance. 'It's difficult to convey how enormously romantic the atmosphere was in Simla,' says Iris Portal, 'the warm starlit nights and bright, huge moon, those towering hills and mountains stretching away, silence and strange exotic smells. Very often coming home from dances the current boyfriend used to walk by the side of the rickshaw, murmuring sweet nothings and holding hands over the side of the hood, nothing much more than that, but it was very romantic. Everything was intensely romantic – and a lot of people were lonely.' As an army officer explains: 'When they were bored and we were bored we used to meet up together. There was no harm done. There weren't many scandals and ninty-nine per cent of those little liaisons in the Hills were as harmless as you can think of.'

Yet there was 'a frightful lot of chitter-chat – most of it completely bogus'. One constant belief was that at the Charleville

Hotel in Mussourie 'a separation bell was rung by the manager at four o'clock in the morning'. In actual fact, within this permissive atmosphere 'a strong sort of Edwardian morality prevailed. If a young officer wanted a bit of fun he would pay court to a married woman, not to a girl.' Unmarried girls, 'brought up in an atmosphere of innocence', were not considered 'fair game'. There was also the fact that 'you were looking for a husband – and so you knew where to draw the line.' It was what Iris Portal describes as 'the last remnants of the Kipling business. I was never allowed to go out with a young man alone. It always had to be in a party with at least one married woman in it, even though she might be only a few years older than oneself and certainly not terribly moral or virtuous. That didn't matter a bit, provided she was married. The married women had an edge on one because they could go out alone with a man and they could give parties as they pleased. And they did very often pinch the most attractive young men.'

But for most people these sojourns in the Hills were brief and uneventful. Many wives came down to join their husbands in the plains at the earliest opportunity and without waiting for the rains to end, 'then there was the main exodus in about September or October when everything was wound up in the Hills and they all came down'. Those who had stayed on in the plains waited for the first signs of change. 'Every year there seemed to be a miracle. After humid nights and weeks and weeks of rains you wake up one morning, go out on the verandah and there's just that hint of freshness. The rains are ending, the autumn is coming.'

13

THE COLD WEATHER

The arrival of a cargo (if I dare term it so) of young damsels from England is one of the exciting events that mark the advent of the Cold Season.

LADY FALKLAND *Chow Chow* 1857

The Cold Weather was heralded by greenfly hatching in millions, autumn breezes and the 'cold weather line' that appeared in the plains at sunset, 'this long flat line of smoke just above the tops of the houses, and as you passed you would get a waft of something, a whole range of scents'. It was the time of year when 'one could think of planting seeds, because those were the months when one could grow English flowers'. For India autumn was the season of festivals, beginning with *Dashera*, which in Gurkha regiments was celebrated with animal sacrifices: 'British officers were supposed to attend and did attend but nobody liked it very much. If the bullock's head was severed with one blow that meant good luck for the regiment for the rest of the year.'

But the British had their own autumn rituals. The first was the arrival in September of the catalogues, sent round in good time 'to enable customers to choose what they would like despatched from London for Christmas'. In October this was followed in the larger stations by the already familiar ritual of dropping cards: 'We started off by going to Government House and writing our names in the book there, then we went on to the Deputy Commissioner's wife, and on down the ladder to the Colonels' wives and Majors' wives and so on, dropping our pasteboard cards into the little wooden boxes hung outside the gatepost of each house.' This annual ceremony had its origins in the days of the old East India Company 'when all the people who had been senior enough and wealthy enough to move up to the hill stations to avoid the unhealthy hot weather came back in October. The ones left alive among those who had had to stay down in the plains went to call on them at the beginning of the cold weather to show that they were still alive – and this became a tradition. On the fifth of October you put on your morning suit and you went and called on them.' Accompanying this formal acknowledgement of autumn was an abrupt change of attire from light summer to heavier winter wear.

Next came the arrival of the Fishing Fleet and the changing of partners: 'In the hot weather you took out what was called the "B" class girl, usually Anglo-Indians, who were dears in every way and the greatest fun. But the moment the cold weather started they were taboo, because all the young girls from Roedean, Cheltenham and the great schools of Britain came out in the P & O liners and you were expected to toe the line. You kept your nose clean and if you were unwary you caught yourself a wife.' In the cities and the larger stations the cold weather's sporting and social activities were 'absolutely endless'. Nobody enjoyed them more than the young girls fresh from England. 'I lived in a whirl and I thoroughly enjoyed it,' remembers Deborah Dring. 'Every day we went to something, a tea dance or a dance or a ball or a dinner party.'

With six months of almost perfect weather ahead, elaborate 'weeks' could be planned: 'Most stations had their "weeks" during which various dances and balls were held and various games were played, polo and hockey tournaments, tent-pegging and pig-sticking and so on.' The season reached its peak with Christmas week, distinguished in Calcutta by the visit of the Viceroy. At Belvedere, the old Viceregal Lodge, there was always a fancy dress ball and a children's party where Father Christmas entered on an elephant.

Christmas in India was celebrated by the European community in its own style. 'Everybody made an effort' at Christmas; the Christmas dinner and the Christmas cake followed the familiar pattern, although pea-fowl – 'beautifully white flesh but very, very dry' – frequently took the place of tinned

162

turkey. Christmas up-country was often spent in camp in or on the edge of the jungle, sometimes in tents, sometimes in *dak* or forest bungalows. These camps were mostly simple affairs; 'usually two or three families would join together and bring their tents and elephants – if they had any – and pool things to eat.' There would be rough shooting by day, then 'a bath in the round tin tub at the back of the tent,' followed by quiet suppers – '*dal* and rice perhaps, with a poached egg on it' – round a roaring camp fire. The campers slept surrounded by the sounds of the jungle, hearing 'the rasping saw of a panther prowling round the camp'. This was 'the natural India' that many loved.

Other camps were more sophisticated; governors' and vice-roys' camps that remained highly formal, and maharajahs' camps that were lavish in the extreme, as Geoffrey Allen recalls of Darbhanga Raj: 'Hundreds of tents were put up and the guest house was absolutely full of VIPs. People from hundreds of miles all round Bihar were asked. Hospitality was lavish. Firpo's, the caterers from Calcutta, used to come up and very good food and drink was laid on, with Firpo's servants, dressed up in livery, passing the food round. Hall and Anderson's, the furnishing firm from Calcutta, used to bring up literally hundreds of wardrobes, beds, mirrors and dressing tables by train to furnish all these tents.' Instead of rough shoots there were elephant drives against big game with 'elephants and beaters all out in a very long line, driving through the long grass, with dozens of cars coming and going, bringing food and provisions in and out of the camp. In the evening there was usually a big dance and for these dances, of course, one changed into even-ing dress. The men always wore stiff, white shirt fronts and the ladies all had to wear gloves. The band used to come up from Calcutta to play.'

The cold weather provided maximum opportunity for move-ment in comfort and style. If 'the key note of British rule was indeed personal rule' it was best characterized by the Tour. Not only was this an essential duty for every official in the district, but it featured in one form or another in nearly every trade and occupation; policemen, canal workers, *box-wallahs*, missionaries – even soldiers – had their tour or its equivalent.

Sometimes its purpose was obscure: 'It was never explained to me,' declares Penderel Moon, 'what you were supposed to do, so I had to invent objects for myself.' Yet the end result was very clear. 'It allowed two widely separated cultures to meet in friendship and affection,' and it depended for its effect on slowing down to meet the pace of India, 'the pace of the bullock cart'. The motorcar remained 'an alien thing' in India; roads were strewn with hazards and pock-marked with holes gouged out by the steel-rimmed wheels of bullock carts. In hot weather the wooden spokes of the wheels of the earlier motorcars tended to work loose and 'one had to tie a special kind of grass around them and keep it wet the whole time'. Wherever possible 'you reverted to the coaching age'.

The duration of the tour varied with occupation and district. 'I'd go out on tour for four or five weeks,' says Cuthbert Bowder, who worked in the irrigation branch of the PWD in the United Provinces, 'and then come back to my base for about ten days' rest. Then I'd be off again. I should think that I toured for about nine months of the whole year.' The same pattern was followed by those working in the forest or agriculture services or in other branches of the public works department. Elsewhere it was a matter of weeks rather than months: 'Some skimped it a bit, others would make every possible excuse to extend the period for as long as possible.' Some used the tour for sport, arranging it so as to cover the best parts of *shikar* in their districts; others used it as a way of adding to their incomes 'because there was a system of extra payment for travelling allowance or, as we called it, TA. If you went on tour you used to say, "I'm going hunting the TA bird." ' Very few failed to enjoy it, perhaps because 'you were completely independent'. For Percival Griffiths it was 'the best part of one's life in one's early days. You camped outside a particular village for four or five days, dealing with all its problems and its disputes, and then moved on to the next village perhaps ten or fifteen miles away. In a district where the paperwork was heavy, it would follow after you, probably by bullock cart, and when you'd done your active work during the day you sat up at night and disposed of your file.'

BRITISH OFFICER'S DISTRICT TOUR 1936—37.

బ్రిటిష్ అధికారి జిల్లా పరిటను ప్రణాళిక.

Place.	స్థలము	Date. తేది	Time. సమయం	Address.	బంగళా
Rajahmundry	రాజమండ్రి	30-10-36	0900—1300	Traveller's Bungalow	ప్రయాణముల బంగళా
Cocanada	కాకినాడ	31-10-36	0900—1600	,,	,,
Samalkot	సామర్లకోట	2-11-36	0800—0930	Railway Station	రైల్వే స్టేషన్
Pithapuram	పిఠాపురం	2-11-36	1100—1600	Dy. Tahsildar's Office	డిప్యూటీ తహసీల్దార్ ఆఫీసు
Tuni	తుని	3-11-36	0900—1100		
Anakapalli	అనకాపల్లి	3-11-36	1400—1700	Traveller's Bungalow	ప్రయాణముల బంగళా
Vizagapatam	విశాఖపట్నం	4-11-36	1100—1600	,,	,,
		5-11-36	0900—1200	,,	,,
Vizianagaram	విజయనగరం	6-11-36	0900—1200	,,	,,
Chipurupalle	చీపురుపల్లి	6-11-36	1530—1700	,,	,,
Chicacole	చీకాకోల్	7-11-36	1300—1600	,,	,,
Ichapuram	ఇచ్చాపురం	8-11-36	1300—1600	,,	,,

I hope that all ex-service, and serving Viceroy's Commissioned Officers, N.C.O's and men, who wish to, will come and meet me at the above places and times.

All should bring their Discharge Certificates and Civil Employment Forms with them when they report to me, and correspondence connected with grievances where necessary.

It is emphasised however that while I will be pleased to see any ex-soldier, there is no obligation for men to come unless they have grievances or suggestions to make or prospective recruits to bring forward.

సూ చ న.

సూరాలనుండునట పనిచేయు సైనికాధికారులు, వైసిరాయి ప్రకటించ సొమ్మును పొందునట్టి సైనికులు మొదలగు వారందరను

కోరునవారు, పైనూచించిన తావులకు, వేళలకు వచ్చి నన్ను కలసుకొనవలసినది.

వారందరు తమ డిశ్చార్జి సర్టిఫికేట్లను, సివిల్ ఎంప్లాయ్మెంట్ ఫారములను తీసుకొని నావద్దకు రావలసినది.

ఈ విషయమై ప్రకటించుచున్నది. నాకు ఉపదేశములు చేయనెంచినవారు మాత్రమే రావలసినది.

H. E. M. COTTON, Lieut., R.E.,
Q. V. O. Madras Sappers and Miners.
Q. V. O. మద్రాస్ సాప్పర్స్ అండ్ మైనర్స్.

Bangalore,
October 1936.

British officer's Cold Weather Tour, Bangalore, 1936

166

Modes of transport varied from district to district. In the Sind, as David Symington recalls, it was the camel: 'As an assistant collector I used to have seven baggage camels and a riding camel. They were all provided by a contractor, and the contractor was also the man who had the honourable job of driving my riding camel. These camels were hired out on a peculiarly Sind idea of the rate for the job; the assistant collector used to pay seven rupees a month for each camel, the collector used to pay nine rupees and the commissioner in Sind used to pay about ten or twelve rupees. This seemed absolutely right to everybody!'

Accompanying her husband from one camp to another, Norah Bowder often travelled on an elephant 'with the baby and the ayah and the cook and the bearer. We used to all sit back very comfortably on one elephant. Sometimes the *mahout* would have the baby sitting in front, on the elephant's head. When it got warm it would fill its trunk and spray us with water to keep us cool, and if we were eating an orange it would put its trunk back and take the orange and eat it. It would stand there and my little boy would put his bricks underneath the elephant and nobody ever worried. Ayah used to sit leaning up against the elephant's leg.'

Up on the North-East Frontier Geoffrey Allen toured the Himalayas on foot:

You carried all your rations and took hundreds of porters with you, and you went out into areas which were unmapped. You recorded the names of the villages and the populations. You tried to make friends with sometimes hostile tribes, and generally showed the flag. You handed them a little pinch of salt and you took a little on your finger, ate it and said, 'This is Government salt. Would you like to become a Government servant? You eat salt, too, if you want to be friendly to Government.' And normally they ate the salt.

A lot of your tour consisted of dropping right down very steeply into a valley and then climbing very steeply up the other side again. We lost quite a number of porters over the years who slipped off the track and fell with their loads into the rivers below. The usual method of crossing rivers was over a thick, twisted rope made of plaited canes stretching from high up on one bank to low down on the other. There was a thick wishbone-shaped piece of wood made from a tree root, and suspended from this was a leather thong in which you sat. You backed into this, sat in it very uncomfortably, put your hands above your head and held on to this wishbone. Then they gave you a push and you shot down this sloping bamboo cable, with the cane rope smoking furiously, to the other side. They were very clever at landing without bashing their brains out on the other side. Eventually you got quite used to crossing in this manner.

In contrast, most touring in the plains was carried out in some style, as Cuthbert Bowder describes:

As soon as you had had dinner on the night before all the kitchen was packed up, with only sufficient pots and pans left out for breakfast the following morning. Your office equipment was also packed up and loaded on to carts or camels and they travelled during the night to your first stopping place, about ten miles distant. After breakfast the following morning the remainder of your gear was packed up, and that reached your destination at about five or six o'clock in the evening. When you arrived at your office table the following morning everything was exactly as you'd left it before leaving. If you had been reading a book, for instance, on some abstruse point of canal law, it was there again at exactly the same angle on the table.

The tents were rather like big tops. The floor was strewn with straw and over the straw you had a *dhurri*, a cotton carpet. They were well furnished with easy chairs known as Roorkee chairs, and when it was cold enough for a fire there was a stove in the tent which made it extraordinarily comfortable. After breakfast you got on to your horse and you rode off to inspect the canals. Then you came back at about one o'clock and lunch would be ready for you. You'd probably have a pink gin or something just before, and then you'd read the papers and rest until half-past two when you went to your office table and conducted interviews with various people, peasants and the landed gentry, until four o'clock. At four o'clock you took the gun and a couple of men and you got the odd partridge or pea-fowl or hare, just enough to keep the pot boiling, without any trouble at all. Then you came back and had a grand tea of hot buttered toast before a roaring fire. The sunsets were very beautiful but very short-lived and almost immediately after darkness clamped down. After tea, back again to the office table where I used to work until dinner, and very often work again after dinner.

On tour the district official was never off duty, as Philip Mason explains: 'When you were walking round in camp in the evening a villager would come to one with some story he wanted to tell. He would try to ingratiate himself in the first place by telling you that there were some duck on a pond a little way off, or that a partridge was hiding in the next bush. But after a bit you would say, "Now tell me, what's the story? What's it all about?" Sometimes the only thing to do was to sit down on the ground and say to him, "Sit down, brother," and then it would all come out.' Contact was also to be made in other ways. 'We used to have two little rival surgeries, my wife and I. My prescriptions were usually rum, castor oil and aspirin, and hers were quinine and aspirin – and we did a little very rough surgery.' In return the official could be sure of the warmest hospitality. 'They would probably offer you refreshments, almost certainly hot milk or a boiled egg, which the headman would peel with rather grimy fingers as a special mark of honour and offer to you.' This hospitality reached an extreme on the North-West Frontier, where travellers might be required to sit and talk 'while a goat was slaughtered and cooked'. Even where there was no food to be offered there were other forms of hospitality, as George Wood discovered when he sat down with a circle of village headmen and found 'one rolling up the trouser of my right leg and one rolling up the trouser of my left leg. Then two pairs of horny hands began to massage my muscles as a traditional welcome to the tired traveller.'

Sometimes hospitality – often with a mis-spelt WELLCOME writ large upon a triumphal arch – was a little more formal. Kathleen Griffiths remembers how 'many a time when we've been on a long, weary tour and are returning very late at night, a little primary school has heard that we were passing and they've had the whole school decorated with marigolds and garlands, and they have kept open because they knew that we could not pass them by. I cannot count the number of times I have listened to the repetition of the story of the Maharanee Victoria.' Only in one respect – Penderel Moon saw it as a 'grave defect' of British rule – was this personal form of government visibly at fault: 'There was all this emphasis on village touring but it was never suggested that you should do what I call urban touring. Yet it was in the towns that there was most discontent with the British Raj. There was nothing to bring officers into direct touch with the city populace.'

Both the British and the Indian Army had their forms of touring. The Indian Army had the recruiting tour, undertaken by its officers in the area from which the regiment drew its recruits: 'It gave one a chance of keeping one's finger on the pulse,' explains Reginald Savory, 'and we got to know our own men very well indeed, not only those serving but their fathers and, in some cases, their grandfathers and their uncles.' A measuring-stick – 'almost as much a sign of India as the spinning wheel' – was always carried, 'the kind of thing vets used to use for measuring horses. We used to measure our men in the same way. You knew how tall they were but they liked being measured, and if you thought they were good enough then the local sub-assistant surgeon would feel the man to see if he had an enlarged spleen and then he was told to come along behind us.' As the recruiting tour proceeded it would assume the proportions of a triumphal procession:

At the entrance to the village you'd probably be met by the local village band, big drum, pipes, side-drums, many of them retired drummers from the regiment. Then you'd be received by your head host, generally one of the senior ex-army officers, and brought out under the great village tree, the peepul tree, under which the whole village would come and sit and keep out of the rain or the sun. There'd be a table with a white cloth on it and I would sit there with the senior Indian ex-officer and hear complaints, because our job was not only to pick up recruits but also to keep in touch with the recruiting area, so one was able to do a tremendous amount.

In front of the recruiting officer there was always a bottle of whisky. They'd pour you out enormous tots into very thick glasses and they saw to it that you drank as much as you possibly could. While you were turning away talking to a chap on your left your glass was being surreptitiously filled. You'd turn round and find two or three glasses waiting for you. Eventually one got to know what was happening and one used to hand one's glass over to somebody else. But it was a very, very warm reception. We'd sit and we'd talk and we'd discuss old friends and all the old times, all the old regimental stuff that nobody else could understand, but it was the breath of life to these chaps.

When I left in the morning they would all come out. They'd take you off with the band to the village boundary and as I left they'd all cry the Sikh war cry, '*Sat Sri Akal!*' and I would shout back, '*Sat Sri Akal!*'

There was also the route march, common to both armies; movements from the plains to the Hills and vice versa, from one station to another, to and from the North-West Frontier – often along the Grand Trunk Road, one of the lifelines of India upon which soldiers had marched since the days before the Mutiny and which had altered little since Kipling's day, with its 'traffic of bullock carts, of cattle being driven to pasture, the continual stream of pedestrians, staging posts usually marked by the *dak* bungalow, and the groves of mango trees which gave shelter from the sun.' The route march might well cover a distance of five hundred miles 'which at fifteen to twenty miles a day would take a month. After the first day or two the blisters wore off and it was sheer enjoyment, and, of course, we saw much more of the country moving at a walking pace.'

To the British soldier the extended route march was certainly 'no joke'. Many BORs dreaded foot-slogging in India. 'Your feet would be so blistered they felt like hot water bottles,' recalls Ed Davies. 'As you walked along a fine dust would rise in vast clouds and get up your nose, into your eyes, into your ears. Drinking water on the march was taboo. It was strictly forbidden. I used to suck a pebble all the way, which is what my dad told me to do, and found it very soothing. The officers used to ride up and down seeing everyone was all right saying, "Are you all right, Smith? Are you all right, Jones?" and we used to rally round and continue the march. Sometimes we used to carry the equipment of someone who'd weakened. We'd say, "Here y'are, Smudger, let's have yer bundle, let's have yer rifle, or let's have yer pack."' To help pass the time the regimental band played and in both armies the traditional songs – 'very repetitive and most of them unprintable' – were sung. Francis Dillon recalls how the troops in his Indian Mountain Battery sang 'the famous Pushtu song called "The Wounded Heart": "There's a boy across the river with a bottom like a peach but, alas, I cannot swim."'

For all its discomforts the route march was one of the 'great experiences' of India and there was always the feeling 'that you were with friends,' as Charles Wright describes:

You fell in with your rifle and pack by company, mules in the rear and bullocks with the baggage waiting behind, and you marched at the rate of three miles an hour. The first halt was always twenty minutes after leaving camp when the troops relieved themselves on the side of the road. That was march discipline: always go out on the left of the road, take off your pack and rifle, sit there until two minutes before you were due to fall in. The whistle would blow, you'd don your pack and rifle and fall in in threes. The band would strike up and you'd march happily along for fifty minutes, off for ten minutes, on again until you arrived at camp. You passed flat expanses on either side, fields of sugar cane, a village on a high mound with the well worked by a bullock or a camel where all the villagers used to collect to bring the water in. They would pull their saris over to hide their faces and sneak into their huts, but the children would come out to dance along with you. On the road bullock carts passed by, axles creaking and groaning, the boy drivers shouting at the beasts, prodding them with sticks. We'd arrive in camp, each man absolutely red, the dust caked on his face with the sweat. The tents would be unloaded and placed on their respective places and when everything was ready the commanding officer would blow a whistle and all the tents would come up like a lightning stroke, as if a little town had sprung into being at once. The mess marquee and odd tents here and there were pitched and the campers settled down to housey-housey or a snooze in the sun. You'd finished your day's marching, you'd have a couple of beers in the canteen and lay down your bedding roll under the stars. Night would come very suddenly, velvet night, very peaceful – and it was marvellous!

14

THE MESS

Have you had any word
Of that bloke in the 'Third',
Was it Southerby, Sedgewick or Sim?
They had him thrown out of the Club in Bombay
For, apart from his mess bills exceeding his pay,
He took to pig-sticking in quite *the wrong way.*
I wonder what happened to him!

NOËL COWARD
I Wonder What Happened to Him 1945

'India was the soldier's paradise. If you were in the Army you
could do anything.' The British officer in India had privileges
of rank and regiment, rare opportunities for sport and action
in the field. But from the civilian's point of view his life was
circumscribed. 'The Army in India led a life which was quite
different from ours,' says David Symington. 'They lived in
messes, and they had their troops to drill and exercise and look
after. They lived in a smaller world than ours.' This smaller
world centred on the military cantonment: 'Cantonment life
and village life had certain similarities. An Indian Army regiment in cantonments lived very, very much unto itself. It did
not encourage visits from outside. In fact it discouraged them.
The moment a stranger appeared in barracks a report was sent
at once to the adjutant.' This insularity was heightened by the
code by which the British officer lived. 'The British officer was
very different from his contemporaries in civil life,' says George
Wood. 'By force of circumstance we were separated from our
contemporaries and as time went on foreign service broke childhood friendships and replaced them with service friendships.
The result was that we became ingrown, we were godfathers to
each other's children, we had the usual family quarrels and

special friendships. We felt ourselves more and more a class apart, a samurai class. We were a family of brother officers, and there is no other word to express our relationship.' It was an attitude that the army wife shared – as far as she could: 'It was that lovely feeling of being part of a very closely knit family. They weren't strangers. Some you liked better than others, but they were the family, so that was that.' In the Indian Army the word extended to include the men as much as their officers. 'It was very much a family affair,' echoes Claude Auchinleck, 'and that was the charm of it. Son followed father and nephew followed uncle. That was what made the Indian Army so popular and so beloved by the British officers who served in it; because they felt they belonged to the family.' This sense of family – *bhai-bund* – was brought home to Rupert Mayne, not an army man himself but nevertheless a Mayne, on the centenary celebration of the 6th Lancers, known as Mayne's Horse: 'In the midst of the pensioners a very old man came up to me, buried his white beard in my chest and sobbed. I could not make out what he was saying so I patted him on the shoulders – and then the truth came out. He pulled up his trousers and showed a very badly wounded knee. And he explained to me that in a charge in Mesopotamia he had been hit by a Turkish bullet, had fallen off his horse and that my uncle had dismounted and carried him off the field.'

Before joining an Indian regiment the 'unattached' subaltern had his year to serve with a British regiment. He studied Urdu, learnt the ways of India and was 'vetted' by the regiment of his first or second choice. This could involve an invitation to stay with the regiment for a few days. 'I thought I'd try for the Guides because they had cavalry and infantry,' recalls Reginald Savory. 'That would have enabled me, if I fell off my horse too much, to swap from one to the other. The Guides were one of the most famous regiments in the Indian Army, they were *It*. As my second string I put down the Gurkhas; they were also very smart, very *pukka* indeed, and I spent a week with them in their mess. However, I was not selected – and I only found out the reason why after I had retired. I sent them a cheque in payment of my mess bill and I forgot to sign it. It was sheer forgetfulness but I think the Gurkhas thought, "Here's a pretty crooked sort of chap, we don't want him!"' For Lewis Le Marchand the procedure was rather easier; he joined his uncle's regiment, the 5th Royal Gurkha Rifles: 'At last, after years at Sandhurst and another year in a regiment which, as much as you loved it you couldn't call "My regiment", you found yourself in your own regiment, allowed to wear its button, its uniform, its mess kit, its particular flashes on the topee and its shoulder badges. You spoke of it as "My regiment. I joined my regiment," and, after a number of years, that is the first thing that you have.'

Whichever regiment you joined the same institution dominated the cantonment. 'The Officer's Mess was the centre of regimental life,' recalls John Morris. 'Here the unmarried officers spent a great deal of their time and had their meals and in particular, dined together every night.' Most messes conformed both architecturally and socially to the same pattern. The 3rd Gurkha Rifles Mess at Landsdowne was no exception: 'It was completely jerry-built, with bricks, wood, bits of stone, and without architectural merit of any kind whatsoever, designed by the officers and built by the troops themselves. And it was furnished similarly, with every sort of local-made jerry-built furniture. One entered the mess through a foyer which was furnished with rapidly decaying heads of animals which had been stuffed. On one side was the billiard room, the walls of which were also adorned with stuffed animal heads. All round the walls of the dining room were arranged the portraits of previous commanding officers. We always used to talk among ourselves and say that when an unpopular commanding officer left we would in no circumstances allow his portrait to be hung in the dining room – but tradition always won.'

Attached or unattached, joining one's first mess could be, as Reginald Savory recalls, a pretty 'rigid' affair: 'I remember the night we joined after a long and dusty train journey from Calcutta. We were allowed to dine in the mess in our plain clothes because we hadn't had time to unpack our mess kit, but we dined in what was in those days called the "dirty dining room". The mess was pretty stuffy. I was terrified of the commanding officer, we all were. I was equally terrified of the majors. The captains we treated with some respect and the senior subaltern put the fear of God into us. Altogether we were a little bit – to use a civilian word – regimental, but then all this was pre-1914, when the army was a little bit more blimpish than it was later on. The war taught us a thing or two.'

But even after the Great War there were routines that remained set and unbending, as John Morris describes:

One arrived in the Mess about half-past seven, dressed in full regimentals – stiff shirt, skin-tight trousers, skin-tight jacket and all the rest of it. One had a glass of sherry and as soon as dinner was ready the mess sergeant or mess havildar saluted the senior officer and announced that dinner was served. Then we trooped into the dining room in order of rank.

Dinner in the Mess was a most extraordinary meal because although we were living in fairly primitive surroundings we always had a most elaborate dinner. You invariably started with what was called a first toast. This was generally a sardine or half a boiled egg on a piece of soggy toast. You then went on to tinned fish. Then you had a joint and then pudding and a savoury, which was more or less the same as the first course and was called the second toast.

As soon as the last course had been served the mess sergeant placed three decanters in front of the senior officer; port, madeira and marsala. These were circulated and on Saturday nights, which was guest night, it was obligatory to drink the health of the King Emperor. After the royal toast the regimental pipe band was brought in and paraded round the table. The noise was absolutely deafening but it was considered the done thing to say how good it was. As soon as the senior officer had lit his cigar or cigarette or cheroot, one was free to smoke. But one was not free to leave the table until the senior officer did so and this frequently resulted in a great many boring evenings, especially with some of those old gentlemen who insisted on telling their stories of prowess in the hunting field which we'd heard innumerable times.

Conversation was informal but a certain protocol was observed: 'It was assumed automatically that a captain was more intelligent than a lieutenant, and a major more than a captain and so on. As for expressing an opinion which differed from the general point of view, that was almost unheard of. It would have been considered very bad manners not to agree with the senior officer and, of course, one was not allowed to mention a lady's name. If you mentioned a lady by mistake you had to pay for a round of drinks. The usual topics at table were the goings on in the regiment; who had done well in the football competition, who had shot well and so forth. This sort of thing was necessary for good discipline in a good regiment.' At breakfast the conventions took a different form: One just wasn't supposed to speak to one's fellow officers at breakfast time. In front of each place was a wire reading frame on which you could prop a book or newspaper. They weren't much use because the newspaper didn't arrive until the late afternoon. We subscribed to various papers and magazines in the mess, the chief of which was the *Field*, which was regarded almost as a sort of bible of sport. But one day it was discovered that we also subscribed to the *New Statesman*, so a special meeting was called and *La Vie Parisienne* was ordered in its place.'

The mess was where the unmarried officers ate and slept and so a certain easing of formality was quite in order: 'The mess is your home, so a subaltern has as much right as a senior major or the colonel. Whereas on parade you'd be addressed by your surname, in the mess you're Pat or George or whatever the name might be. It's your home and you do exactly as you please in it.' But it was 'home' with one important qualification: 'Except on guest nights women were not allowed in the mess.' For the army wife the mess was 'a place to which you did not go. In the same way, you did not walk about the parade ground. That was holy ground.' So while the mess was 'a place of refuge for the bachelor officers of the regiment, it was also a refuge for married officers who wanted to get away from their wives'. Nor were ladies necessarily welcome on guest nights, which were welcome opportunities to 'let yourself go'. After the band had played off and the anteroom had been cleared, games were played: 'High-Jinks', described as 'a fairly rowdy affair', or 'High Cockalorum', which began with six or eight people bending down and a similar number jumping on their backs; cock-fighting, with 'two officers sitting on the floor trying to throw one another over,' or contests that involved 'people jumping from ibex's horns on to the mantelpiece and then on to a bison's horns and so on all the way round the room'. Senior officers were always fair game. Visiting generals would be shot off the ends of mess tables wrapped in blankets and if, in full flight 'you could not succeed in striking a match it was a misfire and you were shot again'. Occasionally limbs were broken – and quantities of furniture. In John Cotton's Light Cavalry Regiment 'the Mess had a ballroom which used to be cleared and used as a race track for bicycle races. This nearly always ended with a large number of windows being broken. The following day we would persuade one of the senior officers to certify that there had been a storm the previous night.' Guest night was also the occasion for 'a good deal of drinking. Drink was very cheap, with whisky at about six rupees a bottle, but that was offset against the small salaries we were all paid. Nevertheless, the senior officers certainly drank a great deal more in those days. What always surprised me was their capacity for holding their drink. One might have a very riotous guest night, finishing at three in the morning, but at six o'clock mounted parade the same officers would be there, impeccably turned out and able to sit on their horses without any sign of having been the worse for wear a few hours earlier.'

Before joining the 15th Ludhiana Sikhs, Jackie Smyth spent his unattached year with the Green Howards, who 'played hard and drank quite hard – at guest night you were always charged for two glasses of port even if you didn't drink any'. As a new officer and guest of honour, he created an enormous sensation when he asked for a lemonade: 'Everyone looked up as though some sort of strange animal had been introduced into the mess.' Certain regiments – British or Irish rather than Indian – prided themselves on being 'hard-drinking regiments'. Reginald Savory remembers one such regiment, 'hard-drinkers to a man, from the colonel downwards'. On the night before their departure for Europe in September 1914 they were 'drunk to a man. The next morning I went to the railway station to see them off. They were led by their band – poor devils, how they managed to play I don't quite know. They were followed by the colonel and his adjutant on horses, and about twenty or thirty private soldiers. The rest were either carried along behind the regiment in bullock carts or left drunk on the parade ground. They were shovelled into the train and some of them, who were more drunk than the others, actually died in the train on their way to Karachi.'

Every regiment had its own standards. In the Bengal Lancers a high price was put on horsemanship: 'The absolute height of success was if you were a good polo player and played in the regimental team. Nothing else really mattered, neither your military competence nor anything else, but if you played in the regimental polo team you were tantamount to a god!' Whatever its code, regimental esprit was dependent upon shared values: 'There was always this threat that if you didn't conform you'd be shunted off somewhere.' Those who fitted in got on, the misfits were quickly eased out: 'When it became noticed that a young officer was never going to make it, it was suggested to him that he should transfer to one of the Service Corps or the Remount Depot, where he would find a larger scope for his slightly different personality and talent. Many people transferred, generally for financial reasons and without being misfits, so it was no disgrace.' The greatest crime of all was letting the regiment down – and the final arbiter was always the colonel, who was, as Lewis Le Marchand explains, 'the man that keeps you on the straight and narrow. I remember my colonel saying to me, "I don't mind a bit what you do on leave out of this country, but what you do in this country is my concern and the regiment's concern. Any dud cheques, any unpaid club bills and any foot wrong socially in this country is very much my concern and the concern of the regiment." The Indian Army officer's word must be his bond, his behaviour must be beyond all criticism, because if it isn't he won't get the best out of his men.'

The honouring of bills was regarded as all-important: 'No

officer was allowed to let the seventh of the month pass without paying his mess bill.' Despite that, 'most young officers lived beyond their means. The Army hadn't recovered from the idea that to be an officer in the Army you had to have private means. The result was you pretended you had private means and you lived as if you had, but you hadn't.' Sometimes the only solution was a visit from the regimental *banya*; 'Very, very surreptitiously so as not to let anyone know – but of course they all did – you would arrange for him to let you have a thousand rupees. He'd come round to your bungalow in the evening through the back door. Your bearer would say, "There's a gentleman to see you," knowing full well who he was. The *banya* would bring out wads of notes from his pocket and you would sign a chit and you probably wouldn't even ask what interest was going to be paid.' The general impecuniosity of junior officers was only one of the impediments to early marriage: 'You didn't get a marriage allowance until you were twenty-six years of age. If you got yourself embroiled with a young lady as a young officer the colonel would put his foot down and say, "You're not getting married yet." ' There was also the question of suitability, 'In my regiment,' recalls John Morris, 'it was customary to ask the colonel's permission to marry. There would be a great many questions asked as to who the lady was, her background and so forth. In a small, closed community it was desirable that anybody coming into it should fit in with the people already there.' Sometimes the advice of other members of the regimental 'family' was also sought. 'In Lansdowne we had the most superb example of a memsahib you could find anywhere in India. She was the widow of an officer and had gradually become over the years the sort of super-colonel of the regiment. Nothing was done without reference to her and she provided in her day a great many wives for various officers – nieces and so on brought out from home. Nobody would have been so bold as to get married without asking Mrs Fizzer's permission or advice as to the suitability of the proposed bride.'

Marrying into the army required a major readjustment on the part of the bride. The army was a male-oriented society, dominated by military discipline, where 'wives tended to acquire the rank of their husbands. The colonel's lady regarded herself as a sort of colonel and certainly she commanded all the other wives of the regiment.' Although she was now part of a 'close-knit family' the army wife lacked a positive role to play. Only in the last decade of the British Raj did the military memsahib – largely through her own perseverance – really establish herself within the military community and find a genuinely creative outlet for her energies. Until then, many probably felt, as Vere Birdwood did when she married into Probyn's Horse, that at least 'it was a total loss of the quality of life, at any rate for the women. The life itself was excessively boring, trivial, claustrophobic, confined and totally male-oriented. The army wife was not expected to do anything or be anything except a decorative chattel or appendage of her husband. Nothing else was required of her whatsoever. She was not expected to be clever. It didn't even matter if she wasn't beautiful, so long as she looked reasonable and dressed reasonably and didn't let her husband down by making outrageous remarks at the dinner table. She certainly had wonderful opportunities for riding and for participating in all sorts of horse sports, but apart from that and looking after her children and running a fairly decent dinner party, there her role ended.'

Life was made no easier by the frequency of military postings and the long separations that came with active service. With two years as the average duration of a posting the army wife had little opportunity to put a home together. She had also to endure the absolute lack of privacy in regimental life where 'every facet of your life was known – with the side result that there was virtually no immorality whatsoever because of the extraordinary communal life that we lived. So it had a sort of bonus of an extremely moral existence – but, oh my goodness, it was dull!' Not all military life was so dull – or so moral. The 'Fornicating Fifth' was said to be blatant in its wife-swapping, but elsewhere a discretion prevailed. 'There were love affairs going on in every station,' declares Frances Smyth, 'but it was a question of . . . "You mustn't be discovered."' Vere Birdwood recalls the 'very strong unwritten law that regimental officers could have little affairs with wives of other regiments, but to do so with a wife in your own regiment was much frowned upon. So strongly was this law obeyed that in a Frontier station, when the husband was away campaigning, it was generally considered wise for the wife left behind to have a young officer to sleep overnight in the bungalow as a guard. As far as I know this privilege, if you can call it that, was never abused.'

Yet military life had many compensations. There was always that 'tremendous sense of community that you get from being one of a crowd, of the same lot and the same spirit.' What wife could fail to respond to the splendour of a ceremonial march past – 'and of course, if your husband is leading the parade – this very handsome man, beautifully dressed and waving a sword – it is extremely moving.' And for the husbands themselves, there was 'no finer feeling than being at the head of six hundred men, all marching behind you, probably fifteen miles and nobody falling out. You never feel it again after you leave a regiment.'

15

THE BARRACKS

The men could only wait and wait and wait, and watch the shadow of the barracks creeping across the blinding white dust.

RUDYARD KIPLING *Soldiers Three*

'We used to think of India as a place of stations, never as a place where people had homes and where they lived.' Of all sections of the British community the circumstances of the BORS had changed least since Kipling's day. They remained the least privileged and the most restricted. A German businessman visiting India just before the Second World War remarked to his host that on his journey from Calcutta he had failed to see a single British soldier: 'Where are all your troops? How do you rule here?' The answer lay partly in the 'great segregation' that Stephen Bentley became conscious of when he and his comrades in the Seaforth Highlanders first landed in Bombay and which they were 'going to feel in ever-increasing intensity as life wore on'. It was a characteristic of British rule in India that 'the military were never to the fore' and, in fact, they were spread very thin across the land. As far as possible the military cantonment was self-contained – with its own approved bazaar – and access to the local community limited. 'The first order that appeared when you got to a new station usually stated that all Indian villages, Indian shops, Indian bazaars and the civil lines were out of bounds to all troops.' The BOR was thus all but confined to barracks, barracks which were 'the same everywhere, drab, very widely spaced with no signs of greenery around to break the monotony. Just sand, sand and sand again.'

Within these confines military duties continued in the usual way: 'You paraded for your meals. You paraded to see the doctor. You paraded to draw your rations. You paraded to draw your stores. You paraded to draw your ammunition. You paraded on Sundays because Church Parade was compulsory. It was parades 365 days a year. Any hour of the day or night the call would come up, "On Parade, On Parade."' But parades and military duties took up only a small proportion of the BOR's time. Most of his off-duty hours he spent in his 'bungalow'. These were not bungalows in the usual sense 'but more in the nature of aircraft hangars, very solidly built, about 250 feet long, about 100 feet wide and between 30 and 40 feet high. They were very light, very cool and well ventilated. The cook-house, latrines and other parts of the barracks were all separate. In many cases the cook-houses and the latrines were as far as two hundred yards away from the bungalows.'

Since the bungalow was shared by a platoon of anything up to fifty men, the ordinary soldier had little privacy: 'All he could lay claim to was perhaps one hundred cubic feet for ninety per cent of his life.' He had his own bed and his own kit box. 'This bed was the centre of his life. He used it for everything. He used it as a writing desk, as a cleaning room, as a work bench, as a card table, and when he wasn't doing anything on the bed he was sleeping on it. A great part of the time in India he slept, principally because he had nothing else to do.' The kit box contained all the soldier's worldly goods. 'You weren't allowed to have anything that couldn't go into that kit box. It had always to be locked and your lock had to be burnished and always shining brightly because it was inspected every day.' A vital item of equipment, as Ed Davies, a soldier in the Dorset Regiment explains, was the 'mozzie net' with 'four poles at each corner of the bed and reclining over the top and right the way down a net like a queen's bedchamber. We used to lower it down before the mozzies came in the evening after the sun went down and keep it well tucked all the way round.'

The tedium of daily routine for the ordinary soldier was softened by the services of the camp followers, known as *wallahs*, the first of which began before reveille, with the visit of the *nappy-wallah*: 'He'd shave you and you never had an idea until you woke up all nice and cleanshaven and with a face like a baby's bottom, and he'd charge you at the end of the week.' With sun-up came reveille and the sound of the morning gun, which used to 'echo all round the quiet barracks and startle the crows. You'd hear "Boom . . . quark, ark, ark!"' The *charwallah* came round with a big silver urn and poured out tea into the mugs at the side of each bed. This was paid for by the annaworth and was reckoned to be 'good stuff'. Then came physical training on the barrack square, cold showers and a change into uniforms 'pressed the night before by one of the *chokras*'. These 'boys', often elderly men, looked after the needs of a number of soldiers in return for a rupee a week from each man. Breakfast was usually 'what we called a khaki steak, very tough meat worked to a frazzle' and had to be fetched from the cook-house and taken over to the dining-hall, with the ubiquitous kite-hawks waiting to swoop down upon some unsuspecting rookie out from Blighty: 'He'd come out so unconcerned, whistling, with his plate of grub in his hand, and all of a sudden the kite-hawk would swoop down and leave him with nothing.'

Army rations were not thought to be adequate. 'All the years I remained in the ranks,' recalls E. S. Humphries, who served in the Royal Scots, 'I spent the whole of my money to provide myself with sufficient food to prevent malnutrition.' Vendors were always on hand to make up the deficiencies. 'The egg-*wallah* frying eggs in a large pan, the *dudh-wallah* with his little pats of butter and milk, and the ham-*wallah*, a fellow with a board with a roll of ham on it which he cut.' The most exotic of the vendors was the sweet-*wallah*, 'usually a fat and cheerful man who would announce his arrival by chanting in a loud, strong voice, "Jimmy Kelly good for belly, take and try before you buy. Sweetie! Sweetie!" He would put his tin box on the verandah and before one's very eyes display vast amounts of white, sugary sweets mixed with coconut, all for the price of four ounces for one penny.' All the camp followers had to be licensed by the regimental quartermaster. Some were specialists of rare degree:

You'd get the fellow who came round the verandah of the bungalow shouting 'Corn-cuttit *wallah*!' He'd cut your corns with a nice, horn-shaped little tube that was put on the corn and would draw it out. If the battalion was on the move you'd get a fellow coming round who'd call out, 'Names-to-put-on-the-kitbag *wallah*' and he would paint your name and number on your kit bag. There was the Bombay-oyster *wallah*. He'd bring round raw eggs which he'd break into a glass with vinegar or sauce and which used to be swallowed with a gulp. As well as the dhobi, who took the weekly washing, there was also the man known as the flying dhobi. If you were going on guard that night he would pick up your drill in the morning and bring it back that evening beautifully laundered and starched ready to put on.

The net result of these auxiliary services was a remarkable improvement in the turn-out of the British soldier. Under the Indian sun 'a speck you got away with on parade at Aldershot was like an ink stain on the parade ground at Poona.' Yet the almost unlimited workforce allowed 'bulling' to reach new heights: 'The turn-out of the battalion when I first saw it dazzled me. I had never seen such smart soldiers, because I had never seen soldiers whose uniforms were washed and ironed every day.' On top of this the British soldier in India enjoyed considerable status: 'He was the soldier-*sahib* and was addressed as such by the humbler Indians and insisted on being addressed as such.' The effect on the BORs' morale was considerable: 'After about a year in India they were four feet off the ground.'

One group of camp followers earned a special place in the affections of the British soldier. These were the *bheestis*, the regimental water-carriers whose reputations Kipling had done much to enhance, and the sweepers – known as *mehtars* – whose virtues remained unsung. The *mehtar*'s job was a vital one: 'Latrines in those days used to mean a hole in a board behind corrugated iron sheeting. Occasionally whilst sitting there you'd find a black arm snaking out from under you and taking the tin away. This was a bit frightening at first but you got used to it.' Waste from the latrines was collected by the sweepers and removed in a conveyance drawn by a pair of oxen and known as the 'Bombay milk-cart'. Because it served several bungalows the privy was an important social centre as well as a haven for scroungers, since 'when you were in the privy you were inviolate'. A certain fellow-feeling grew up between the British soldier and the sweepers, 'the only caste of Indian that we had the opportunity of meeting or conversing with'.

The interaction between the British soldier and the camp-follower led to a strange mixture of British and Indian camp slang that both sides mispronounced and mis-used. For the most part such communication took a brisk and no-nonsense approach, as Ed Davies explains: 'If you wanted one of the vendors for something you used to say to him, "*Idder ow jeldi*" – come here quickly. It had to be "*jeldi*" because he got a kick up the backside if he didn't run. We'd say to him, "*Kitna pice?*" – How much? He'd probably say "*Das anna, sahib*" which is ten pence, and we used to say "*Das annas? Hum marcaro jeldi*" – in other words, "I'll give you one across the skull." If you were determined to let them know you weren't going to let them muck you about you used to look them straight in the eye and say "*Malum?*" and that was enough. They'd say, "*Achah*, sahib, *malum*".' Amongst themselves the BORS frequently used their own Anglo-Indian argot: 'If anybody got a bit obstreperous we used to say to him, "Don't be *bobbery* – don't be mad," and we used to say, "What about cleaning your *bundook*, then?" That's his rifle. And, "Oh, I see you've been *charpoy*-bashing again," sleeping on your bed.'

As a rule, military duties were not arduous. In the hot weather activities were restricted to early morning parades and sports and exercise in the evening. Thursday was always a buckshee day, or old soldiers' day, when all parades were cancelled and the day given over to sport and other leisure activities: 'We had one great weapon against boredom. The answer was sport, sport, sport. We were games mad and that was an enormous help.' After games the men showered: 'then you'd don long slacks, khaki shirts with sleeves right down to your wrists so that the mozzies wouldn't get at you, and a side hat, and away you used to go to a club or a bar for a couple of pints, or to your own canteen.' Beer was cheap – about two or three annas a pint – and it was good and strong, but the troops knew that 'when they came out of the wet canteen they didn't have to be offensive, they didn't have to be uproarious, they didn't have to be helpless, they just had to stagger and someone on duty outside the canteen would put them in the guard room for being drunk'.

More adventurous activities beyond the cantonments, even if allowed, were restricted by lack of money. 'When I first enlisted,' remembers Ed Brown, 'the pay was 8d a day, less stoppages. One week I would draw 3s 3d, the next week 2s od and the funny part about this was that as you came away from the pay station the orderly sergeant would stop and ask you if you wanted to buy any war loans. You were then marched to the canteen where you were compelled to spend tenpence on cleaning materials.' Stoppages were a perpetual source of grievances among the BORs. 'There were some legitimate stoppages such as laundry and shoe repairs, but there was one which was neither fair nor reasonable called "barrack damages". It recurred month after month and this was one of the causes of the soldier drawing such poor pay in India.'

The BOR was entitled to a fortnight's leave every year – if he could afford it: 'He was stopped by one element alone and this was money.' As a result most troops stayed put with their regiment. A few made the effort and got away on leave: 'We used to team up with two or three mates, making it a foursome, and save up like billy-o to get the fare and the amount that the hotel wanted and enough spending money for a few fags.' YMCA hotels and the Sandys Homes for Soldiers provided cheap lodgings, even if in return you had 'to sing a couple of hymns – which we used to do out of courtesy.' Staying in a Sandys Home in Landour, E. S. Humphries recalls that 'there for the first time I learnt something of the graces of good living, of kindly culture and good manners'. But such homes – and such hospitality – were few and far between. 'We'd served in Sudan before coming to India,' remembers George Wood, then an officer in the Dorset Regiment, 'and the men were very bitter on the subject of the kindness they had met with in the Sudan from the civilian population, as opposed to the way the British population in India ignored their existence.'

In the absence of support from outside, the regiment looked to itself – and to its officers. 'An officer's life we knew was the finest thing that was ever invented, but we never felt jealous,' says Ed Davies. 'During my whole service in India I never heard one person say, "Look at old Smith, he's living a life of luxury, look at what we've got." ' The reason for this deference was that 'the private soldier was taught to believe that the officer was a better man'. The officers came from 'the privileged classes and the common soldiery from the common people of England. These people were born leaders and born gentlemen. They never did a thing that transgressed the code of gentlemen. I've seen these officers in action on the Frontier. They were always in front. It would've been a dereliction of their duty not to have done it, and their duty was always paramount.'

As a child in army barracks, Spike Milligan very soon became aware of the superiority of officers. 'I really thought they were the gods and never got very close to them without being terrified out of my life. They had very loud voices, very proper, were very well turned out and always on horses, always taller than me, doing things with tremendous panache. If you heard the click of heels you knew the officer was somewhere near and somebody was standing to attention. They used to stand to attention like ramrods. I watched my father salute and I thought his arm would drop off with the ferocity of his salute.' Even more remote than the officers were their wives, 'always very pale and very beautiful and well-gowned and never moving very fast if they were on horses'.

The remoteness of women was perhaps the most frustrating aspect of a soldier's life in India: 'Complete segregation, not only from British women but from any sort of woman.' Ed Brown states that 'when I got home – apart from perhaps three women in the married quarters who were the wives of the bandmasters or band-sergeants – I hadn't spoken to a woman for nearly nine years'. This was certainly no isolated instance.

'I suppose I was in India for five or six years without speaking to a woman of any sort,' declares E. S. Humphries. 'We were inclined to place women on pedestals and this provided a sort of barrier against our licentious thoughts. Those of us who could not restrain ourselves were lectured by our unit medical officer regarding the dangers of venereal disease. He would beg us, if we were unable to withstand our desires, to go to our brothels, saying that "if you go trundling off into the village fields it will bring you calamitous results."'

Although illicit, military brothels existed and 'regiments did make discreet arrangements with the contractor for sexual relief'. Nevertheless, 'the ghost of Lady Roberts and various churchmen still persisted in India, compelling us to make these arrangements in the most secret manner'. The red light districts in the larger cities – 'in Bombay it was known as the Cages, in Poona it was called the Nadge' – were strictly out of bounds. 'If any white soldier was seen in the area whistles were blown by the police, all traffic came to a standstill and the soldier would, of course, be caught.' Periodical medical checks, known as 'short arm inspections', ensured that any man who availed himself of the 'tree rats' or 'grass *bidis*' was properly dealt with. 'He was given a severe ticking-off, had his pay stopped and was sent to Number 13 Block, which was the dreaded treatment centre.' Many turned, as a last resort, to the 'five-fingered widow'.

The ordinary soldier was only permitted to marry if circumstances allowed: 'The most jealously watched list in the regimental archives was the married quarters roll, which permitted a soldier not only to have his wife with him but guaranteed a quarter for her. Naturally the warrant officers, being great men, were all on the married quarters roll and then it filtered down, fifty per cent of sergeants, twenty-five per cent of corporals, ten per cent of the privates.' This privileged section of the community was known as the 'Hunting Clan'. Some BORs fought both army regulations and prejudice to marry Eurasian girls, usually encountered at the Railway Institute dances that did much to lessen the isolation of the British soldier: 'Whenever you were dancing with an Anglo-Indian girl the first thing she did was to assail you with a great puff of garlic and cheap perfume, but you stuck to her, because she was beautiful and in any case probably the only girl available.'

There was one inevitable side-effect of enforced segregation: 'It wasn't widespread but it was there, it was practised and it did more good than harm.' The attitudes of other soldiers towards the 'Darby and Joans' of the regiment was generally good-natured and sympathetic. Spike Milligan records the case of a young soldier 'desperately in need of sex who ravished the sacred cow at the temple. The Hindus took great offence at this and he was prosecuted – and the officer who was representing the Crown opened the case by saying, "On the day of the alleged offence my client was grazing contentedly in the field."' The case was apparently dismissed when it was pointed out that 'the cow had been cited in a previous case'.

In fact, a great deal of the soldier's affections were transferred to dumb animals: 'Puppies, kittens, monkeys, parrots grew in profusion in these regiments and to see a G.S. wagon going to camp with about 20 dogs, 15 parrots and 14 monkeys was really something.' Nearly every soldier had a dog, with inevitable results, as Mrs Lee the wife of an army sergeant remembers: 'Every now and then it would come in Army Orders that all dogs had got to be on parade. They'd parade all their dogs and then they were only allowed to keep one each. All the others had got to be got rid of and the chief marksman would shoot them. One soldier had been out for a walk somewhere and he came back to find his dog had been put up to be shot. So he went up to the officer in charge and said, "Anyone shoots that dog, I shoot them, sir." The officer asked him how many dogs he had. "Only that one." "Oh well, take him off."' The same rule applied when the regiment moved to a new posting. 'It was a strict order that only the regimental dogs would be allowed and they'd march off in the morning with only regimental dogs. But once you got to the other camp then you'd suddenly find dogs, cats, mongoose, monkeys – the whole lot was there, brought up by the bearers in the rear of the column.'

Time passed slowly for the British soldier in India: 'It was

Barrack Room PETS!

"One Monkey per regiment is sufficient," said a well known Commanding Officer, some years ago, when the question of "pets" in barracks arose, "Undoubtedly". he continued, "the animal said to be the nearest to man in its mannerisms, makes a very fascinating pet, but off its chain it's the devil's own mischief itself."

India offers an extensive choice of pets to those who love them, and in and around the various barracks (apart from the dignified "mascot" pets which sometimes accompany the band) may be seen strolling leisurely about the troops' bungalows, young deer, fully grown and long-horned "Black Buck", Nilghi (Blue Bull) or perhaps a stately Sarus, a grey, long-legged, five-foot bird of the stork family, with a scarlet head and an eighteen inch beak like a bayonet.

Tiger Cubs and young Bears are sometimes seen, but as they mature their ferocious nature asserts itself and the order comes "Get Rid of IT."

Smaller animals such as the Mongoose and Squirrel also make delightful pets if procured young. Parrots, of course, get their share of Government Quarters, and the daily morning screech "Wake up Gunner, make the tea, a cup for you, and a cup for me," is as good as any "reveille."

Fowls and pigeons, too, find a place on the pet's roll. But last though not least comes our canine pet the dog. There are always a dozen or more dogs of all sizes,

Advice on pets in barracks;
cigarette manufacturer's leaflet, 1940

too hard a life in those days and the slightest thing used to stand out as a delight. A delight was being able to get off parade, being able to go sick and say that you'd got three days excused duties, or meeting up with someone you hadn't seen for years.' But the men were still held together by common interests. Housey-housey was played regularly and 'on countless occasions we sat up until two or three in the morning playing either crown and anchor or pontoon by candlelight for cigarette coupons which were negotiable in the bazaar for three annas a thousand'. Occasionally troupes of dancing girls 'with bells on their ankles and wrists', Chinese contortionists, jugglers, fortune-tellers or snake charmers would visit the camp; 'one in particular had a pencil-thin snake which he put through his nose and drew out through his mouth'.

Sundays were marred, from the troops' point of view, by church parades: 'Totally unnecessary, really a matter of showing-off to the native population.' Nevertheless, they were significant occasions, as Irene Edwards observed when in Peshawar: 'It was a sight to be seen when the Army marched down the Mall, the band leading; the sun always shining, the trees on either side all in flower. The *chokra* boys flocked and cheered and we Anglo-Indians swelled with pride because we were part of the British.' The Sunday ritual included arms in church. 'Even in my day,' explains Ed Davies, 'we still had to go to church with rifle and bayonet and twenty rounds of ammunition, with flags flying and all the natives looking on. The troops used to file into church with their sidearms and rifle and we had to place them into slots specially made for the purpose. When a long address was given and the troops got bored we used to rattle our rifles, very soft at first. And the more the parson carried on the more we rattled them. All the officers and the officers' wives used to look round, and if looks could kill we'd have died on the spot.'

This ready availability of arms and ammunition on Sundays sometimes had unforeseen consequences: 'I remember two tragedies that occurred during church parades. The chaps were very low in spirit, I suppose. They'd say they were not very well and "please, could they be excused," and they'd go back to the barrack room and blow their heads off.' Suicides among BORs in India were far from exceptional: 'Besides these two shootings we had a young boy who'd only been out two weeks before he hanged himself, and another lad, only seventeen, who considered himself tormented by the NCOs and drove himself insane and blew his brains out.' There were occasional desertions, rarely successful, and 'a new sort of disease that came into the language and was called "doolally tap", not so much a disease as a mental condition in which men went mad, went on the rampage, smashed things up. Or they would stand outside shouting at the sergeant-major, "I want to bloody well shoot you the moment you come out."'

England never ceased to beckon. 'We thought England was the greatest place on earth,' says Ed Davies. 'We were always talking about home and it was a glorious moment when the mail call was sounded. We used to call it "Letters from Lousy Lou, Letters from Lousy Liz," but it meant everything to everybody. The corporal in charge of the bungalow used to shout out, "Come on! Mail up, boys!" and we used to rush in and he would shout out, "Davies, Smith, Jones, Brown, Green." Some chaps would never have any, of course, and we'd say, "Cheer up. Better luck next time."' Everybody in the regiment looked forward to the mail, perhaps nobody more than the army wives, as Mrs Wood describes: 'On Sunday morning after church parade we met under the trees on the lawn, the band played and it was very pleasant. Then at twelve o'clock the mail from home arrived and everybody would vanish. You would race back to your bungalow and there would be those longed-for letters from home, possibly photographs of a four-year-old on an English beach. You lived for that letter day.'

Towards the end of their tour of duty the men would become 'utterly apathetic'. Their officers would go to England for six months every two years while they had no option but to soldier on: 'They'd got no time for anything but this one fact, and it used to recur every minute of the day. No matter what little problem arose, they would meet it with, "Roll on the boat, roll on the boat." You would hear this from morning till night. That one phrase was used in India more frequently, with more force and vehemence than any other.' Another over-used phrase was 'Roll on my seven and five,' because 'a man's service was seven years before the colours and you usually landed up in India doing five.'

Finally the time came when the return draft was called. 'The draft paraded on the square and the whole regiment turned out and escorted us off, with beer and whisky and what have you.' The band played 'Rolling Home to Dear Old Blighty' and the draft marched off to the railway station: 'If you used to go with Indian girls they'd all congregate as you were marching away and sing a little ditty called "Oh doolally sahib", which means a mad gentleman. They'd sing:

Oh doolally sahib, fifteen years you've had my daughter,
and now you go to Blighty, sahib.
May the boat that takes you over
sink to the bottom of the *pani*, sahib!

They'd all sing that and then roll up with laughter.'

16

THE FRONTIER

Probably no sign until the burst of fire, and then the swift rush with knives, the stripping of the dead, and the un-hurried mutilation of the infidels.

GENERAL SIR ANDREW SKEEN *Passing It On:*
Short Talks on Tribal Fighting in the
North-West Frontier 1932

There were two frontiers of India, the North-West – 'full of romance and danger and deeds of derring do' – and the North-East, virtually ignored and, in many areas, unexplored up to the Second World War. The former had long been the scene of constant political and military activity, with 'this little air of danger, where there was always the chance of a stray bullet'. As a result it retained a powerful hold over the imaginations of the British both at home and in India.

To a great exponent of mountain warfare like Claude Auch-inleck the Frontier was 'the one place where the new officer could hope to get on active service. Anybody who had a certain amount of ambition wanted to serve there. And you had to be on your toes the whole time. I never enjoyed anything more.' To a 'political' like Olaf Caroe, last in a line of great frontiers-men, there was much more: 'I remember Lord Ronaldshay saying that "the life of a frontiersman is hard and treads daily on the brink of eternity". That was the sort of feeling one had about the landscape there, which was sometimes gloriously beautiful, green and lovely and verdant, and sometimes stark and horrible and beset with dust storms. The stage on which the Pathan lived out his life was at the same time magnificent and harsh – and the Pathan was like his background. Such a contrast was sometimes hard to bear but perhaps it was this that put us in love with it. There was among the Pathans something that called to the Englishman or the Scotsman – partly that the people looked you straight in the eye, that there was no equivocation and that you couldn't browbeat them even if you wished to. When we crossed the bridge at Attock we felt we'd come home.'

Few failed to respond to the picturesque figure of the Pathan, 'a great chap for swagger'. Walter Crichton, who served four years on the Frontier as a medical officer and very nearly ended his days there, saw the Pathans as 'very fine looking men with long bobbed hair and untidy looking turbans tied loosely with loops coming down round their necks; then sheepskin push-toons which they wore in winter, baggy trousers and sandals – and a fearsome looking bandolier full of cartridges either slung across the shoulder or round their waists – and, inevitably, a rifle.' Like so many of his countrymen he found them 'a very nice lot of people on the whole, whom we liked because they were tough fighters – whether they played the game according to our rules or not – and very good marksmen'.

The North-West Frontier Province consisted of a belt of administered territory and, beyond that, an unadministered tribal area, based on 'a kind of instinct that we didn't want to have a common frontier of administered territory next door to another power'. Administration of the tribal areas was 'merely designed to see that the tribes did not commit nuisances either in India or in Afghanistan'. These nuisances came in many forms; some as manifestations of the 'blood feud' which accounted for three hundred murders a year in the Peshawar district alone, some based on the long-established custom of raiding for cattle, women and guns, and some politically motivated. Following ancient Moslem ethics rather than the Indian Penal Code, the political officer tried wherever possible to make use of the tribal *jirga*, which was both a jury and a tribal assembly: 'They sit round you in a circle of two thousand men and you sit in the middle and have to talk. You have to be able to speak the language well enough to take up a running argument, make speeches and even know the proverbs.' Sometimes outside intervention became inevitable: 'We did interfere whenever they were a nuisance to us, and interference had to be by force.' Force came in the form of a punitive foray, a light bombing raid after advance warning or, as a last resort, a military column involving several brigades.

Life on the Frontier had its own special style, ranging 'from excitement to boredom and back again'. Entry into the tribal areas was by permit only, with special restrictions on women. Those who stepped off the government roads on to tribal territory did so at their own risk. Down these roads came the *kafilah*, the caravans from Bokhara and Samarkand, as Dolly Rowe describes: 'They come down head to tail, these camels, tramping along, plod, plod, plod, bellowing away, supercilious, some with bags round their faces, and froth . . . There are buffaloes, there are donkeys, there are sheep, and then the women; they tinkle, tinkle, tinkle as they walk past you, wearing huge earrings that wingle and wangle about and gold and silver on their fingers. Sometimes there's a woman in front, sometimes there's a man and sometimes there's a tiny little child, and away they go down to Peshawar.'

Despite opposition from family and friends, Irene Edwards went to nurse in Peshawar – 'the city of a thousand and one sins' – in 1929: 'The fort was on one side of us and the city on the other. It was very comforting to see the Union Jack flying on that fort and to see the British soldiers on the parapet. We used to have the wolf whistles but it was all very cheering and comforting, especially when the trouble started and the anti-British feeling grew. When the Redshirts started shouting "Up the revolution!" we used to look at those soldiers and that fort and really feel safe.' Nursing on the Frontier was unusual in many respects: 'I had heard about the family feuds, now I was to see the results. You would get a case coming in with all the intestines sticking out. They used to get the skin of a chicken and wrap the intestines in this skin to keep them fresh. We used to have to cut out parts of the intestine, pick out shrapnel and pellets from gunshot wounds and sew them up. We used to have jealous husbands cutting off their wives' noses, breasts amputated, even pregnant women with their abdomens ripped open.' Even the gardeners were out of the ordinary: 'Our gardeners were prisoners. These men had heavy chains round their waists, down each leg and round each ankle. The clanking of these chains used to be our waking bell as they came into our verandah watering the pots in gangs, always with an armed guard.'

Peshawar was a colourful and, for the most part, peaceful city, a family station 'where you played your games and lived the ordinary cantonment life'. But when trouble spilled down from the Hills, as it did in the Red Shirts Rebellion or the Peshawar Riots of 1930, then it could be as dangerous as anywhere on the Frontier. Walter Crichton recalls:

I was walking through the bazaar with my sub-assistant surgeon, a very nice little Hindu whose name was Tir' Ram, and going through these narrow crowded streets we were held up for a moment by a train of mules carrying timber. I bent over to talk to a little boy who was pounding chillis on the ground and in that instant I suddenly felt a blow, a terrific sock right in the back, and I thought that one of these mules had lashed out at me and caught me with its hoof. But when I turned round to see what had happened I realized it was not a mule at all, but that I was at the end of an axe which was stuck in my back and held at the other end by a rather fierce-looking Pathan who was doing his best to dislodge this axe from my back. Tir' Ram looked around, or I may have cried to him, and promptly leapt at this man, jerked the axe out of my back and then twined his little legs round him and tripped him so that they both fell to the ground in a cloud of dust. I staggered about in a rather drunken fashion with a lot of blood streaming down my back and into my boots. Then members of the militia came running up and seized the fellow and brought him away. They tried to carry me to the civil hospital but I said I'd walk. When I got there I more or less collapsed on to a *charpoy*. They got my clothes off and by the aid of a series of mirrors I told them what I thought should be done – and I was then stitched up.

In surviving the attack 'Crit' Crichton was luckier than one of his predecessors, a Captain Coldstream. Irene Edwards relates how she and he were having coffee and talking about golf:

He knew that I was very keen on golf and asked me if I'd like a lesson from him. I said yes, I'd be very grateful, and he arranged to pick me up at five that afternoon. Then he went downstairs. When he got to the bottom he waved to me and said, 'I'll pick you up then, at five.' I said, 'Right,' and I turned round to walk back to the duty room. Then I heard a peculiar sort of scuffling noise. Suddenly I heard shouts of 'Sister, Sister, come quickly!' I rushed to the top of the stairs and looked down and there were two of the *babus* carrying Captain Coldstream upstairs. I could see blood streaming from his neck and I said, 'What has happened?' 'He's been beaten,' one *babu* said. The other *babu* said in Hindustani, 'No, he has been knifed.' I looked down at Captain Coldstream and I knew that he was dying. When assistance came I went back into the duty room and I saw our coffee cups. I looked at Captain Coldstream's coffee cup and I picked up mine, which was still warm. I sat there and cried and cried, till another sister came and put her arms around me. We then walked out on to the verandah and we saw Abdul Rashid, the orderly, standing there with blood pouring down his arm. I went up to him and said, 'Oh, Abdul Rashid, have you been hurt?' and they all looked at me queerly. I thought Abdul Rashid had gone to Captain Coldstream's assistance. Actually, he was the murderer.

Further up the Frontier there were smaller family stations such as Palantrana, where 'the European community consisted of the political agent and his wife and the OC of the Corps of Militia and about half a dozen officers and the Agency Surgeon.' Here the dangers of Frontier life were obvious. Crit Crichton had a nice bungalow, 'large and commodious with a very nice garden – but it was whispered to me as I got there that my predecessor and his wife had actually been murdered there by Pathans from across the border. On one occasion my wife was fishing, and on the other side of the river there was a battle going on between two sections of Pathans.'

In tribal territory there were non-family stations only, fortifications or large camps surrounded by barbed wire, where life was 'great fun but terribly frustrating, and on occasion frightening'. For all that, every soldier jumped at the chance: 'It was an adventure to go there and the British soldier was proud to go there. Only good British regiments were sent to the Frontier and they went there with a feeling of professional pride.' Separations and hardships 'on the grim' – as the Frontier was known to the British Ordinary Soldier – were inevitable. 'Before we could leave,' recalls Reginald Savory, referring to his own regiment of Sikhs, 'all the women had to be told to go, and they were put into special carriages in one of the local mail trains and sent off under the escort of trusted elderly men, because the Sikh is a lusty chap!' On active service on the Frontier officers got three months leave a year on full pay – 'but we earned it. The remaining nine months were spent surrounded by a barbed wire fence, away from your wife, longing for the post to arrive. I lived that kind of life for ten out of the twenty years which separated World War One from World War Two.'

When Ed Brown's Royal Warwicks moved up to Landi Kotal they followed the usual practice and marched: 'We could see on the horizon a kind of battleship shimmering in the heat. This was a fort, looking just like a gunboat or a warship, shimmering grey in the heat of the day. And we never seemed to get much nearer to it, we had to keep on marching and marching. We passed a caravan, a thousand head of animals I should think, camels and donkeys laden with carpets from Persia and Afghanistan, and a lot of followers. We saw one of the men beating a woman with his camel whip and we had to suffer the sight of this poor lady being whipped cruelly as we left her in the distance.' After a night at the fort they continued to march: 'Horrible looking hills loomed nearer and nearer and then you saw some sort of crack going up through the hills – and this was the Khyber Pass; great slabs of rock towering up on either side of you.' Finally, at Landi Kotal itself, 'as you went through the gate there was a notice which read, "Abandon hope all ye who enter here," and that just about put the lid on it.'

The restrictions of life on non-family stations were considerable yet George Wood, who spent two years on the Khyber as brigade-major, remembers that the British soldiers were never happier. Nevertheless, their isolation created certain difficulties: 'As we were all behind barbed wire, the ordinary punishment for defaulters seemed rather inappropriate. However, with the assistance of our engineer I set the defaulters to work

---

Major G. Humphries of the Telegraph Department is permitted to visit Torkham on 12th February 1930 on duty.

It is clearly to be understood that no one except on duty is allowed to accompany him and in no circumstances whatever are any ladies allowed to proceed to the border.

w. a Ganltn

P.E.S.H.A.W.A.R.   Lt.Col.,
12th February 1930.   Political Agent, Khyber.

Travel permit, North West Frontier, 1930

with pick-axes and cold chisels to level a large area of virgin rock to a perfect level over which was spread a coating of fine cement. The contractor was then told to produce all the roller skates in India, fairy lights were slung over this area and all through the cold weather the British troops roller-skated and roller-skated.'

Campaigning on the Frontier required a rigid and constant adherence to a system that had been tried and tested for more than half a century. 'The advance into hostile country was an absolutely stereotyped performance,' explains Claude Auchin-leck. 'Your line of advance was always up a river valley. As the column went along, the advance guard would put people up on either side of the valley on peaks or ridges from which the enemy might fire on the main column, and if it was properly done you got through. When you got to your camping ground pickets built themselves little forts with stone walls all round the camp to prevent the camp being fired into. Then you pro-ceeded to make camp like the Romans did, with a wall all round it of stone and, if necessary, dug in a bit. If you failed to know how to picket the route – what places to put your men – then you were always liable to an attack on the baggage column or the transport mules by perhaps fifty or one hundred men who came down unseen. It was purely a matter of ground. You always had to have high ground and you had to know exactly where to put your men.'

Even on the best regulated operations there were risks – 'the danger was there and it was an invisible danger.' Only when you were at your most vulnerable did the enemy show itself and that moment came most often when the picket was being withdrawn. 'The Pathan would very often be waiting in dead ground where you couldn't see him,' explains Reginald Savory, 'and when you were just ten yards or so off from the picket the Pathan would jump on top and have a shot at you at short range. So the moment the last man was off you brought down covering fire. The last man was generally your fittest man and carried a yellow or a red flag and as he got down below the crest he waved his flag and ran down the slope as quick as he could. When he was about twenty yards away the fire came down on the top. Withdrawing pickets along a ridge and run-ning uphill to the next peak, with the enemy shooting at you from behind, was one of the most unpleasant experiences I've ever known. One used to get most frightfully conscious of the little dip between one's shoulder-blades.'

Those who failed to observe the rules of mountain warfare invariably paid a price, as John Dring witnessed when, as political agent in South Waziristan, he accompanied a punitive column into hostile territory: 'The hostiles were out in very large numbers; they got above the military pickets and disaster followed. Every single thing went wrong. One regiment came literally running from the hills into camp. We got bogged down seven miles from Razmak, all wires were cut and I spent no less than four and a half weeks in a hole in the ground utterly cut off. On that short march the column suffered at least eighty killed, including the British colonel of one of the regiments.' Sniping – 'the odd bang, bang at night and the whang of a bullet' – was a constant and trying feature of Frontier campaigning. Regiments new to the Frontier frequently returned fire: 'We used to rush and mount the Lewis guns, fire Verey Lights and spray the outside of the wire with fire and, of course, when the machine guns opened up they just slid back behind the ridge.' More experienced regiments held back: 'It was accepted practice in the Indian Army never to return fire. It was a sign of steadiness not to shoot back, to look for and spot the man but never fire back. If a regiment shot back against a sniper it was a mark against them – "Oh, they're the chaps who shoot back at snipers."'

Few regiments were as skilled in mountain warfare as the Gurkhas, and none more experienced than Lewis Le Marchand's 5th (Frontier Force) Gurkhas. After being subjected to sniping every night – 'not many casualties, but very annoying' – they retaliated by 'sending out the usual working party of possibly thirty odd men, Gurkhas in their off-parade clothes, baggy trousers and so on. They went out and cleared a little bit of the countryside and then came back after about an hour's work, but instead of thirty of them coming back, only twenty-five did. We left five men with rifles concealed in their long trousers hidden up where we thought the sniping was coming from. And sure enough, that night at about ten o'clock or so a couple of rounds of sniping started, and then there was a volley of shots and our five Gurkhas came in bearing the corpses of two Mahsuds, dead as mutton. The political agent came to see them the next morning and said, "Good God, I dined with that fellow last night!" It was one of the local Khans. He'd given the political agent dinner first and then decided to go down and have a few shots at him.'

It was a precept of Frontier warfare never to lose a rifle. 'The loss of a rifle was regarded as the most heinous crime and it generally meant a court of enquiry and sometimes a court martial. You were never allowed to forget it. You'd hear people say, "Oh, that regiment – oh yes, weren't they the ones who lost those rifles in Tirah in 1894?" That was the kind of disgrace which one feared much more than losing one's life or getting a bullet in the groin.' The Pathans coveted rifles greatly and were prepared to throw lives away in order to secure one. Most attempts, as in the following incident described by Reginald Savory, were unsuccessful: 'I was sending some men up to picket one of the heights when they were charged by a group of young chaps with knives. They went for them with the bayonet and killed the lot. We laid them out in a row – such a good-looking lot of young chaps they were – and one of the village elders came along, an old grey-bearded man. I showed him these four or five boys lying by the roadside and I don't think I've ever seen anybody quite so broken-hearted in my life.' More often rifle thieves, known to the BORS as 'loose-*wallahs*', naked and greased all over, attempted to steal rifles by night. To prevent this 'every man had to sleep with his rifle chained to him. The chain went through his trigger guard and round his waist. If you hadn't got a chain you dug a little pit the length and width of a rifle, you put the rifle in it and you slept on top of it.' Sometimes not even the most elaborate attempts to safeguard rifles were enough. 'We had to have folds stitched into the end of our blankets,' remembers Ed Brown. 'We used to thread the rifle into the fold and the sling outside it round your arm. But still they broke into the camp and stabbed a man numerous times to make him release his rifle. Eventually he did – and although that man was stabbed and hurt so badly he had a court martial. He was told that he should never have lost the rifle but in view of the circumstances his only punishment would be that he'd have to pay for the rifle. Eighty-one rupees, eight annas they charged him for it. He accepted it. It was all part of the way things were.'

The Frontier was never merciful: 'The Pathan is an attractive man but he had a very, very cruel streak in him, and if you left a wounded man behind he was not only killed but frequently mutilated in the most obscene manner. It became, therefore, a point of honour with us never to leave a wounded man behind. So if one of our men was wounded we counterattacked in order to get that wounded man back.' But above all the Frontier tested the man: 'To run away or to show cowardice on a Frontier campaign and come back and wine or dine with your brother officers in the evening was a far worse punishment than risking death.' There were occasional failures. 'I've seen a British officer lying in a hole and pulled him out of it – but not very often,' says Claude Auchinleck. 'Before one went into attack one was frightened, there's no doubt about it. You just had to put it away somewhere and go ahead.'

17

THE LAND OF REGRETS

*Sooner or later the lurking shadow of separation takes
definite shape; asserts itself as a harsh reality; a grim presence, whispering the inevitable question; which shall it be?
. . . the rival claims of India and England; of husband and
child.*

MAUD DIVER *The Englishwoman in India* 1909

Throughout its history one generation of British men and
women was always absent from the Raj: 'There were no old
people among the British in India. A man of sixty was probably
the oldest that one was likely to meet.' Early retirement was
only partially responsible. Of the ten young officers who went
out with H. T. Wickham in 1904 to join the Indian Police,
two died within five months and another six within the decade.
Twenty years later India was still taking its toll of the misfit –
and the unfit. 'I made two friends on the voyage out,' recalls
Philip Mason, 'one of them died in his first summer. He wasn't
happy in India at all. Just before he reached Bombay he said to
me rather sadly, "I suppose I shall never again feel really well,"
and he didn't. He was not merely critical of the society he
found himself in, but he felt he had to express his criticism. He
went out on Famine Duty in the hot weather in June, and he
got an appendix and by the time they got him into headquarters, a two day journey in a bullock cart, that was that.'
Similarly, an acquaintance of Rosamund Lawrence 'hated
everything about India. She didn't like the servants and she
didn't like the weather, she didn't like the food and she didn't
like the people. She wouldn't learn to ride and she wouldn't
learn to drive. She just grumbled all day long and hated everything. And then one day the doctor told me that she was ill. I
said, "Oh, what's wrong with her?" and he said, "I don't know,

but she's very ill." The next day she was dead. Her idea of happiness was a suburban villa.'

Sometimes India – and the standards that were demanded of the young men who went there – was too much for even the stoutest character. Olaf Caroe recalls an instance when he was governor of the North-West Frontier Province:

In Waziristan there was a political agent who was the son of a man who had been in Waziristan before him. He was kidnapped and held by the Mahsuds and I had to harden my heart and take air action. It was taken and he was released. He came and stayed with me in Government House and I said to him, 'I think you'd better be moved. It's not fair to send you back again to this place.' And he begged me almost on his knees, with tears in his eyes, to send him back. He said he would never be able to stand up to himself or to anybody if he wasn't sent back. So I said, 'All right, I'll send you back for a short time, and then we'll move you on.' So I sent him back to his original station in South Waziristan and after six weeks or so I wrote him a letter and said, 'I think you've been there quite long enough. You must feel that you've proved yourself now, and I propose to move you to such and such a place.' Two days later I was rung up and told that he had shot himself, and my letter was lying unopened on his desk. He had found it too much for him.

Apart from the misfits, India took its toll in other ways. Speaking of the turn of the century, Mrs Norie recalls that 'life was so very short. When anybody got ill and died – and lots did – they were buried the same day. It made the parting so sudden and it made an awful impression upon people.' Nevertheless, it was characteristic: 'Everything is sudden in India, the sudden twilights, the sudden death. A man can be talking to you at breakfast and be dead in the afternoon – and this is one of the things you have to live with.' The old cemeteries of Calcutta and the UP, crowded with the graves of young men, younger women and their even younger offspring, were reminders of the fate that could still overtake those who failed to take the proper precautions.

While there were many noble and devoted exceptions – pioneers who fought through improvements in health and welfare in the face of hostile and even dangerous opposition, whether it was improving rickshaws in Simla or campaigning to stop cows being kept in houses in Delhi – the stock of the medical officer was not high. When Iris Portal fell ill up-country, her car was sent fifty miles for the nearest doctor: 'When it returned my husband was absolutely horrified to see emerging from the car first an enormous red nose, then a very pock-marked face, and then a very drunken doctor who said in muffled tones, "It must be malaria, or typhoid, or cholera. It obviously isn't cholera or typhoid, so it must be malaria. Give your wife thirty grains of quinine a day." Then he tossed the pills on the table and was driven away again. When I got back to headquarters I had various tests and was told that I had had typhus.' But whether good medical attention was available or not, 'gippy tummies', dengue and malaria continued to make life uncomfortable. 'We always used to take two grains of quinine every day,' remembers Kenneth Warren, 'and anybody who didn't take it was bound to go down with malaria.' For all the precautions, malaria in one form or another was virtually endemic in some areas. Kenneth Warren had the intermittent variety: 'I had two good days and then on the third it used to come on at about a quarter to twelve. I didn't want to be caught wandering about out of doors with this ague, so I used to go back to the bungalow just in time and then in about ten minutes I shook all over, my teeth chattered and I sweated. By next morning it had gone.' Even memsahibs took malaria in their stride: 'You go to dinner and you know your temperature's up at about a hundred and something, but you just don't bother.'

An abundance of insects added greatly to the general discomfort, not only those that bit or stung or stank when squashed, but others that destroyed – bored through books and ate through furniture. The bottoms of leather trunks fell away when lifted up and 'if you left your boots on the floor at night you lost the soles by the morning'. There was the potential threat of snakes, even though 'in nine cases out of ten the snake would try and avoid you and it was only when you were unfortunate enough to tread on it when it was asleep, or something like that, that you suffered any evil consequences'. It was even possible to spend a lifetime in India and never see a snake. 'I can remember months and months of not seeing a snake at all,' says Raymond Vernede. However, he was required to kill a cobra in his bathroom on one occasion and a krait was found under a cushion in the sitting room on another. For want of a better place to put it the latter was left tightly curled up in the calling box and forgotten. The following day the sweeper, 'a curious, inquisitive gentleman', opened the flap and 'the krait expanded and leapt out and there was a most fearful shriek'. The memsahib was rather more vulnerable than her husband. 'I hated snakes,' recalls Mrs Symington, though with some reason: 'The children's toy box had a snake in it one day and when I opened it out it popped. On another occasion I'd been sitting on a chair that had a loose cover, and when I got up the nanny went and sat on it and I suppose she was rather heavier than I was because a snake slithered out and went straight across the room to my little girl who was sitting in her chair.' Others had a more blasé attitude towards snakes. The men in Ed Brown's regiment, for instance, when stationed in the Rajputana desert, found numerous snakes sheltering in rat holes: 'We used to tee off with hockey sticks and golf balls and try and hit these snakes when they put their heads up out of the holes. Some of the snakes were cobras and I remember one of our fellows catching one with a piece of rag by letting him strike and catch his teeth in it. He put it in a bath of water in the wash-house and everyone crowded round to see what it was and whether it was dead – which it wasn't. It put its head over the rim of the bath and I've never seen such a stampede!'

The Pax Britannica gave both British and Indians a quite remarkable degree of safety in their daily lives. Hot weather after hot weather thousands of Europeans slept nightly out of doors, undisturbed and in perfect security. Nevertheless, the North-West Frontier had no special monopoly on violence.

Violence directed against individuals was rare and isolated – but it occurred. When Percival Griffiths took over as magistrate in one particular district in Bengal, he did so in the knowledge that his three predecessors had all been shot by terrorists: 'It was rather sad because of those three, two were specially known for their fondness for the Bengali and for the tremendous amount of public work that they were doing for the Bengali. The shooting was not directed at them as persons, it was directed at them as representatives of the British Raj.' Even in the worst years, when the non-co-operation movements and the *swaraj* demonstrations were gathering in strength, few Europeans were in real physical danger. 'We were left alone,' says Mrs Symington. 'I never had any rudeness or hostility or was ever frightened about anything. When my husband went away to quell a disorder or a riot I used to feel a bit nervous but I never felt that any harm would come to him. The whole house was always open, because we never felt that we were going to be attacked.'

This was only part of the picture. Half a century earlier, when Claude Auchinleck had come out to India, the attitudes of many memsahibs were very different. The Mutiny had not been forgotten. Claude Auchinleck's father had himself fought in the Mutiny as a subaltern and 'it had left scars on the communal memory. So far as the men were concerned, the Mutiny meant nothing to them. But the Englishwomen out there remembered the Mutiny and they influenced to a certain extent the behaviour and the feelings of their menfolk.'

The English memsahib came in for a great deal of criticism. 'Most of them started out as perfectly reasonable, decent English girls,' states John Morris, 'and many of them in the course of time developed into what I can only describe as the most awful old harridans. And I think they were very largely responsible for the break-up of relations between the British and the Indians. In the early days, before the Englishwoman went out to India at all, British officers spent much of their time with Indians, got to know them better, got to know the language well and so on; whereas once the Englishwoman started to arrive in India she expected her husband to spend his time with her. She couldn't communicate with anybody except her cook who knew a few words of English, so she was forced to rely almost solely upon her husband for amusement and company. I don't think that she realized what a menace she was.' Others were also critical of the memsahib, but for different reasons. 'At one stage of my life in India,' recalls George Carroll, 'I was very much against the white women because I considered that they were apt to let us down in prestige by going off to the Hills every Hot Weather and leaving one down below. The general understanding was that they went up there to lead a life of immorality, and in many cases it was true.'

But even the critics agreed that attitudes were changing: 'Womenfolk before the First World War were definitely more reserved and more concerned with preserving their separation. After the war that began to disappear.' As hot weather conditions improved, more and more wives chose to stay down in the plains with their husbands. None the less, the image stuck – 'the mythical picture of the British memsahib which was started by Kipling and has lived in the annals ever since'. Frances Smyth argues that this was a generalization with only a certain amount of truth in it: 'British women in India were like British women anywhere else, they were a lot of individuals. But there were certain attitudes which you took up, perhaps, from all the others. Such as, you don't mingle with Indians too much; you remember that you're British; and in the way you treat your servants. The older women would get together with you and say, "You know, you won't do your husband any good, my dear, by going and doing those sort of things," in a disapproving way. And so, if you were a good little wife, you probably thought, "Well, I'd better not."' Such pressures were by no means the same everywhere: 'There was a great difference between the civilian wives and the military wives. The civilians were for the most part stuck out in small stations where the wives took a much closer part in their husbands' work, whereas the military wives really had nothing to do with their husbands' jobs.' It was here and in the big cities where the wives 'who lived a life far more English than the English' were most often to be found – 'more often than not, the real India passed them by'.

Other factors discouraged the Englishwoman in India from playing a full role in the country. As might be expected in this 'very extrovert society' the women conformed to the cultural expectations of the men. 'There was a very strong feeling that women were not supposed to be clever. They were supposed to be decorative and intelligent and good listeners, but they weren't supposed to be clever and, if by any conceivable chance anyone was, they kept it pretty dark.' They were also at a great disadvantage when it came to mixing with Indians, because Indian women 'didn't come into society. They were nearly all in purdah, so your chances of meeting them were fairly rare.' This imbalance remained virtually unaltered right up to Independence and it required considerable strength of character on the part of those many memsahibs who penetrated this wall of male supremacy by giving 'purdah-parties' and establishing friendships with Indian women. There was also the 'generally rather indifferent education given the middle-class Edwardian lady'. Like her sisters at home she was not trained to do more than read good books and run a house well – and in India the latter was very often taken care of for her. Yet despite these many handicaps the exceptions who began to break through the 'Anglo-Indian' ethos in the early twenties were fast becoming the rule by the end of the thirties. Wives were finding useful and valuable roles for themselves, not only in support of their husbands but as individuals and as pace-makers outside the British community, taking up nursing, guiding and many other forms of voluntary work.

The sahibs themselves were equally subject to the 'attempt to push everybody into a mould', and to the feeling of 'sticking together, that you must always back each other up, if necessary'. Some saw this conformity as yet another manifestation of the 'convention-ridden memsahibs, who tended to build up a kind of "little-England" protectively around their unfortunate husbands'. But whatever the cause, it was not an atmosphere that encouraged artistic or cultural pursuits. 'You found repeated the social patterns of the way people lived at home,' asserts Iris Portal, 'and the British were not in those days a very cultured race. It was not fashionable among upper-class people of the type who went into the services to be very cultural, although you did find in the ICS very highly cultured, intellectual people who did get homesick for a more cultured life. I remember a very able member of the Indian Civil Service who shared a house with my father one winter and used to worry him by constantly playing gramophone records of Bach in his bathroom.'

At least one hardship was common to both sexes: 'The heartaches of separation are ever present in India,' declares Lewis Le Marchand. And this was particularly true of the army. 'Although the saying is "If you marry the drum you've got to follow it," there are many times when you simply cannot stay with it and you've got to be sent away. For the wife it is, "Goodbye, husband, I'll take the kids up to a hill station and we'll expect you on leave when we see you." ' Deborah Dring's experience was probably shared by many other army wives whose husbands were frequently 'up the line' on military duty: 'My husband and I were always being separated. I once worked out that in thirteen years we'd only spent three whole years together.'

The worst of these 'unending separations' and 'dreadful partings' were those that involved children. A time came when they had to be sent to England 'by convention, to be educated and to get them out of the Indian climate'. Every mother was forced to make a choice between children and husband – and with a major sacrifice either way. Those who chose to remain with their husbands did so at some cost to their children, as Marjorie Cashmore describes: 'We were told by our bishop that we mustn't keep our eldest child out over the age of five, so when she was only three we had to send her to her granny. That meant that for five years we didn't see her. In those days it took six weeks to get a letter and by the end of the five years when we got her back again she really was a stranger to us.' In the early years of service, separation and loneliness were much accentuated by poor pay and infrequent home passages. The assisted passage to and from England was a comparatively late innovation. Speaking of his own father, John Cotton recalls that 'between 1916 and 1926 he never came back to England at all, nor did we see him during any of those ten years'.

In striking contrast to the salaries of senior officers and – in the ICS particularly – generous pensions, low pay to junior officers was common to all the services in India. One result of this was a 'terrible feeling of insecurity', and one of the most common characteristics of the life of the Raj was 'this feeling that the only possible way of ensuring some kind of security for the family was to save and save and save, and this is what the majority of officials in India did, with the result that the family went short in the early years of the father's service'. Only in one respect was this Spartan code not observed: 'the one thing that was never saved on was the children's education, because this was considered the greatest security of all'.

India was hard on the British and the British were often hard on themselves and on others, never more so than on those who stood uneasily between themselves and India. Irene Edwards remembers as a child that 'there were benches, one marked "Europeans Only", one marked "Indians Only". There were also the waiting rooms marked "Europeans Only" and "Indians Only". As an Anglo-Indian child I never knew which one to occupy.' Attitudes towards the Anglo-Indians varied: 'The lower classes and the Other Ranks welcomed the Anglo-Indians into their clubs and messes. They even married them. But the higher up you went the greater was the prejudice against the Anglo-Indians.' In retrospect these prejudices came to be seen as reprehensible. 'We can never be sufficiently blamed,' declares Iris Portal. 'When I was very young I took the conventional attitude which everybody took – even enlightened people like my parents – of making jokes about "blackie-whites" and "twelve annas in the rupee".' The prejudice came from both sides. According to Irene Edwards, 'the Indians looked down on the Anglo-Indians because to them you were neither one nor the other. They used to call us *kutcha butcha*, that is to say, half-baked bread, and depending on the shade of your colour they used to talk about the Anglo-Indian as being *teen pao*, three-quarters, or *adha seer*, half a pound, if you were nearly white.'

The Anglo-Indians co-existed in their own 'railway communities' beside the local British communities, with 'a deep gulf' in between: 'It wasn't that one was unfriendly; it was a sort of social taboo.' Outside work the point of social contact was the Railway Institute Dance. 'We used to go to these dances in rather a condescending manner,' admits Joan Allen. 'We'd go to be polite to them and it was like moving into a different world, a much more old-fashioned one, because the girls would never sit with their dancing partners but were always taken back to their parents. I'm afraid we used to rather laugh at them because they seemed to be such frumps. They always seemed to be dressed about several years back and never seemed to quite catch up with modern fashions.'

From the British point of view marriages between the British and Anglo-Indian communities were deeply frowned upon – but not from the Anglo-Indian: 'An unwritten rule was for the girls to try and marry the British soldier. Not to propagate the species but to improve the strain, so our aim was to marry British soldiers, not to marry Anglo-Indian men.' Given the isolation of the British soldier and his segregation from unmarried European women, this ambition was often realized. 'I met hundreds of Anglo-Indian girls and I can't think of one that was really unattractive,' declares Stephen Bentley. 'They had the virtues of the two nations. They were all wonderful dancers and you always saw them when they were made up for a dance. You never saw them when they were "off-parade".' The point is echoed by E. S. Humphries: 'The Eurasian girls were experts at making themselves up and the aroma from their bodies was tinged with the wonderful scent of jasmine which made them probably far more attractive than they really were. In some cases they managed to persuade a British soldier to become engaged and ultimately to marry. It was frowned upon by the British Command, but despite all the efforts to quash it a vast number did manage to get married. One of my own soldiers elected to become engaged to a lovely Eurasian who was almost as black as your hat. I took steps to warn him against it, and when he persisted I made arrangements for him to be transferred to another station.'

The Second World War changed many attitudes, including those towards Anglo-Indians. The impetus for this change came from the Anglo-Indians themselves who seized the opportunity to prove both their loyalty and their worth, as Iris Portal's own experience confirms: 'I changed my attitude completely in the Second World War when I went to nurse in the Indian hospitals in Delhi, where the only woman who could help me and came in and worked with me, was the Eurasian wife of a Eurasian doctor who became one of my best friends. And I realized then what nonsense it all was.'

18

THE DAY'S WORK

The life of the 'Anglo-Indian' officials is not all jam. In comfortless camps, in sweltering offices, in gloomy dak bungalows smelling of dust and earth-oil, they earn, perhaps, the right to be a little disagreeable.

GEORGE ORWELL *Burmese Days* 1935

'It was service, service, service every time.' The word runs like a response through the litanies of 'Anglo-India'. Even those outside the military or the civil administration used it when referring to the 'tour of service' by which they were contracted to their employers. It was part of an often unconscious attitude inherited, as David Symington suggests, by all those who made their careers in India: 'We realized that we were members of a very successful race. We belonged to a country that, in the world league, had done exceedingly well for a small island. And we also realized that we were working in a country which was as pre-eminently unsuccessful as we were successful. And I suppose that that produced a frame of mind in which we tacitly – not explicitly – felt ourselves to be rather superior people.' The superiority was stressed by authority at an early age, whether in the office, the tea garden or the court of law, and it was accepted without question. As Assistant Superintendent of Police at nineteen, George Carroll had authority over hundreds of policemen in his district: 'The question of exercising my power never arose in my mind because it seemed so natural that, as an Englishman, I should have power over all my Indian subordinates.'

The prestige of the Raj enhanced the status of all the British in India, *box-wallahs* and BORs as well as those in authority. Its advantages in terms of respect and obedience were considerable, but it demanded a conscious sense of responsibility towards those under you. Geoffrey Allen, working as a junior assistant to a native *zemindar* in Bihar, found that the local population relied on him for justice: 'You were always being asked to try cases which were brought before you. It was much cheaper for tenants to come to you to decide cases than to go many miles away to the civil courts.' From the Indian point of view such authority was founded upon the *ma-bap* principle, as Kenneth Warren illustrates in the context of the tea-garden manager: 'It was customary for a member of the labour force who had a request to make to come to you and first of all address you as *Hazur* – Your Honour, and then *ma-bap* – you are my father and my mother, I have this, that and the other request to make.' While this open paternalism drew its authority from an Indian initiative, it was reinforced by the 'public school mentality' which required the school prefect to look after those under him:

We had an epidemic of ophthalmia in the garden where I was manager and a number of the labour had to come to hospital for treatment, among them a man who was three days in hospital under treatment and was cured. The next thing I heard at my early morning durbar was that this man's child had been taken to the hospital with her eyes burnt out. She had developed ophthalmia and her father, although he himself had been cured in the hospital, said he knew better and that he knew of a jungle cure, a mixture of certain herbs and jungle plants, which he mashed up and plastered on his daughter's eyes and burnt them out. She was a child of about fourteen, a charming little girl, and when I came into the hospital she heard my voice and fell on to her knees and held on to my legs and implored me to cure her saying, 'Sahib, I know you can cure me. You can do anything if you wish to.' It was a most distressing and terrible experience for me. I held the durbar the next morning. I had the father brought up to my office together with the whole of his clan. I told them what had happened and how disgraceful it was and what did they, the clan, suggest should be done. With one accord they said he should be beaten. They put their heads together and discussed it and then the head man turned to me and said, 'Sahib, we think it is right and proper that you should beat him and not us.' So I said, 'Well, if that's your decision all I can do is carry out your wish.' I came down from the verandah and I went up to this fellow and I hit him. I hit him so hard that I bruised my right hand and I had to have it in a sling for twenty-four hours afterwards.

The sense of duty was strongest in the civil administration. Its strength may be gauged by Rosamund Lawrence's comment that her husband was 'like the Duke of Wellington, always talking about duty. My husband's people, the Lawrences, were very religious and they were absolutely immersed in what they felt was their duty to India.' In Henry Lawrence's case the expression of his duty took the form of a *shauq*, an obsessive interest: 'My husband was absolutely heart and soul wrapped up in what he called the Sukkur Barrage. He was obsessed by it, by the amount of people there were and how they were all going to be fed by it, but he was only one of a chain of people, who had started it long before.' Duty of the order exercised by the ICS meant that 'an officer of the Raj could never say that his home was his castle. There never seemed to be a moment when you could be entirely free – unless you were on leave. You would find somebody waiting to see you on a Saturday evening or a Sunday, because he knew that that was the time you were free.' Accessibility to the humblest petitioner was a Mogul tradition inherited and maintained by the British. Its most significant expression was in the early morning queues of *mulaquatis* on the verandah of every district or political officer in the land. '*Mulaquatis* were divided into two classes,' explains Penderel Moon, 'the *mulaquati* proper was a person of some education and standing, an honorary magistrate, a municipal commissioner, a leading lawyer, the headman of a group of villages or a landowner, who'd come in to salaam-*wasti*, to say salaam to you. Generally they had some ulterior motive. I'd ask about their health, sit them down and have a general chat about the weather or the crops or the latest news, trying to bring them to the point as quickly and politely as one could. Then there was the second group, what my *chaprassi* called *feriadis*, which means "the humble petitioners", who simply came with grievances.'

The success of the interview was often dependent on fluency in both native languages and customs, as Olaf Caroe explains:

You had to be very careful in using the right honorifics in speaking to a gentleman. You had to call him Your Honour, 'Your Honour has brought himself to this place,' and you had to know all about *'ijazat o barkhast'*, when to sit down and when to get up, and observe the oriental formalities of behaviour, shaking him by the hand and in the right way and with the right amount of cordiality. If you could quote a hackneyed verse which was appropriate to the occasion you'd probably get what you wanted. Whether it was Urdu or Punjabi or Pashtu, particularly, they had some very racy, meaty proverbs. I remember once someone said, 'You're very patient,' and I said in answer, 'Well, I remember a Pashtu proverb, Patience is Bitter, but the fruit of it is sweet.'

The interview was fraught with hazards. 'One was always very wary,' comments Raymond Vernede. 'Sometimes people came merely to indulge in backbiting and to insinuate against their enemies. Many people came because others would notice that they had been, and they could go back and say that they had seen the District Magistrate. I suffered a great deal of flattery, which I had to get accustomed to. You had to recognize that it was the tradition of the country. You were the God, the sun and so forth. "Defender, preserver of the poor," was a stock expression, but it was like saying "sir". I disliked that sort of thing but never paid very much attention to it.'

The administrative system of the Raj had its origins in Mogul rule and was based principally on the collection of land revenue. But this was only a part of the Collector's or Commissioner's work. He was also responsible for the administration of justice, either in makeshift form in the open air or in a proper court of law, often referred to as 'the halls of chance'. Many covenanted officers found work in the courts frustrating and tedious, most criminal complaints being 'either false, frivolous or futile' and with 'witness after witness telling obvious lies'. Some even felt that the British legal system was 'totally unsuited to India and had been completely perverted'. The sanctity of the law meant very little to most Indians. 'It was really rather a game,' asserts Percival Griffiths, 'and in order to win the game you had to get witnesses. As the people of the country were pretty poor, you didn't have to pay a very great deal to get a man to come and give evidence the way that you wanted. In fact, there used to be a Bengali saying, the *tetul gacch shakshi*, which means the tamarind-tree witness, because there was always a tamarind tree outside the court and the witnesses would be gathered and coached there under the tamarind tree before they came into court.' Most cases that came up before the sub-divisional or district officer concerned property – or criminal assaults arising out of disputes over property: 'The usual kind of story was that a buffalo had wandered into somebody's sugar-cane and a quarrel had arisen and someone had taken a stick and hit somebody over the head.' In the Sind crime arose from '*zana, zar, zamin*; *zana* meaning women, *zar* gold and *zamin* land,' and usually took the form of murder or cattle-thieving, which was 'more or less the national sport'. Armed with sessions powers as a special assistant agent in Madras, Christopher Masterman was sentencing men to death while still in his mid-twenties: 'The accused would invariably plead guilty. You asked him, "Did you kill this man?" He said, "Yes." "Did you mean to kill him?" "Yes, of course. He was stealing from my palmyra tree." Then you said, "Well, was he armed?" "Oh no, he wasn't armed." "Then why did you kill him?" "I killed him because he was stealing from my palmyra tree," and you couldn't get away from it.' Death sentences were invariably commuted to terms of gaol or transportation over the *kala pani* to the Andaman Islands.

The Indian court was more than a seat of justice. 'The courts were to the Indians the equivalent of the cinema to us,' explains Raymond Vernede. 'They were fascinated by it all, and they listened quietly in most cases. In the hot weather I'd go to the court in khaki shirt and shorts. Some of the police prosecuting officers would be rather overdressed in their uniforms and perspiring very unpleasantly; the lawyers would have their gowns but it was all pretty informal. In my day we had overhead fans which made it possible – except on bad days – to survive. But tempers could be rather short after sitting several hours on a difficult case.' Having heard all the evidence, the district magistrate was then required to respond with a judgement that would support the truth. This required getting to the *kutchchahal*, 'the raw state of the case, what it was like before they'd prepared it for court', resorting if necessary to arbitrary methods that went beyond the rules of jurisprudence. 'When I was in doubt I did not hesitate to make extra-judicial enquiries from the police investigating officer,' admits Penderel Moon, 'or from other responsible people in the locality as to what they thought the truth of the case was – and I used to take into consideration these extra-judicial opinions in forming my judgement, which was quite irregular.' Nor was he alone in making his own adjustments to a much-abused system. 'I also made rules of the most arbitrary nature,' declares Philip Mason. 'I said that I wouldn't allow anyone to call more witnesses than the other side had called. I also said that nobody could cross-examine for longer than the main evidence. It was high-handed and arbitrary but one was so certain that one was doing the right thing that one didn't have any doubts.'

A certain prejudice in the courts was inevitable, showing itself most obviously in 'a bias on the side of the cultivator, the man who actually drove the plough, as against somebody rather distant who collected the rent from him'. In the ICS there was traditionally 'a division between the people who protected the poor, the *gharib-parhwas*, and the *amir-parhwas*, the protectors of the rich'. Philip Mason recalls the case of a *banya* who 'didn't dare go into his village because he was so oppressive that they hated him. He came and asked me to pass orders against all the villagers because they wouldn't let him into his village and I said, "I'm going to pass orders against you, because you must have done something to provoke them." It was rather unjust, I must admit, but it showed my social bias at the time.'

A major impediment both to legal and social progress in India was corruption. *Dastur* – 'the custom of the country' – was a Mogul inheritance, perfectly acceptable to Englishmen in the days of John Company but combated thereafter with fierce Victorian zeal. Victorian ethics of 'honour, decency, truthfulness and running a good show' persisted in India to a quite remarkable degree. 'I would have no hesitation in saying that during the years I was in India, bribery and corruption were unknown among the British,' asserts John Morris, one of the fiercest critics of the moral codes of the Raj. It is an assertion that few have challenged – except in degree – and a great many have confirmed. 'It never entered my mind that lowness of pay or lack of cash could ever influence any British officer to take a bribe,' maintains George Carroll. 'It never entered my mind, and I was always quite convinced that no British officer would ever take a bribe of any sort. Once when I was a superintendent of police a man who was accused in a certain case approached my bungalow and placed in front of me a large bag of cash. When I realized that he was offering me a bribe I chased him out of the compound. He ran like a hare to my gate and got into a tonga which was waiting and he got away. Had I caught him he would have had a jolly good thrashing.' One explanation of this innocence – the public school attitude – has already been offered. There was also the belief that 'we had inherited high standards which we had to maintain. Living in the public eye you felt you couldn't really afford to take risks – even if you had been tempted – which would not escape notice and would lower that standard.'

Such attitudes created an administration that was 'probably the most incorruptible ever known. A source of great amazement to many Indians but one that gave rise to a very great trust.' The truly remarkable feature of this incorruptibility was the background against which it was maintained. 'I was always amazed,' declares John Cotton, 'at one's moderation in the face of temptation – which was always present.' Some found corruption and bribery among the subordinate levels of the administration appalling. 'I was perhaps much too hot in trying to check it,' recalls Penderel Moon. 'I ran in a large number of people of almost every rank for corruption, from the highest to the lowest. Tips I didn't object to. It was harassment, refusing to do a thing unless the palm was greased.' For their own protection all government officers were subject to the *phal-phul* rule, by which they were forbidden to accept presents other than fruit and flowers. 'There was a comic aspect to this,' comments Percival Griffiths. 'If there were four or five European officers on a station and it was known they were all men of complete integrity who wouldn't accept presents, a chap would bring an expensive present along and offer it to the first man, knowing that he would say no, and then take it to the second and then to the third and then to the fourth. So he would get the goodwill resulting from offering presents to all of them, knowing that it wouldn't cost him anything in the end!'

Others attempted to get round the *phal-phul* rule in other ways. The presentation of trays of fruit and nuts, known as dollies, was deemed to be acceptable and was a special feature at Christmas time. But sometimes the dollies or the bouquets of flowers concealed something more, as John Morris recalls: 'I remember on Christmas morning the man who supplied the troops with food appeared to pay his respects to me and presented me with a cauliflower as a Christmas present, and I noticed when I took the cauliflower that out of it fell a gold sovereign. This was an understood practice, but it was also understood that one accepted the cauliflower or whatever it was and returned the sovereign.' Efforts to subvert were also made through the memsahib or the children. 'An old lady came to see me,' relates Rosamund Lawrence, 'and she brought some little varnished toys for my little boy which must have cost a few annas at the most. My boy was delighted with them so I sent a note in to Henry saying I was sure she would be terribly offended if I didn't take them, so what was I to do? "Better not," he said. The very next day there came a letter from her asking that a most valuable piece of land on the banks of the river should be accorded to her nephew.'

Raj gossip sometimes liked to hint that British residents in the native states did on occasion accept bribes from the rulers.

Conrad Corfield's account of a new Resident who was presented with a Christmas dolly illustrates how such allegations could arise: 'An enormous dolly was brought in looking quite beautiful. He started picking at it and at the bottom of the tray he found one hundred and one gold mohurs. He was staggered and went into his office and wrote a furious letter to the Ruler. The Ruler wrote back and said, "I'm dreadfully sorry, but one hundred and one gold mohurs is what has been presented to the residency every year at Christmas and if the amount is not enough will you tell me what is?" Then they started to make enquiries and found that five of the gold mohurs were always kept by the servants of the residency and the rest went back to the state office, where it was distributed – while in the lists was put "Towards Christmas present for the Resident, 101 gold mohurs." '

In the business community bribery and corruption was quite a different matter – although there were always the established companies, well-stocked with public school boys, where it was virtually unknown. 'One would hear rumours that so-and-so was making a lot of money on the side,' relates Rupert Mayne. 'I can remember one man always known as "corkscrew" for the simple reason that he was in on it; and another person who earned some sixty rupees a month before the war and retired with a hundred thousand pounds which he made during the war.'

Elsewhere in business the moral code was 'something akin to that which existed in England at the time of Pitt. It was not considered immoral to have a cut in every contract.' Speaking of the railways, Eugene Pierce recalls that 'my father was a very honest man by any standard but he got so many thousands of rupees before a brick was even laid, when he gave the contract to the right parties. For orders to supply rails or sleepers or cement, contractors presented him with money and gold bangles and my mother was given jewellery. Stations used to be virtually sold. Your stationmaster used to give you a bribe to be placed at that particular station. His salary was negligible but the stations were allotted wagons which were the gift of the stationmaster to give to the merchants who booked them, so his income was enormous. He paid the district traffic super-intendent and the company inspectors who'd go down their district once a month – when a brown envelope was slipped into their hands containing this tip.'

Despite its high standards, 'Anglo-India' was not a place of great religious principle or practice. That particular function was delegated to the missionaries, who were given a limited role on the fringes of 'Anglo-India' and were, by and large, left to their own devices. Few worked in India for more altruistic motives or faced greater difficulties. 'Travancore was a great centre for missionaries,' recalls Christopher Masterman, 'CMS, SPG, Canadian Baptists, American Missions, Medical Missions, Roman Catholics, Belgian Priests – and there was a great rivalry between the different sects. If the CMS had a beanfeast of some sort, half the SPG lot would go and join the CMS, and vice versa. I don't think they ever converted a caste Hindu but they got the scheduled classes, the depressed classes and the untouchables.' Yet, as Bishop Cashmore describes, in other parts of India the rivalry was less acute : 'We would not go into an area that the Baptists had or the Methodists or the CMS had without their permission, and they wouldn't come into ours without permission. So there was no sheep stealing.' In terms of genuine conversion, the missionaries made few inroads into Caste Hinduism or Islam, but their pioneering in education and medical work – in the face of widespread apathy and even hostility – was one of the great achievements of British India. Rosalie Roberts' account of midwifery in Bengal exemplifies the difficulties faced by pioneers in the field :

They would wait five or six days with the woman in labour, hoping it would come all right. They didn't want to bring them into hospital. So I used to go out on my cycle, off into the jungle. I started going out in my white uniform but I soon stopped because all the cows and buffaloes in the jungle chased me and I changed over into khaki. Practically all the midwifery cases were on the mud floor. I tried to manage with as little as possible so as to show the village midwife that she could do it with what she had at hand. In some cases it was very difficult – while I was attending to the woman they'd be tying charms on her hair – but as time went on I got to know the village midwives and we got quite friendly and by the end of the five year period the delay had got down to two days or even one day, because they weren't afraid any more.

The missionaries had no monopoly on privation and hardship. Many young men suffered long and lonely first tours of duty that lasted four years and more before a home leave and provided as severe a test of stamina as any. There were a handful of men in the Forest Service or the Survey of India who spent month after month in the forests or in the mountains and for whom loneliness and discomfort were the norm. Arthur Hamilton recalls how, after a long season of surveying, 'I was just longing to meet a European to talk to him. The vastness of the mountains overcame me and I had an awful feeling that I must throw myself over a cliff.' But for the great majority actual hazards and privations were limited in duration and interspersed with generous periods of leave and a great deal of leisure. When not on active service officers in the Indian Army observed a far from uncomfortable routine. An early morning parade was followed by breakfast and a change into mufti before 'regimental office' when charges and grievances were dealt with. Lunch was usually followed by a long siesta: 'Then in the late afternoon you either played games at the club or, if you were so inclined, you played games with your own men. Thursday was a whole day holiday. Saturday, of course, was a half-holiday and Sunday was a holiday. You had as a right ten days absence every month and you were also entitled to an annual holiday of two months. Every three or four years you got eight months furlough at home. So it really cannot be said that any of us were greatly overworked.'

These were all the occupations of the minority. The ICS itself was never more than 1,300 strong – of which many were Indians – and although the Indian Army rose in wartime to be the largest volunteer professional army in history, its British officers were very few – no more than twelve per regiment –

and growing fewer each year as 'Indianization' slowly began to take effect. The majority of the British in India – a fast-increasing majority – were, in fact, businessmen, some contracted to the old-established trading companies or to newer industrial concerns, some working in the large city emporia, others working as managers or engineers in tea or coffee or jute. It was often said that theirs was not the 'real' India, but in terms of numbers they were in fact the most 'representative' of the British in India; young men who came out as junior assistants and probably spent one hard and uncomfortable tour in the *mofussil* before promotion to the company's air-conditioned offices or the chambers of commerce in Calcutta or Bombay. Again, it has to be remembered that most sahibs in India spent most of their working hours in darkened bungalows, sitting at desks surrounded by files, *babus* and *chaprassis*, contending with inordinate amounts of paper work and, in particular, with a system of minuting said – quite wrongly – to be derived from Lord Curzon, by which 'everybody from the lowest Indian clerk right up to the final authority wrote a minute enlarging on what had gone before'.

Until the air-conditioner turned the office into a refuge from the hot weather it was more often a shuttered, silent and somnolent place, where the only sounds were the creak or the whir of the *punkahs*, the fluttering of papers under large quantities of paper weights, the scratching pens of the *babus* and the soft padding of the *chaprassis'* bare feet as they circulated files or cups of sweet, milky tea. Extended lunch breaks and long siestas divided the day into manageable stints and the work itself was made easier by the presence of 'the most efficient and wonderful clerks in the world. If there was any grinding work to be done at a file, all this work could be done for you by your clerks and everything would be neatly set out on paper, and if it was done properly you had merely to reach a decision at the end and say either "Yes" or "No" or "Thanks very much".' The routine life of the office-*wallah* was not one of great remark or circumstance. It was often tedious and certainly not much fun – but it was undoubtedly the most common experience of a working life in the Raj.

19

INDIANS

The Indian gentleman, with all self-respect to himself, should not enter into a compartment reserved for Europeans, any more than he should enter a carriage set apart for ladies. Although you may have acquired the habits and manners of the European, have the courage to show that you are not ashamed of being an Indian, and in all such cases, identify yourself with the race to which you belong.

H. HARDLESS *The Indian Gentleman's Guide to Etiquette*
1919

'I remember once returning from leave in England in the twenties,' says John Morris, 'I went on to the train in Bombay and discovered that the other berth was occupied by an Indian. I am sorry to say that by that time I had become affected by the mentality of the ruling class in India and I said to the station-master, "I want to have the gentleman ejected." He spoke absolutely perfect English and he could have taught me a great deal about India. It is one of the incidents of my life of which I am most ashamed. But you have to remember that in those days army officers did not associate with Indians of any class other than the servant class, to whom they just gave orders. I think that one of the chief reasons for the curious attitude of the British towards Indians – it may have been quite unconscious – was the fact that they were regarded as a subject race.'

The attitudes of the British towards Indians varied greatly according to the social circumstances of the parties concerned. It was frequently asserted that prejudice against Indians was greatest amongst those who came into contact with them least – that is to say, in the British Army and in the commercial community – and least amongst those who worked in close proximity to Indians up-country. Yet, there were many exceptions to the general rule: Anglo-Indians who made a point of referring to Indians as 'niggers' and, conversely, BORS who fraternized with the lowliest of the cantonment *wallahs*. In fact, BORS' attitudes were curiously ambivalent, for 'if a soldier was seen joking or talking to an Indian, especially the same Indian two or three times, he had to be jeered at and called a "white nigger".' Yet there was still a special camaraderie between British troops and certain Indian Army regiments, the Gurkhas in particular, who were 'full of jokes and fun and more like us in a way'. E. S. Humphries recounts how 'it was their great joy when they greeted a British soldier to hold up their little finger and, giving the full length of it as a measurement, say to the British soldier, "Aha, look, British Tommy so big!" Then, taking off a quarter of an inch from the bottom they would say, "There, Gurkha soldier nearly so good as British soldier!" Finally, putting their thumbs still higher up the little finger until it almost touched the nail they would say, "This is the other Indian soldiers!"'

Attitudes changed with time. Those who went out to India in the early years of the century found a marked lack of familiarity between the races, the strongest prejudice coming from 'senior officials, old die-hards and hesitant partners', with what Claude Auchinleck describes as 'an attitude of ensuring what you might call "white superiority". Supposing you were on leave in the Himalayas and riding along a mountain track. If an Indian came along the other way riding his mule or his pony, he was supposed to get off. Similarly, an Indian carrying an open umbrella was supposed to shut it. It sounds ridiculous but that attitude was still being imbued into the newcomer to the Indian services when I first went out.' The attitudes of the womenfolk in earlier days were similarly exclusive: 'We didn't mix with the Indians at all,' remembers Mrs Norie, who returned to India as an adult in 1893 and lived there throughout the prewar period. 'You mixed with a very high-up family perhaps, but you didn't really bother about the Indians.'

The changes brought about by the Great War emphasized the difference in attitude between the older generation and the new. 'Much as I loved and respected my father,' records

Rupert Mayne, 'I abhorred the attitude adopted by my fore-bears, which culminated in him saying that he would never per-mit me to go into the Indian Army and serve under what he always called a native officer.' Frances Smyth, who returned to India in 1925, found a parallel between this change of atti-tude and the emancipation of women in England: 'In my day in India it was rather like that. We were just beginning to accept Indians as equals – just.' In one respect change was not for the better. Improved communications between India and Europe, assisted passages and the establishment of commercial airline services broke the close threads of communication be-tween India and the Englishman, hitherto isolated by long periods of time from home. By bringing England nearer it drew India and British-India apart, breaking rather than making the necessary connections.

The psychology of the two races was often described as complementary rather than matching: 'The Indian was pliant and would say "yes" to everything whether he was going to do it or not, whereas the British were more obstinate, more ob-durate people and they wouldn't undertake a thing unless they could see it through.' But if the British were 'a bit Olympian or perhaps a little squirearchical, this was complemented by the attitude of the Indians towards us. They expected the Euro-peans to be rather superior, encouraging us to behave in that way.' Sycophancy was not something the British enjoyed. 'There was certainly a lot of sucking-up to the British,' states Ian Stephens. 'All sorts of tricks which one had to be wary about. But the wariness itself was a danger because it mightn't be what you thought. What was being misconstrued might really be genuine affection. A genuine desire for normal, human contact.'

Differing standards of morality and what often appeared, from the British point of view, to be a perverse sense of right and wrong in such matters as *dastur* often led to 'a lot of shout-ing and a lack of sympathy'. Nor was the Moslem or Hindu culture thought much of. Nineteenth century evangelical atti-tudes effectively blocked any widespread study of Indian art and culture. Hindu art, in particular, with its close association

with Hindu religion, was found to be particularly repellent
Rosalie Roberts recalls how she once visited a missionary col
league in South India and was duly shown the local sights:
'After we'd had a meal she took us down to a temple. It was a
wonderful temple, very old, with hundreds of carvings and on
every ledge was a tiny lamp. All these little lights were flicker
ing and this huge gateway, like a four-storey building, was li
up. It looked like fairyland it was so beautiful. The next morn
ing she took us inside the temple – and it was revolting. All the
little niches had idols where there had been sacrifices and the
blood was spilt there. There was the stench and the darkness
just the flickering light by the idols, and that was the picture
inside.' The ethics of Hinduism did not appeal to the Christian: 'In Hinduism I saw no compassion. A beggar would
come to the door and their religion would make them give
alms. But if that beggar, through want of food or illness, collapsed on their doorstep, they would do nothing. They wouldn't
touch him. Their religion forbade them to. They would lose
caste.'

The Indians, in their turn, found aspects of British culture
incomprehensible and, on occasion, shocking, as Iris Portal
illustrates: 'When my husband commanded the Governor's
Bodyguard in Bombay I had a great time with all the wives of
the troops, Sikhs and Mohammedans. I used to spend a great
deal of time with them down in the lines, not only doing child
welfare and first aid and hospital work, but just chatting. They
used to give me their views about life and I used to give them
mine, and I remember the wife of the *Jemadar* saying, "The
Jemadar-Sahib tells me that English ladies run about in their
underpants. Is it true?" I said, "Oh, no, of course they don't,"
and she said, "Oh yes they do. The *Jemadar*-Sahib says that
he's been to the Willingdon Club on duty and he's seen them
running about in pants. I think it's absolutely disgusting." Of
course, they were just innocent English girls playing tennis in
shorts.' Immodesty of dress and behaviour were not the only
British habits that Indians found indecent. There was the
Maharajah who 'refused to allow the railway from Bombay to
Calcutta to pass through his capital, because travellers might

234

be eating beef in the restaurant car'. There was the occasion, recalled by Charles Wright, during a British Army route march when the regimental cook slaughtered a cow and there was 'a terrible rumpus. The natives got to know about this and nearly stoned the camp and we had to turn out in a hurry to disperse them.' The British had also to be aware of other dietary prohibitions: 'The orthodox Hindu would not eat meat but was quite content to drink any liquor that you might offer him, while your Mohammedan friend would eat any kind of meat other than pork but, strictly speaking, would not drink any kind of liquor.'

Undoubtedly the greatest social stumbling block between the British and the Indians was purdah: 'If you can't have a *partie a quatre*, it's rather difficult to get to know people. If you only invite the man you don't make the same equation with people.' The bolder memsahibs gave 'purdah parties' or tea parties with screens erected on the lawns to protect the guests from male view. Others visited and encouraged: 'I had a great friend in Hyderabad whose husband was a close friend of my husband's,' recounts Iris Portal.

He was a very Westernized, very cultured, sophisticated man and she was old-fashioned and completely in purdah and didn't know any English at all. It took me a little time to make friends with her, chiefly because my Urdu was not good enough for her, but we did make friends eventually and we saw a good deal of each other. I used to go and visit her and have a *pahn* with her and smoke a cigarette. Then she wanted to meet my husband, so I arranged a meeting. We all sat round the tea table and she never spoke because, of course, a well brought-up Indian lady won't speak in front of her husband. I didn't speak much for the same reason. The men were very, very embarrassed and it wasn't a very lively party. But after it was over I asked her husband, 'What does *Begum-Sahiba* think of my husband?' 'Oh,' he said, 'I'm afraid all she will say is, "Very large and red!"'

Only in the very last years of the Raj did Indian women

emerge into society. It was 'a revolutionary change and if it had occurred fifty years before the whole history of India would have been different'.

The movement towards Independence was characterized by the slow, often reluctant but inevitable progress towards power-sharing. The Amritsar Massacre of 1919 and 'Anglo-India's' support for General Dyer's determination to punish, created an undercurrent of feeling on both sides that was never really eradicated. The 'Indianization' of the ICS and the Indian Army had been put on a more open footing immediately after the ending of the Great War, but in the Indian Army it was not sincerely applied. To avoid having British officers serving under Indians, special segregated units were set up. In Claude Auchinleck's opinion this had 'a very bad effect on Indian feelings. The Indian officers themselves realized that they were being put into units which might be reckoned as inferior to the British officers' units. The only result was that these Indian regiments became objects of contempt.' The establishment of an Indian 'Sandhurst' did much to improve matters. 'I regard my time at the Indian Military Academy as a watershed,' states Reginald Savory, one of its first instructors, 'not only in my military career but in my political thinking. For the first time I met young, middle-class Indians on level terms and I found all these young men fascinating. They were very outspoken, highly intelligent, and one of the first remarks I had levelled at me was this, "You British officers of the Indian Army don't know India. All you know are your servants and your sepoys."'

In commerce, as much as in the services, the lack of suitably qualified Indians and the fear of lowering standards was often cited as the reason for slow Indianization. It was said that 'Indians did not always produce the best managerial material'. As a result, putting Indians into higher management jobs was held back in the thirties in favour of 'the young Britisher who was prepared to take responsibility and was prepared to take his coat off and get on with the job. The feeling persisted that the young Indian was much more inclined to look round for someone menial to do the dirty work and wouldn't get on with the job in the same way that a young Britisher would. The astonishing transformation was after Independence when the young Indian was prepared to do all the things that one expected of a young Britisher. India now belonged to India and Indians were prepared to do whatever was required for India.'

In most spheres an initial reluctance was followed by a general acceptance of Indians as working partners. 'In the Bengal Pilot Service we had one Indian,' recalls Radclyffe Sidebottom, 'who joined in the teeth of what was anticipated to be great opposition. But so strange is the service and so deep is tradition that the moment he joined the vast majority of the pilots took no notice of the fact that he was Indian at all. After that there was fairly rapid Indianization.'

These were the general attitudes that concealed minor variations and exceptions. From the British point of view the maharajahas and princes whose domains were for the most part outside British India, were themselves above the usual conventions. Many were of extreme sophistication, 'Brindians' with English standards and interests, often great sportsmen and great hosts – and more than equals. Even those who were not were left to indulge their own peculiarities of behaviour. The opening words of the political officer's rule book suggested that the good officer left well alone. Only in instances of gross maladministration or outrageous public conduct did the Resident openly interfere with the ruler and the running of his state. The maharajahs were free both to accumulate wealth and to spend it lavishly. Richest of them all was the Nizam of Hyderabad who was renowned both for his meanness – 'he used to go to auctions and bid for second-hand gramophones' – and for his bouts of spending. He was once observed buying up the entire stock of shoes at Spenser's in Madras so that he could choose the pair he wanted at his leisure. The Maharajah of Darbhanga was equally capricious in his spending habits: 'He would see that a particular dog had won at Cruft's and he would immediately buy this dog and import it into India. He was very keen to show you his dogs and a man would follow regularly behind with a bottle of methylated spirits and a rag to wipe over the place as soon as the dog had left his calling card. Some of these bits of furniture – the most beautiful modern furniture – smelt terribly. It was really very sad because five or six dogs in favour at the time lived in the palace and were made a great fuss of, whereas the dogs that had been favourites last year were relegated to the kennels and never came out again. You'd see thirty or forty beautiful pedigree dogs in these kennels which were never bothered about.'

There were maharajahs who were great practical jokers, who enjoyed squirting guests with concealed lawn sprinklers or leaving wet paint on chairs. One ran a toy railway on his dinner table which carried wines and cigars round to his guests and which he speeded up occasionally, leaving 'a thirsty guest with an empty hand outstretched'. Some, like the Maharajah of Kashmir, made up their own rules of cricket, as H. T. Wickham relates:

At three o'clock in the afternoon that Maharajah himself would come down to the ground, the band would play the Kashmir anthem, salaams were made and he then went off to a special tent where he sat for a time, smoking his long water-pipe. At four thirty or thereabouts he decided he would bat. It didn't matter which side was batting, his own team or ours. He was padded by two attendants and gloved by two more, somebody carried his bat and he walked out to the wicket looking very dignified, very small and with an enormous turban on his head. In one of the matches I happened to be bowling and my first ball hit his stumps, but the wicket keeper, quick as lightning, shouted 'No Ball!' and the match went on. The only way that the Maharajah could get out was by lbw. And after fifteen or twenty minutes batting he said he felt tired and he was duly given out lbw. What the scorers did about his innings, which was never less than half a century, goodness only knows.

British attitudes to other sections of Indian society were rather less tolerant. The British concept of benevolent paternalism ensured that a distinction was made between those 'whom we regarded as completely educated and the half-educated'. Shopkeepers, moneylenders and *vakils* were disliked principally because 'they were profiting from the lower classes and exploiting the rustic'. Equally disliked were the caste Hindus in areas such as South India where strict Brahminism clashed with good administration, as when non-caste Hindus were forbidden to drink from the same wells as caste Hindus. It was also the fashion to denigrate the *babu* type: 'We used to make fun of them, very unfairly, because they were interpreting rules which we had made.' *Babu* jokes, based on the English language either wrongly or over-effusively applied, were a constant source of amusements for all 'Anglo-India'. Coupled with the denigration of the *babu* was a traditional distrust of the Bengali – 'litigious, very fond of an argument' – who was frequently seen as a trouble-maker: 'He doesn't appeal to many British people in the same way as the very much more manly, direct type from upper India.' Following directly from this general dislike of trouble-makers was a widespread antipathy towards politicians and Congress-*wallahs*, not only because of their aspirations for *Swaraj* or the methods by which they sought to effect those aspirations, but because 'they were often people of very poor mental calibre. It was very hard on the young Indians who had got into government service to find themselves put underneath people whom they regarded as layabouts and scallywags and failures.'

Then there were the preferences. 'One did find oneself liking the hillman more than the plainsman,' admits Philip Mason. 'British officers in colonial situations always do like the simple, unspoilt people. In the plains children would come out of school quiet, sober little creatures walking home, while in Garwhal they used to come out like puppies tumbling out of a basket. They would come roaring out, racing and fighting and pushing each other about just as children might do in England.'

Much the same attitude affected that unique and devoted relationship between British officers and Indians that characterized the Indian Army. 'It bordered on paternalism,' agrees Claude Auchinleck, 'but the difference was in your relationship with the men off duty. After a parade in the morning the men immediately got into their own native clothing. In the evening the officers would go down in plain clothes, in mufti. The dis-

cipline, the saluting and all that sort of thing was just the same
but the atmosphere was quite different. There was no question
of ordering them about. They were yeomen really, and that
made all the difference.' Being head of the family, as F. J.
Dillon explains, entailed certain responsibilities. 'From the day
a man joined his unit and came under your command he became yours in a much more personal way than in the British
Army. You knew all about him, where he came from, what his
family was. You probably visited his village and actually knew
his parents. And he certainly relied on you if ever he was in
trouble. There was a pretty general custom in the Indian Army
of durbar, when the Commanding Officer would meet the whole
of his Viceroy's Commissioned Officers and NCOs and any of
the men who wanted to attend. Any man could raise any question he liked there.' The Viceroy's Commissioned Officers were
the middlemen, 'God's own gentlemen,' who stood at the elbow
of every inexperienced British subaltern; the *subadars*, *risaldars*
and *jemadars*: 'They feel absolutely for you and help you all
along the line, but if they think you can do it without help
they'll jolly well make you do it.'

The men themselves, the sepoys, represented the diversity
of India, coming from what were held to be the martial races,
each with their own characteristics:

Generally speaking the Gurkhas were very, very fine mountain soldiers. The Sikhs were very tenacious, very brave, and
would carry out orders to the letter. The Punjabi Mohammedan troops, who formed something like fifty per cent of
the Indian Army, were very biddable, very leadable and
easily trained but never quite up to the standard of the Sikh
or the Gurkha. Then came the Indian troops from further
south; the Jat, very heavy, solid and wonderful in defence,
very similar in outlook, speech and everything else to the
Norfolk man. Then came the soldiers from the foothills, the
Dogras, the Garhwalis and after them a big belt of soldiers
from much further south based on and around Poona; the
Maharattas, very brave and to be reckoned with but not quite
as at home in the hills as the troops from further north. Then

you got the Sappers and Miners, the Engineers, some from the Punjab, some from the UP and some from Madras, like the Madras Sappers and Miners who were descendants of our old Madras Army – all of them excellent troops.

After the Mutiny these racial groups had been split into mixed units, the idea being that 'if you had four companies of different religions there would be very much less chance of a mutiny'. Claude Auchinleck's 62nd Punjabis were one such mixed regiment, with 'a company of Rajputs, the descendants of the famous warrior tribes of Rajputana, a company of Sikhs from the Punjab, a company of Punjabi Moslems from the hills north of Rawalpindi and another company from the Frontier. Four completely separate companies. The Sikh never cuts his hair; he's allowed to drink but he's not allowed to smoke. The Moslem shaves his head and shaves his body and he smokes but doesn't drink. The Rajput smokes and drinks. They wouldn't eat together and each company lived its own separate life, but they got on very happily together.' Other regiments – principally those which had supported the British during the Mutiny, such as the Sikhs and Gurkhas – retained their racial unity and were known as Class Regiments. It was in these regiments, easier to command and administer, that the fiercest devotion grew up between officers and men and a terrific sense of pride that enabled the British officer to declare with absolute confidence that the men under his command were the best soldiers in the world. 'They were well known as being the finest mountain troops in the world,' asserts Lewis Le Marchand, describing the Gurkhas as 'very proud, very gay, very simple. He's as brave as a lion and he'll obey any order you like to give.' It was the same with Reginald Savory's Sikhs:

They are physically as fine a race of men as the world can produce; one of the most interesting races of men in the world and one of the most difficult to command. I always felt that when they were shouting and you could hear them running about the place, then they were happy, they had something to do with themselves. When there was a silence in the line then I always had an idea that something was brewing and I used to send for an Indian officer and say, 'You go down to the lines, it's too quiet for my liking, something is hatching.' And very often it proved to be true.

The Sikh with his turban and his long roll of beard is a man to whom personal looks mean a tremendous amount. You would see him looking at himself in the glass, picking his teeth or rolling his moustache and generally making the most of his looks. Sikhs use their conceit to show off to their rivals. For instance, it's a challenge to any other man if, as you walk down the platform of a railway station you twirl your moustache and say, 'Hmm, hmm,' to the man as you pass. We had many cases in the regiment of chaps who came to blows, very often with hockey sticks, broken heads and heaven knows what. You'd say, 'What's the trouble! Why did you hit him?' 'Oh,' he says, 'I was walking down the platform and he twirled his little moustache and went, "Hmm, hmm!"'

Until he knew you he was a little bit stiff. He stood to attention and he'd say, 'Yes, sir, no, sir.' But when you did get to know him and when you could reach the stage of being able to pull his leg and get a smile out of him, then you had him absolutely in the hollow of your hand. They had that spirit in them which was a wonderful thing amongst men you command. No wonder we were so proud of them.

20

'QUIT INDIA'

*It is only when you get to see and realise what India really
is – that she is the strength and greatness of England – it
is only then that you feel that every nerve a man may strain,
every energy he may put forward cannot be devoted to a
nobler purpose than keeping tight the cords that hold India
to ourselves.*

LORD CURZON, Viceroy of India, 1899–1905

'There was a judge in Bengal, who was greatly loved by all the
people of his district. He was their *ma-bap*, and they all came
to him with their troubles. He loved India, he was devoted to
India and like so many other men he worked long hours for
India, and yet he met his end at the hands of two girls in saris.
They came along to his bungalow and told his servant that they
wanted to see the judge-*sahib*, as they had a petition to present
to him. The judge came out on to the verandah and directly
he got close to the girls with his hand out to receive the petition
one of the girls pulled a pistol from her sari and killed him.'
Like many of her compatriots, Marjorie Cashmore found such
actions incomprehensible and sought an explanation from an
Indian friend in the Congress Party: ' "Here you have devoted servants of India, giving their lives, sacrificing everything
in order to serve your people. You have others who come out
from England and don't understand India. They've only come
out for a few years and they abuse the Indian. I can understand you wanting that type of person out of the country, but
this person is serving you, doing more than anybody else for
your people and yet you kill him." And he laughed and said,
"Don't you understand? The judge and those like him are
hindrances to our getting Home Rule. The other man we

needn't bother about because he gives us a cause for kicking out the British." '

Self-government for India was an issue that pre-dated the Mutiny, yet the average Englishman in India did not look upon Indian nationalism with favour and, until the Great War forced the issue, did not give self-government much thought. Claude Auchinleck records the pre-war army view: 'I don't think the average subaltern thought much about British rule and, indeed, took it for granted that it would go on forever. I do remember when one of our Indian officers from the hills in the north said to me, "What is going to happen when the British leave India?" I looked at him and said, "Well, of course, the British are never going to leave India." ' Even to the young men joining the ICS, such as Christopher Masterman, it was not a serious issue. 'When I first went to India it never entered my head that India would one day be independent, but I saw a sign when the Montague-Chelmsford Reforms were introduced in 1921. I certainly felt then that Independence would come but I don't think we realized that it would be coming so soon. After the 1935 Act everyone realized that Independence was coming and was coming quite soon, and I don't think we resented it.'

The young men who joined the ICS after the Great War had very different views. 'I went to India clearly thinking that we were going there to lead India on the way to self-government,' declares Philip Mason. 'Although one constantly lost sight of this in the rough and tumble of a district, because you're always thinking all the time of stopping Mohammedans and Hindus from knocking each other on the head, or getting your land records right or getting your court up to date in it's work, or stopping some oppression, none the less, I don't think one *really* lost sight of it.' Yet the tendency to be above politics was there: 'Political changes and political advancement had very little relevance to the happiness of the ordinary chap that we were dealing with, and it was his happiness that was our chief concern.'

A certain escapism also affected those outside government: 'If we thought about Gandhi at all it was really that he was just a bit of a nuisance and slightly absurd.' Vere Birdwood quotes from a series of minutes which she saw in 1941 added to a file: 'The most junior officer had written, "I don't think we'd better start this project, there may not be time to finish it." His senior officer had minuted on the file, "What nonsense. I was told this in 1919." And the most senior officer, the Governor, had minuted on that same file, "Absolute nonsense. I was told this in 1909."'

The inevitable consequence of this tendency to overlook India's future was that 'Indians never really believed that Britain had any intention of handing over power at all. They were convinced right up to the end that we were going to find some trick to avoid handing over power – and that was the foundation of their Non-Cooperation Movement.' Campaigns of non-cooperation and civil-disobedience grew in strength and frequency as the century proceeded. In urban areas it was impossible to ignore the changing circumstances, as Edwin Pratt remembers: 'When I first went to Calcutta you could walk down Chowringee and the Indians walking in the opposite direction would just get out of your way. Time came when they just continued to walk where they were and you got out of the way.' A very few met hostility, infrequently and uncharacteristically. During the Second World War Iris Portal cycled daily from her bungalow to the hospital where she was nursing: 'One day, bicycling along the road in a nurse's uniform I came on a row of young Indian boys who were right across the road arm in arm shouting "Quit India!" It was the first aggression that I had ever met in India, so I put my head down and rode straight at them on my bicycle, ringing the bell violently.' Many others remained untouched and virtually unaffected. In Bengal, where officials and policemen were being regularly assassinated, the Roberts could still feel untroubled 'for the first twenty or thirty years. We were on our own there, sleeping out on the verandah. The house was more or less open but I don't think we felt uneasy at all.'

Those who did meet trouble were the ones appointed to deal with it, and it came most often not in the form of political disturbances but in the 'endemic' inter-communal strife between Moslems and Hindus. This was 'the bugbear of a district officer. Once it broke out and you got Hindus and Moslems going for each other hammer and tongs really all you could do was turn out the police and try and separate the parties and drive them away from one another.' A great deal of effort was devoted to trying to anticipate the incidents – most frequently processions – that provoked these religious conflicts: 'There was a record kept in the police station which it was part of one's duty to keep up to date. This recorded all the customs in connection with festivals; the route which the *Mohurram* procession would follow, whether it went near a particular temple or not, whether it went near some particular peepul tree which might become holy in the course of time. You had to see that they followed the exact precedent.' It required only the slightest deviation, infringement or supposed provocation to create a full scale riot: 'Some stupid little thing would happen, a rumour that Pathans were abducting Hindu girls, or that somebody had killed a Mohammedan. Usually it was quite untrue, but then the trouble, which was always smouldering in certain cities, started. You'd get some stabbing incidents at night, and then everybody was out trying to keep the score up; if five Mohammedans were stabbed one night, six Hindus would be murdered the next.' The conflict between Hindus and Moslems was a long-standing one. 'There was no answer to it,' declares Penderel Moon, 'you couldn't prevent it, but you might if you were sufficiently prompt and on the spot at the time, prevent it assuming a very serious form. I was a great believer in the maximum display of force at the very beginning to try and overawe people. I was also a great believer in using force effectively if you had to use it at all. I didn't believe in firing one or two rounds; I used to say to my magistrates, "If you ever have to open fire, fire at least five rounds. If you open fire make sure that it is effective, so that people are seen to fall and the mob takes fright.' It didn't occur to me as ruthless. It occurred to me as plain commonsense.'

Raymond Vernede was district magistrate in Benares in 1939 when widespread rioting broke out during the Moslem festival of *Mohurram*:

246

I set out with a platoon under a very junior, recently joined subaltern and we found, as I'd rather feared, that the trouble had broken out in the most dangerous area in the city. Here there was a minority of Hindu spinners living right in the middle of a large number of Moslem weavers. We turned a corner and there in front of us all the houses were on fire. You couldn't hear anything for the roar of the flames, but outlined against the flames were literally hundreds of men looting the houses on both sides and throwing the stuff down to their friends below. It was impossible to issue the stock warnings to the crowd – nobody could have heard – so as pre-arranged with the subaltern I said I wanted him to fire to disperse this crowd. So he told a corporal to take three steps forward and fire one shot. He fired and although there were literally hundreds of men milling around, the shot went right through the whole lot without hitting anyone. But the effect was electric. The crowd was gone and the whole street was empty within a minute. We just went round the corner, about ten yards, and there the whole thing was repeated – flames and hundreds of men silently looting. So I said, 'You've got to stop this now, another round.' I pointed out to the corporal, who was their marksman, a man outlined very clearly against the flames on the cornice of a roof and I said, 'You shoot him.' The officer ordered him to shoot, because I couldn't order him to shoot, and he shot and killed the man. He fell off into the street and there was an absolute stampede. Within fifteen minutes the news of the firing was all round the city and had an astonishing effect.

Political demonstrations and the great majority of civil disobedience campaigns were of a very different order, being based on the Gandhian concept of *satyagraha* and passive resistance. In some instances the mere presence of the sahib was enough. 'I never allowed anyone to shout "Mahatma Gandhi" without giving him six on the bottom with a stick,' declares John Rivett-Carnac

I found that if I went down myself, making quite an imposing figure in full uniform with a helmet and a revolver on each side and riding boots, I could overawe the crowd. I did this really through boredom and the desire for excitement, and considered it rather fun in a way. These mobs of about one or two or three thousand would converge on the market place. They would all have numerous flags and banners and would be shouting about Mother India, and they'd advance up to where I was standing. I would order a halt and tell the constable to take away all the flags and banners. I would then read out the names of five or six of the leading non-cooperators and they would be taken off with all the flags and banners by the constable, leaving myself with the sub-inspector. I would then speak to the foremost man and say to him, 'It's time for you to go home,' and he would refuse, whereupon I would give him a medium-sized blow on the chin. After about the second or third butt he would stagger off. I then did the same with the next man and the third man would turn and start retreating and I might help him along. Then the whole crowd would bolt out of the market place. This, as a rule, was a Hindu crowd; the Mohammedans I found very much more dangerous, but it never crossed my mind that I could be killed under these circumstances.

Another policeman, F. C. Hart, who served in the Special Branch, recalls how it was possible to restrain the enthusiasm of local Congress leaders in Bihar by dumping them naked by the roadside rather than affording them the prestige of arrest and gaol: 'In those days everybody wanted to get a gaol ticket. Their whole political future depended on it.' The Indian sense of modesty also gave the police an advantage when dealing with women demonstrators: 'On one occasion in Patna City a number of women laid themselves down on the ground right across the street and held up all the traffic. When the Superintendent of Police arrived on the scene he was at first nonplussed. If they had been men he could have sent in policemen to lift them out bodily, but he daren't do it with women. So he thought for a bit and then he called for fire hoses and with the hoses they sprayed these women who were lying on the ground. They only wore very thin saris and, of course, when the water got on them all their figures could be seen. The constables started cracking dirty jokes and immediately the women got up and ran.'

Only when it was quite clear that the police were unable to contain the situation would the military be called in. 'We didn't have to shoot anyone,' Charles Wright explains, 'when the crowd were getting very angry and very unruly and pressing up against us we would ease them back by gently dropping the butts of our rifles on their toes, which did eventually move them back'. This was usually followed by what was known as 'showing the flag': 'The schoolmasters of the villages would parade all the children outside to shout as we passed by, "Three cheers for the Black Watch Regiment!" and keep on repeating this till we got through the village. However, I'm sure they didn't like us there.'

That the army did not relish 'coming to the aid of the civil power' is well illustrated by Reginald Savory's letters, written during the civil disturbances in Peshawar in 1930: 'I wrote to my wife on May 10 and said, "These civil disturbances are most unpleasant for both sides, and for me, I'd far rather be back in Gallipoli." On June 14 I wrote saying, "I'm wondering what the future has in store for the Indian Army; whether you and I will be in this country in four years' time," and ten days later I wrote to my wife in the following terms, "At times I feel like chucking it and taking my first pension. Living in a country in which, through no fault of one's own, one is hated, has few attractions and the future will probably deny us what little status we have at present."'

It says a lot for both sides that throughout this penultimate chapter of the Raj friendships between individual British and Indians not only survived but frequently prospered. David Symington recalls that 'the relations of members of my service with the Congress leaders was quite surprising. There was a time in 1942 in the Quit India Movement when we did experience a certain amount of unpleasantness, but that didn't last long. For all the rest of the time, although the Congress leaders were supposed to be in open hostility to the Raj, they would meet us on ordinary occasions as friends and we would exchange jokes about what they were going to do next. I remember the Congress leader in Sholapur who was going to offer individual *satyagraha* came along to me and said, "Oh, sir, I've come to say goodbye." I said, "Why, what's happening? Are you going away?" "No, I have got to offer myself for imprisonment today." So he said goodbye to me very politely and went out and got himself arrested on the road. They would go along shouting, "No help for the wars. Not a man, not a rupee!" and in due course, when they'd got it off their chests, the police would take them in and they'd be hauled up before a court and sentenced to a short term of imprisonment.' Anne Symington's friends in Congress included a leading political figure, Mrs Sarojini Naidu, with whom – even during the height of the Quit India troubles – she frequently had tea: 'I met everybody that was anybody in the political world there and they used to say, "Is it all right to speak in front of Anne?" and she'd say, "Oh yes, perfectly all right."'

Another leading figure of the Congress Party was Pandit Nehru, with whom Raymond Vernede had a brief but illuminating encounter:

I received a coded telegram from the Government to say that they had released Pandit Nehru from gaol in Dehra Dun and they were sending him down to Naini Tal where his wife was also in prison and seriously ill. She had had a bad turn for the worse and they were very anxious that he should be released to see her – but they were not prepared to release him unless he would undertake not to take part in any political activities or make any political speeches while he was out. In the telegram they used the expression 'Release on Parole' and I was to use my discretion as to how to put this message across. Nehru arrived at about midnight at the narrow gauge station outside Allahabad and he was obviously very tired and very tense. I came up and met him and said I'd been deputed by the Government to meet him and that the Government wanted to release him on parole so that he could see his wife. It was the first he'd heard officially that his wife was seriously ill. I then plunged into my delicate task, saying that they would release him on parole provided he gave an undertaking. Immediately he stiffened and said, 'Oh, but I could never agree to that. It would be against all my principles to give such an undertaking. I have been in gaol for nearly three years. I want to be with my wife and the last thing I want to do is join in politics and make speeches – but I am not prepared to give an undertaking to the government.' All along the platform there were the shapes of Indians lying asleep in their white clothes and we walked up and down this platform for over half an hour, carefully stepping over these bodies, with a little group of bewildered policemen standing at the back wondering what it was all about. I tried to point out that releasing him on parole was an act of chivalry, that it was the highest honour you could pay your enemy. 'That may have been all right in the Middle Ages, but it doesn't work in India,' he said. 'It doesn't apply any longer. It stinks.' Then I suddenly had a brainwave. I said, 'Well, look, if you won't give an undertaking to the Government, what about coming to a gentleman's agreement with me?' He stopped in his tracks and he looked at me and a delighted smile came over his face and he said, 'Ah, a gentleman's agreement with you? That would be different. I think I could accept that.'

As Independence approached, the changing political circumstances often placed former political prisoners in positions of authority over those who had gaoled them. Early in the 1930s Olaf Caroe was involved in the gaoling of the two Khan brothers, Dr Khan Sahib and his younger brother Abdul Ghaffar Khan, known as the 'Frontier Gandhi'. Within a few years both had become his close friends and 'when I was Governor and Dr Khan Sahib was my Chief Minister I remember we had a terrific quarrel once and he more or less lost his temper with me. So I said to him, "Doctor, if you don't retract that I shall put you in gaol again!" He looked at me in fury for a moment and then burst into laughter and embraced me.'

In the last years of the Raj 'the awful portent of Pakistan

began to arise, and from 1939 this danger appeared before us and we could see no clear way of averting it'. To nearly all the British in India 'the idea of partition was horrifying'. Many saw it as 'the biggest disaster of the whole of British rule' which 'undid the greatest thing we had done during the Raj, which was to unify India'. Few had any doubts as to who was responsible. 'I first realized that partition was something more than a talking-point,' explains Percival Griffiths, 'when I dined with Mr Jinnah and he expounded his two-nation theory. He said, "You British people, you're good administrators, but you are very bad psychologists. You talk about Indian nationality but there is no such thing. I don't regard the Hindus as my fellow nationals at all, and they don't regard me as their fellow national. You talk about democracy, but you know there was never any such thing as democracy in India before you came. You have introduced a kind of democracy as a passing phase. It will pass with you."' The contrast between Jinnah and Nehru was marked. Olaf Caroe, who knew both well, found both arrogant, but Nehru's arrogance was 'shot through with charm, which Jinnah's certainly wasn't. He was very arrogant and very immovable and he is certainly not one of my heroes.' It was said at Viceregal Lodge that Jinnah was always five minutes late, whereas Mahatma Gandhi was always five minutes early.

Nowhere was partition more bitterly resented than in the Indian Army: 'To us it was the heartbreak of heartbreaks. We felt it beyond credence. We had united these dozens of different castes, creeds, colours, beliefs under one flag. We had united them under one regimental colour. It took us two hundred years to build that up, and for that to go literally at the stroke of a pen – it was something that one will never get over.' Perhaps no one felt this loss more than Claude Auchinleck, whose duty it was to divide the Indian Army into two: 'All Indian Army officers hated the idea but we did as we were told. They had to be split and then all the equipment had to be split with everything else. What it meant was that regiments like my own, half Hindu and half Moslem, were just torn in half – and they wept on each other's shoulders when it happened. It was moving for me and I think it was moving for them. The older officers like myself undoubtedly felt a sense of loss. You felt your life's work would be finished when what you had been working at all along was just torn in two pieces.'

With the exception of one battalion, the divided army remained 'staunch' through all the horrors that accompanied Independence. The slaughter that began in Calcutta in 1946 in what became known as the 'Great Calcutta Killing' was only the extension – on a much greater scale – of what had been going on between the rival communities of Hindus and Moslems for years: 'You could almost know that it was going to happen by a peculiar silence,' declares Radclyffe Sidebottom. 'But as tension grew the voice pitch went up and the high-pitched screaming of the rioting crowd was something that you could never forget. You'd hear the screaming coming towards you, they would commit some horrible act and then patter away without a sound. But it wasn't so much the sounds, it was the smell of fear – and you'd get the smell of fear not necessarily from those who were being killed, but from the rioting mobs that are doing the killing. The moment the crowd decided that one of the opposite religion had been killed, then everybody in one form of dress would turn on the others and in a matter of forty-eight hours there were three hundred, four hundred deaths a night. If you saw a man literally writhing in agony and you stopped your car and got out to help him – then you were finished.'

From the safety of a boat on the Hoogly River Radclyffe Sidebottom witnessed another side of the killing:

You could see a crop of one religion or another who had been captured and tied, brought down to the *bund* which went down to the river, being pushed down the bank into the water where dinghies with poles were pushing them under. You could see them being laid on their faces with their heads poking out over Howrah Bridge and being beheaded into the river, their bodies thrown in afterwards. After the riot the river was literally choked with dead bodies which floated for a while, sank for a while and then, when the internal gasses blew them up, floated again after three days. They were carried up and down the river by the tide, with vultures sitting on their bellies or their backs according to whether they were male or female – one floated one way, one floated the other – taking the gibbly bits and leaving the rest to float ashore to be eaten by the pi-dogs, the jackals and the ordinary vultures.

Another witness was Ian Stephens who, as a journalist, found himself numbed almost to callousness by the 'putrefying corpses stacked to the ceiling' in the morgues, but could 'never quite eradicate from the memory – though it was so small – a Hindu *chaprassi* who came to deliver papers to my bungalow, a funny little thing with a huge moustache. I remember his smile and, within five minutes, he'd been knifed to death in the street outside.' Mary Wood recalls a similarly personal, but happier incident: 'I was drying my hair when all hell was let loose outside my bedroom door. I shot out on to the balcony in my curlers and there was my poor little sweeper hanging on to one end of a long pole, while at the other end of the pole were four or five of the rest of the household who were intent on beating him up – and would certainly have done so except they were so startled by Memsahib gibbering with fury in hair curlers, that they fled. And I was left with my poor little sweeper who had flung himself at my feet and assured me I'd saved his life. I'm sure I hadn't, but one wonders what happened to people like that after the British all . . . went?'

21

TOPEES OVERBOARD

The Englishman in India has no home and leaves no memory.

SIR WILLIAM HUNTER *The Old Missionary* 1895

When asked at his initial interview why he wanted to go to India Philip Mason had replied, 'Because it's such an exciting place politically. We have succeeded in devolving power to Canada, but to do this in India, where you have different religion and different culture and different race, is a very much more hazardous and difficult experiment, and it seems to me very exciting and I should like to be in on this.' Thirty years later this 'hazardous and difficult experiment' was completed – but not without a great many misgivings. 'I felt that the last chapter hadn't been worthy of the one hundred and fifty years that had gone before,' declares Olaf Caroe, echoing the feelings of many of his colleagues. 'The thing had been much too hurried.' Indeed, Independence Day came with such speed and in the midst of such turmoil that there was little opportunity either for preparation or reflection: 'We were at the centre of a vast typhoon which was going on all round us, but of which we were curiously unaware at the time.'

From the outbreak of war in 1939 the writing had been clearly on the wall – and yet a curious sense of timelessness had persisted: 'It seemed as if it would go on for ever.' Vere Birdwood had seen the change coming when the splendid cavalry regiments – 'pennants flying from their lances, their horses tossing their heads' – were hurriedly mechanized: 'One began to see that all that had gone before was a sort of dream. When we saw these splendid looking men crouched over the wheels of buses, driving round and round and trying to master gears when all that they had really mastered was how to ride a horse, it really did seem as if it had all been something that would never come again.'

Perhaps the least prepared were the Anglo-Indians, as Eugene Pierce describes: 'I don't believe any of us ever visualized that British rule would come to an end and certainly not as abruptly as it did. When it was announced that India was to get her independence we were very jittery about it. We immediately started discussing what we were going to do.' Now Anglo-Indians were called upon to decide once and for all where their loyalties and their identities lay. 'It was the end of our world,' asserts Irene Edwards, 'I remember once sitting on a platform in Mhou. You could just see the fort in the distance with the Union Jack flying, and a group of little India *chokras* were sitting and talking near by and one said to the other, "Do you see that flag up there? Do you know, there are a lot of people that want to see that flag come down? But that flag will never come down." And I, in my foolishness, agreed with them; I thought the flag would never come down. We were proud of being British. My father, when he heard "God Save the King" being sung, even away in the distance, stood up and we had to stand up with him. That is what we thought of the British Raj and it came as a shock to us when it ended. Now we did not know where we were, whether we were Indians or British or what.'

August 15, 1947, was celebrated in an atmosphere of remarkable good will. 'The day came,' recalls Rupert Mayne, 'and I can remember going round to the Viceroy's house in the evening. There were tens and tens of thousands, millions in the street, everybody patting you on the back and shaking you by the hand. We were the British heroes, the British who had given them Independence.' But with Independence came the great exodus, and with it the 'competition of retaliation' that ended with some one and a half million dead. Sylvia Corfield recalls how she waited in Simla for a military convoy to take her to safety, 'standing above the Mall just outside Christ Church and seeing all the shops being looted. I remember standing on the verandah of the United Services Club, which had opened its

256

doors to women, standing there with the Bishop of Lahore and hearing the rickshaw coolies' quarters in the lower bazaar being bombed. We felt quite helpless listening to their cries and the dull thud of the explosions. We couldn't do anything.'

Rupert Mayne, travelling near the border between the two new countries, found himself equally helpless:

Amritsar was like one of the towns in Normandy after the bombardment. It was more or less decimated, and between there and Lahore there was mile upon mile of people going East and going West carrying their belongings. The Hindus and the Sikhs from Pakistan moving on one side of the road, the Mohammedans on the other. Every now and again some goat or something would run across the road and then there would be a beat-up trying to get it back again. Even the bark of the trees had been eaten up to a height of ten feet, as high as a person could stand upon another person's shoulders. The incident that, in my mind, epitomises the tragedy was when we stopped and were watching the people go by when a figure came out from the huge line of refugees, stood to attention and asked me to help him. He then said that he'd been with the 4th Indian Division through the desert and in Italy. What could I do to save him? All I could do was look at him and say, 'Your politicians asked for *Swaraj*, and this is *Swaraj*.'

'When I left India in December 1947 I felt we were leaving a task half finished,' declares Reginald Savory. It was a feeling that many shared. 'Our intention in India was to hand over a running show and I believe that if we could have held on for another ten years that would have been the case.' An extra decade would certainly have allowed the process of Indianization to have been completed – but 'the will was lacking'. By 1947 most officials and army officers had put up with eight years of extreme working conditions. Few had been able to take home leave and, as Ian Stephens observes, the pressure had begun to tell. 'A lot of them became almost drudges and when the great change of '47 came they were most of them too tired to take it all in. They were disillusioned; much of what they'd served for seemed to be breaking up and they pulled out fatigued and recognizing that they must rebuild their lives somehow and get re-adapted elsewhere.' Not all sections of the British community were required to 'rebuild their lives'. The *box-wallahs*, the businessmen and the planters went on as before, without major loss. The missionaries continued to play a leading role in health and education and many thousands of Anglo-Indians took the plunge to become Indian or Pakistani citizens. Large numbers of officials also stayed on for a year or two until an Indian replacement could be found.

Independence had opened the way for a greater friendship between the races. 'Both Europeans and Indians at that time held out their hands to each other in an extraordinarily easy way.' The new openness lasted and stood the test of distance and time. There was no longer 'that curious barrier that there used to be'.

Most directly affected by the break-up of the Raj were the ICS and the Indian Army; some went home because they had no choice, others because they preferred to. 'Much larger numbers of us would have stayed on and served under Indian governments,' says David Symington, 'if it hadn't been for three things. First of all, everybody was very tired and pretty browned off, disillusioned by all the political failure. Another reason was that the Government made it easy for us to go by offering us compensation. But most important of all was the fact that you either had to serve a Hindu Government or a Mohammedan Government, and you had either to be pro-Mohammedan or pro-Hindu accordingly, and that was contrary to everything that we thought right or possible.' The prospect of leaving India was accepted with fatalism : 'We all knew, like knowing that death is inevitable, that one day we would leave India. Most of us did not look forward to this day, but we knew it would come and, of course, everything was geared to this feeling in a queer sort of way.' A minority went with relief – 'without a thought, without a pang, without a qualm,' and were 'delighted to get away and lose India forever'. Many more were 'glad to get some rest', and eager to see their homes and families again – and yet went with great regret, taking with them 'a nostalgia for sights and sounds and smells and for the nice things' that would grow more acute as the years went by. 'I've only got to shut my eyes,' states Frances Smyth, 'and picture an evening in a village in India, with the smell of wood smoke, which is the most gorgeous smell in the world. There was a very sudden twilight in India always and when the twilight came it was dark and the mist would rise up in a sort of blue haze from the fields – and there would be this gorgeous smell drifting across the fields.' Others recall best the 'spicy, peppery smell of the shops in the bazaar' or 'the smell of dust after a long drought when the first rain falls' or being in the bazaar and 'talking with people, laughing with people, probably hot and sweaty and tired and thirsty – but all so very worthwhile'. For Vere Birdwood 'the most wonderful feeling of all was sleeping out under the stars; you could read by starlight in India'. For all of them India had moved deep into the blood. 'I never really got it out of my system,' declares Nancy Vernede, speaking for many.

Perhaps there was also a less demonstrable nostalgia; for Indian qualities that were not always appreciated in their time; the gentleness of the Indian, his courtesy and heightened sense of hospitality that so rarely allowed an Englishman to feel that he was not welcome in another man's land. 'We were walking back to our camp,' relates Philip Mason, 'and some people in the village we were passing saw us and came running out and said, "You can't go through our village like this, we must get you a bullock cart and you can go on that." I said, "No, no, I want to walk." "We'll get you a horse." "No, no, we want to walk." "Well, you must sit down and have some oranges or milk," and they joined hands and made a circle round us like children at a party and said, "We won't let you go until you have sat down."'

Even less tangible was the 'terrible nostalgia for having lost a skill'. The enormous self-confidence and the rare skills that so many had acquired – 'I went out rather a shy, diffident young man and I came away feeling I could turn my hand to anything' – would be regarded in the future with quite as much suspicion as favour. England itself would seem flat and characterless after India's extra dimensions and its 'sudden revelation of light'. Indeed, England seldom lived up to expectations. 'While I was in India England was always that wonderful country that I had known as a child,' remembers F. J. Dillon, who returned to find that 'the England I had always thought of didn't exist any more'.

Nor was it a grateful mother country that they were returning to. 'The English never cared,' states Claude Auchinleck, 'the politicians especially. I don't think they ever took any interest in India at all. I think they used it.' The lack of interest was not confined to politicians. Vere Birdwood remembers 'the total disinterest of the people in England to Indian affairs. I don't think any of us ever spoke about India for the six months or so we spent in England. We might occasionally be asked at a dinner, "Well now, what's all this about old Gandhi?" or something of that sort. Well, to try and settle down to a long dissertation on Indian politics between the soup and the fish was not really possible, so we just used to shrug our shoulders and our host or hostess or whoever might have felt obliged to put this question thankfully passed on to news of the latest theatre in London.' But even if 'you were a stranger when you came back to England', it was still home. The ties were too strong to be ignored. 'I was very fond of India,' remarks Kathleen Griffiths, 'and I found as the years went on that it grows on you. It becomes a part of your being, almost. But always at the back of my mind there was that thought that at the end of it all I want to return finally to England, back to my own country.'

The Raj had its critics. 'The psychology of the Raj was really based on a lie,' declares John Morris. 'The majority of the British in India were acting a part. They weren't really the people they were supposed to be. They were there for a very good reason; earning a living and making money – nothing ignoble about that – but I don't really feel that most people had a sense of vocation, that they were serving India.' Others also had their criticisms: 'English rule in India was very often called sarcastically *banya ki raj*, the rule of the moneylender, because all our laws enabled him to lend money to the illiterate people at vast interest. It was money for jam for the money-lender and the law was on his side.' Some disliked the Raj for a more basic reason. 'Cheap labour was another jewel in the crown of the Raj,' maintains Ed Brown. 'At the back of the jewel was the squalor, hunger, filth, disease and beggary. Only when I came out of the army could I see what a terrible thing it was that a country had been allowed to exist like this. Such snobbery, so many riches, so much starvation.' It was also said that if India made the British self-confident it was, perhaps, at the expense of the Indians, leading to 'the reduction of Indian self-confidence, to their self-criticism and their despair about themselves and their future'.

Such criticisms come with hindsight and, as such, are best left to the judgement of future historians. At the time 'Anglo-India' did not so much see faults or attributes in the Raj as simply take it for granted. 'I thought nothing about the Raj,' asserts Norman Watney. 'It seemed to me that I had a job, it was a tough one and that was all there was to it.' For those with ancestral roots in India the attitude was much more complex: 'I don't think we ever consciously thought about the British Raj as such. We simply accepted that this was where fate had placed us. We felt that this was our destiny – in many cases the destiny of our forebears – that we were there at some sacrifice to serve India. Those long partings from children were a great sacrifice, the loneliness was a sacrifice. There was absolutely no feeling of exploitation, no feeling of being wicked imperialists. In fact, in those days we didn't think imperialists were neces-sarily wicked.'

Certainly, on the personal level the benevolent paternalism had much to commend it: 'The fashion is to judge India by the few who made money out of it, and forget the devotion of the people who served it. The men who looked after the forests, the people who built hospitals, the people who made roads, who did the irrigation. It was their occupation, granted, but they did it with a love of India, a love of the people, and what they did and what they contributed is now forgotten to a large ex-tent. They were the ordinary, plain little people, the ones in the middle who were never exalted, but who ran India really.' Certainly, it could also be argued that 'if we had not made a Raj in India, somebody else would have – and they would not have made such a good job at it'.

An assessment of the Raj and its worth has no real place in this present informal selection of images. Here let it be said only that the British found in the Mogul vacuum 'chaos and anarchy and the degradation of morals and standards', which they filled in time with a common language and legal system, a civil and administrative machine of rare quality and the 'great civilising effect' of the Indian Army. The Pax Britannica did indeed bring uninterrupted peace – though not prosperity – within India's borders and its power extended far beyond. Kenneth Mason, while exploring deep in the Pamirs, ran out of money and was lent some by a yak owner: 'I wrote out on half a sheet of notepaper to Cox's, Karachi: "Please pay bearer on receipt of this the sum of fifty pounds sterling." It must've been eight or nine months later that I heard from my bankers, Cox's at Karachi, that a greasy piece of paper had arrived and had been presented in the Peshawar bazaar and was said to be worth fifty pounds sterling. That piece of paper had gone from hand to hand all over Central Asia. It had marks of people that couldn't sign. It had thumb marks which had been dipped in ink. It had been to Samarkand and Kiva and God knows where, and it'd come over the Khyber Pass and was presented in Peshawar bazaar and was still said to be worth fifty pounds sterling.'

It could be said that the Raj also conferred indirect benefits upon India; the introduction of 'a new, galvanic impulse that gave Indians new ideas about liberty and a belief in the need for progress', and perhaps most important of all, the creation 'of the concept of patriotism for the Indian nation so that they thought of India as one nation and even talked of Mother India'. The end result was a 'synthesis of Eastern and Western civilizations which makes India different both from the West and from Asia', a synthesis which Penderel Moon saw as 'essentially a partnership; a government by Indians and British working together in close partnership – and its success arose partly from what I would call the intelligence of the Indians, their sense to accept what had happened to their country, that it had been conquered by foreigners, and to get the best out of it they could.' Penderel Moon was always, by his own admission, 'somewhat critical of the British Raj. I thought that many of the institutions we had brought to India were unsuited to India, that we had insufficiently built on Indian tradition and Indian ideas. But I also felt that the British Raj couldn't tackle the main problems of India, which were economic. I felt that a foreign power could not achieve the revolutionary steps that would be necessary to change the Indian peasant life. Then I asked myself, "Should one really try to change it?" I can't answer that question, but obviously Indian intelligentsia wanted to change it. And I felt that the British Raj must give place to Indian Raj if any change is to be effected.' Yet for all that, he concludes, 'the British Raj in years to come is going to be viewed as one of the wonders of the world!' A similarly critical but ultimately affectionate judgement comes from Ian Stephens. 'I'm so fond of it,' he declares. 'It was a great, lumbering, clumsy, brutal thing but, despite its flaws, this fusion, this contiguity between Britain and India worked, and there was much good in it.'

For all their zeal in government and the benevolence of their intentions the British had no lasting place in India. In the last resort, argues Iris Portal, 'you must never take land away from people. People's land has a mystique. You can go and possibly order them about for a bit and introduce some new ideas and possibly dragoon an alien race into attitudes that are not quite familiar to them, but you must then go away and die in Cheltenham.'

And this the British proceeded to do. Most went with a sadness accentuated by tearful farewells from the most trusted of their retinues, who accompanied them on their last journey across India; ayahs who had fostered their children, bearers who had stayed with them for a quarter of a century and more. Pensions and gifts could not eradicate the fears that many felt for their future. Some slipped out ungarlanded and without ceremony, others took a more formal leave-taking. 'I can remember seeing the troops going up the gangway in pairs,' says Rupert Mayne, 'and finally their colonel, Colonel Blaire, standing and facing us, giving us a tremendously smart salute, about turn and up the gangway. Thus went the last British regiment. That was the Black Watch leaving Pakistan forever.'

The final, ritual farewell was made – as always – where the East ended and the West began: 'As we left Port Said and sailed into the open waters everyone was paraded with their topees on deck and at a given signal we all flung our topees into the sea and that was the last of India.'

Lastly, there was England and Home: 'The coast of England was green and white and the most beautiful sight I've ever seen in my life; little villages nestling in the folds of the hills, the white of the cliffs and, after being without colour for so long, the green of the grass – and to cap it all, when we got to Southampton it was snowing.'

NOTES ON CONTRIBUTORS

Geoffrey, St G. T. ALLEN, OBE, MC; born 1912 Cawnpore; ancestors in India since 1799; grandfather founded *Pioneer* and *Civil & Military Gazette*; returned India 1919; Asst. Manager Darbhanga Raj 1933; 2/7 Gurkha Rifles 1939–45; Seconded IPS 1945, Asst. Political Officer, Sadiya Frontier Tract; stayed on in IPS after Independence.

Joan ALLEN (*née* Henry); born 1913 Bihar; father indigo/sugar planter; ancestors in India incl. John Nicholson; returned India 1931; married Geoffrey Allen 1937; Lived in Bihar and Assam.

Field-Marshal Sir Claude AUCHINLECK, GCB, GCIE, CSI, DSO; born 1884; father in Indian Mutiny; joined 62nd Punjabis 1904; Kurdistan 1919; Imp. Defence Coll. 1927; CO 1/1 Punjab Regt. 1929–30; Instructor Staff Coll. Quetta 1930–33; Commander Peshawar Brigade 1933–6; ops. against Mohmands 1933–1935; Commander Meerut 1938; C-in-C, India 1941/1943–47; Supreme Commander 1947.

Stephen BENTLEY, BEM; born 1902; went to India 1927 as 'band boy' in 2nd Battalion Seaforth Highlanders; main stations, Lahore, Jhansi, North-West Frontier; returned to England 1933.

Vere Lady BIRDWOOD, CVO; born 1909; father Sir George Ogilvie, KCIE, IPS; ancestors in India since 1765, was sixth generation to have lived in India; married Capt. (later Col.) Christopher Birdwood, Probyn's Horse (son of Field-Marshall Lord Birdwood, C.-in-C., India) in New Delhi 1931; left India 1945.

Cuthbert BOWDER, C. Eng.; born Bareilly 1902; father Indian Finance Service, grandfather East India Co. service; served in Irrigation Branch, PWD, in UP 1925–47; principal stations Meerut, Jhansi, Bareilly, Naini Tal; Supt. Tari & Bhabar Govt. Estates Div. 1944–7; left India 1947.

Norah BOWDER (*née* Sullivan); born 1903; married Cuthbert Bowder, Bombay 1933, UP; left India 1945.

Ed BROWN; born 1904; went to India as 'band boy' in 2nd Battalion Royal Warwickshire Regt. 1919; main stations Khyber Pass, Bombay, Delhi; returned to England 1928.

Sir Olaf CAROE, KCSI, KCIE; born 1892; Capt. Queens Regt. North-West Frontier, 3rd Afghan War 1916–19; joined ICS 1920; transferred IPS, NWFP, 1923; DC Kohat 1928–9, Peshawar 1930–2; Chief Sec., Governor 1933–4; Resident Persian Gulf, Baluchistan, Waziristan 1937–9; Foreign Sec., Govt. of India 1939–46; last Governor NWFP 1946–7; left India 1947. Numerous publications.

George CARROLL, KPM; born 1899; grandfather Capt. East India Co. in Mutiny; joined Indian Police Service, Central Provinces, 1919; married Mary Strong; was later Guardian to Rajahs of Khetri, Chambra and Chota Udepur and Tutor to prince of Jhodpur.

Bishop Thomas CASHMORE, born 1892; SPG Missionary, Ranchi 1917; Recruiting Indian Labour Force for WWI Waziristan 1917–23; Trustee Lutheran Mission, Chota Nagpur 1917–23; Vicar, St James's and Principal St James's College, Calcutta 1924–33; left India 1933.

Marjorie CASHMORE (née Hutchinson); born 1896; married Thomas Cashmore in India 1919; Chota Nagpur, Calcutta; five children born in India, two serving in Garhwal Regt.

Sir Conrad CORFIELD, KCIE, CSI, MC; born 1893; father CMS missionary, school principal; childhood in India; joined ICS 1920; Lord Reading's staff 1921–2; joined political service 1925; served in Kathiawar, Baluchistan, Rajputana, Central India and Hyderabad; Adviser, Maharajah of Rewa 1933–4; Headquarters, Political Dept. Simla 1934–8; Resident, Punjab States 1941–5, political adviser to Viceroy 1945–7.

Lady Sylvia CORFIELD (née Hadow); born 1900 Dibrugarh, Assam; father solicitor; returned to India 1919, married Col. Daunt, Central India Horse (decd. 1953); married Sir Conrad Corfield 1961.

Sir John COTTON, KCMG, OBE; born 1909; sixth generation to serve crown in India; father J. J. Cotton, ICS Madras; went to India 1929; joined 8th KGO Light Cavalry 1930, stationed Bolarum, Mardan, Lucknow; joined IPS 1934; served Aden, Persian Gulf, Rajputana, Hyderabad, states of West India, Baroda; Dep. Sec. Political Dept., Delhi 1946–7.

Lady Mary COTTON (née Connors), born 1910; married Sir John Cotton 1937; three sons born in India.

Col. Walter 'Crit' CRICHTON, CIE; born 1896; joined IMS 1920; married Dorothy CRICHTON (née Martindale), 1920; joined

Foreign Political Dept. 1930; Agency Surgeon Kurram Valley, NWFP 1932; MOH Simla 1934; Chief Health Officer, Delhi Prov. 1936; active service 1941–5; left India 1945.

Ed 'Jungle' DAVIES, born 1908; joined Dorset Regiment 1924; served in Meerut, Landicotal and North-West Frontier; Regimental Boxing Champion; demobbed 1936.

Brig. F. J. DILLON, OBE, MC, 7 bars to Frontier Medal; went to India 1919 with Mountain Battery; 3rd Afghan War, Waziristan, Mahsud Campaigns 1919–24; joined Indian Mountain Battery 1927; stationed Peshawar, Khyber; Mohmand Campaigns 1935–6; Army HQ, Delhi/Simla 1936–40; stayed in India after Independence.

Edith DIXON, born Quetta 1898; father Col. M. O'Connor, Traffic Manager, O & R Railway; great-grandfather and grandfathers in East India Co.; lived in Rawalpindi, Saharanpore, Simla, Calcutta; left India in 1914.

Lt.-Col. Sir John DRING, KBE, CIE; born Calcutta 1902; father Sir William Dring, KCIE, East India Railway; joined Guides Cavalry 1923; transferred IPS 1927; Asst. Private Sec. to Viceroy; Dep. Commissioner, Dera Ismail Khan and Peshawar; Sec. to Governor, NWFP; Political Agent, South Waziristan; Chief Sec., Revenue Commissioner, NWFP; left Pakistan 1952.

Lady Deborah DRING, born 1899; father Maj.-Gen. G. Cree, CB; ancestor Surgeon-General of India; married John Marshall, 45th Rattray Sikhs, later Maj.-Gen. (decd. 1942); married John Dring, IPS, 1946; left India 1947.

Irene EDWARDS (née Green), Frontier Medal, Afridi Campaign, 1930–1; born Agra 1906; father Railway Officer; nurse, St George's Hosp., Bombay 1925–9; nursing sister, Lady Reading Hosp., Peshawar 1929–34; Matron King Edward Hosp., Indore 1935–6; private nursing, Calcutta; married 1938; left India 1950.

Sir RIDGEBY FOSTER, born 1907; came out to India 1933 with Imperial Chemical Industries, later Chairman ICI (India); married Nancy Godden 1937; lived in Bihar, Calcutta, Bombay; remained in India after Independence.

Lady Nancy FOSTER, born in India 1911; father Supt. Brahmaputra River Steam Navig. Co.; childhood in Narayanganj, Bengal and Assam, with sisters Jon and Rumer Godden; married Ridgeby Foster 1937.

Sir Percival GRIFFITHS, KBE, CIE; born 1899; entered ICS 1922; served Bengal Province, Kontai, Darjeeling; retired ICS 1934 to enter business; member, Indian Legis. Assembly 1937–47; Leader Europ. Group, Indian Central Legis. 1946; Publicity Adviser, Govt. 1941–4; remained in India after Independence. Numerous publications.

Lady Kathleen GRIFFITHS (*née* Wilkes); went to India as governess 1922; married Percival Griffiths 1922; lived in Bengal, Kontai, Darjeeling, Calcutta.

Arthur HAMILTON, CIE, OBE, MC; born 1895; ancestors in Indian Army since early 19th c.; joined Indian Forest Service 1921; served in Punjab, including Himalayan region; Inspector-General of Forests 1945–49; retired from India 1949.

Olivia HAMILTON (*née* Seth-Smith); ancestors in Indian ICS from mid 19th c., including Commissioner NWFP; married Arthur Hamilton 1925; lived in Punjab and Delhi; left India 1949.

F. C. HART, born Amritsar 1904; educated in India; mother baby in Mutiny; ancestors in India (Bengal Pilot Service, East India Co.) since 1806; served in Special Branch, CID, in Bihar and Orissa, 1934–41; joined Indian Army SIB; left India 1946.

Maj. E. S. HUMPHRIES, MC, DCM; born 1889; went out to India 1909 as a private in Royal Scots; served in a variety of stations in North India, including North-West Frontier; in 1911 transferred to Indian Signal Corps and was later commissioned; left India 1934.

Sir Gilbert LAITHWAITE, GCMG, KCB, KCIE, CSI; born 1894; joined India Office 1919; Asst. Private Sec. to Sec. of State for India 1923–4; accompanied Ramsay Macdonald to India Round Table Conf. 1931; Private Sec., Viceroy (Lord Linlithgow) 1936–43, Delhi/Simla; Acting Asst. Under-Sec. of State 1943; Deputy Under-Sec. of State for Burma (1945) and India (1947).

Lady Rosamund LAWRENCE (*née* Napier); born 1878; ancestors in India include Sir Charles Napier of Sind; in 1914 married Sir Henry Lawrence KCIE, descendant of Lawrences of Punjab, Collector of Belgaum 1914; Commissioner of Sind 1916, Acting Governor Bombay Prov. 1926; left India 1926.

Mrs A. LEE, born 1886; went to India as wife of Band-Sergeant G. T. H. Lee, 2nd North Staffs; lived in NWFP (Rawalpindi, Nowshera, Peshawar); summered Murree Hills; four children born in India; left India 1920.

Lt.-Col. Lewis LE MARCHAND, born Guntakal, South India, 1908; father M. M. LeMarchand, Madras & Southern Mahratta

Railway; fourth generation born in India, 1819 onwards; joined uncle's regt., 5th Royal Gurkha Rifles (Frontier Force) 1930; ADC, Governor of Punjab 1933–6; AA & QMG 8th Indian Div. 1945; retired from Indian army 1947.

Prof. Lt.-Col. Kenneth MASON, MC, Gold Medal, RGS, 1927; born 1887; ancestors in civil and military service in India since late 18th c.; arrived India (Royal Engineers), joined Survey of India 1909; Himalayan surveys 1909–14, including Chinese Pamirs; served India Army WWI; Shaksgam Exploration Leader 1926; Dept. Supt., Survey of India, Burma 1931–2; left India for Oxford 1932.

Philip MASON, CIE, OBE; born 1906; joined ICS 1928; Asst., Joint Magistrate, UP (Saharanpur, Bareilly, Lucknow) 1928–33; Under-Sec., Defence Dept., 1933–6; Dep. Commissioner Garhwal 1936–9; Sec. to Chiefs of Staff Committee; Head of Conference Secretariat, South East Asia Command; Tutor and Governor to the Princes, Hyderabad; retired 1947. Numerous publications (also as 'Philip Woodruff').

Sir Christopher MASTERMAN, Kt, CSI, CIE; born 1889; entered ICS (Madras) 1914; Sec. Board of Revenue 1924–8; Collector of Salt Revenue 1928–32; Collector, various districts, Madras 1932–6; Education and Public Health 1936–9; Board of Revenue 1942–6; Chief Sec. Adviser to Governor 1946; Deputy High Comm., India 1947–8.

Rupert MAYNE, born 1910 Quetta; ancestors in India since 1761, including Mayne of Mayne's Horse and many others; returned to India 1932 with jute merchants (Bengal), transferred to oil company 1937 (Upper India); stayed on in India after Independence, founder member UKCA.

Terence 'Spike' MILLIGAN, born 1918 in Ahmednagar; lived in military cantonments in Poona; father corporal rough-rider in British Army; grandfather, Trumpet-Sergeant-Major Kettleband, also served in India; convent education; left India 1927.

Sir Penderel MOON, Kt, OBE; born 1905; maternal ancestors in Indian Army and ICS from 1814; entered ICS (Punjab) 1929; served in various capacities from Asst. to District Magistrate in Multan, Gujrat and Amritsar; left ICS 1944 to serve in Bahawalpur, Himachal Pradesh and Manipur State Govts. Numerous publications.

John MORRIS, CBE, Murchison Award, RGS, 1928; born 1895; transferred 3rd QAO Gurkha Rifles from British Army 1916;

Afghan War 1919 and subsequent frontier campaigns; member 1922 and 1936 Everest Expeditions and explored Karakoram range; retired Indian Army 1930. Numerous publications.

Grace NORIE (*née* Reynolds) OBE; born 1876 in Rookee; father orphaned in pre-mutiny disturbances, later Head of Forests; returned India 1893; married Capt. (later Maj.-Gen.) Norie, 2nd Gurkhas, Dehra Dun 1898; war work in WWI; left India 1919.

Eugene PIERCE, born 1909 Dehra Dun; Father in BB & CI Railway; educated St Joseph's, Naini Tal; followed father on to railways, then into commerce; leading role in Anglo-Indian affairs; left India after Independence.

Iris PORTAL, born Simla 1905; father Sir Montagu Butler, Governor CP, uncles Sir Harcourt Butler, Sir James Dunlop-Smith; returned India 1922; married Gervas Portal, Gardner's Horse, 1927; stationed Poona, Meerut, Ferozepore, Bombay, Hyderabad; nursing in Indian Military Hosps. 1940–2; Girl Guides Commissioner; left India 1942. Publications.

Edwin PRATT, born 1909; came out to India as Admin. Asst. Army & Navy Stores, Calcutta Branch 1928; served in Indian Army Service Corps 1939–45, finally as acting Lt.-Col.; married Kathleen Griffiths 1947; remained in India with A & N after Independence.

Lt.-Col. John RIVETT-CARNAC, MC, KPM; born East Bengal 1888; ancestors in India since General Carnac (1764), including two governors, grandfather judge in Mutiny; joined Indian Police 1909; Capt. 35th Scinde Horse/13th Lancers WWI; returned Indian police 1919, served in Allahabad, Moradabad, Indore, Muttra, Bahraich, Etah, Gonda and Gorakhpur; left India 1927.

Rev. Arfon ROBERTS, born 1906; went to West Bengal 1928 under Methodist Missionary Society; service included Superintendency, Leper Homes, Bankura and Raniganj; left India 1951.

Rosalie ROBERTS (*née* Harvey); born 1902; went out as SRN to West Bengal 1926; nursing Supt., Santal Mission Hosp., Sarenga 1926–31; married Arfon Roberts at Sarenga 1932, continued voluntary medical work in villages, West Bengal; left India 1951.

John ROWE, born 1888; came to India 1889, father in Norfolk Regt.; returned to India with Sappers 1910; went to Civil Engineering Coll., Roorkee; Military Engineer, North-West Frontier; retired 1938 but recalled to Military Engineering Service, Capt. 1939–46; left India 1946.

Dorothy ROWE (*née* Ellen), born 1890; came out to India 1927 to marry John Rowe, Bombay; lived in Peshawar, Simla, Madras, Ootacamund, Jhansi, Lahore, Jhelum, Rawalpindi, Kohat; left India 1946.

Lt. Gen. Sir Reginald SAVORY, KCIE, CB, DSO, MC, born 1892; joined 14th Sikhs 1914; served WWI with Sikhs; North-West Frontier 1921–2; Kurdistan 1922–3; North-West Frontier 1929–30; Instructor, IMA 1932–4; Commandant, 1/11 Sikhs 1937–9; Waziristan 1937; Comd., 11th Ind. Inf. Brigade 1940–1, 23rd Ind. Div. 1942–3; Director of Infantry 1943–5; Adjutant-General-in-India 1946–7; left India 1947.

Radclyffe SIDEBOTTOM, born 1907; from RN and Union Castle Line joined Bengal Pilot Service 1929; stationed in Calcutta; married Helen Law 1934; invalided out as Master Pilot 1946.

Brig. Rt. Hon. Sir John 'Jackie' SMYTH, Bt, VC, MC; born 1893; father W. J. Smyth, ICS; attached Green Howards 1912; joined 15th Ludhiana Sikhs, Loralai; won VC with Sikhs, France WWI; took part in seven frontier campaigns; commanded 45th Rattray's Sikhs 1935, Chitral Force 1937–8, 17th Indian Div., Burma, 1940–2; left India 1942; MP and numerous publications.

Lady Frances SMYTH, born Quetta 1908; father Col. R. Chambers, IMS; childhood in India; returned India 1925; married Capt. Read, 4th Gurkhas, 1927; married Col. 'Jackie' Smyth 1940; stations: Bangalore, Poona, Allahabad, Bakloh, Amritsar, Lahore, Rawalpindi; left India 1942.

Ian STEPHENS, CIE; born 1903; maternal ancestors in India since 1828, incl. two Maj.-Gens. in Mutiny and one famous *shikari* (Col. Glasfurd); joined Bureau of Public Information, Delhi 1930, Director 1932–7; Asst.-Editor, the *Statesman* (Delhi /Calcutta) 1937, Editor 1942–51; left India 1951, returned Pakistan. Numerous publications.

David SYMINGTON, CSI, CIE, born Bombay 1904; father J. H. Symington, merchant of Bombay; grandfather General, Bombay Artillery, great-grandfather Surgeon, Bombay Establishment East India Co.; joined ICS (Bombay Prov.) 1926; Collector, Ratnagiri; last appt., Sec. to Governor, Bombay 1943–7. Publications (as 'James Halliday').

Anne SYMINGTON, born Mahabaleshwar 1904; father J. J. Harker, Bombay PWD; grandfather civil engineer, India; married

David Symington 1929; Ratnagiri, Bombay; left India 1947.

Raymond VERNEDE, born 1905; father A. H. Vernede, ICS (Bengal & Bihar); childhood in India till seven; joined ICS (UP) 1928; served in Agra, Allahabad; District Officer Meerut, Benares, Unao, Garhwal; Acting Commissioner Gorakhpur; left India 1947.

Nancy VERNEDE, born Mussoorie 1914; father Sir Charles Kendall, ICS, High Court Judge, Allahabad (UP); uncles E. J. Mardon, ICS (UP), Sir James Digges La Touche, Governor UP; returned to Allahabad after education; married Raymond Vernede 1937; left India 1947.

Kenneth WARREN, born 1886; father W. Warren pioneer of Indian tea industry in Assam 1858, owned original tea estate; went to Assam as tea planter 1906; served in Europe WWI; married Sybil Twist; member, Assam Legislative Assembly 1923; Retired from India 1926; Chairman, Managing Director Warren Group and James Warren & Co., East Indian Merchants & Agency House.

Norman WATNEY, born 1901; joined Indian State Railways (N.W. Rly) last British-recruited group as Asst. Loco Supt. 1925; Div. Mechanical Engineer, Karachi, Quetta and Delhi Divisions; Works Manager, Supt. Mechanical Workshops, Lahore 1946; Dep. Director, Railway Board, Delhi (1939 & 1946); after Independence continued service Pakistan.

H. T. WICKHAM, born 1884; joined the Indian Police Service (Punjab) 1904; stationed Ambala, Kasauli; transferred NWFP 1906; stationed Mardan, Bannu, Dera Ismail Khan, Hangu, Tank; Commandant, Military Police Battalion, Peshawar 1919; took part Handyside Raid 1922; Persian, Pushtu Scholar; retired from India 1922.

Maj. Gen. George WOOD, CB, CBE, DSO, MC; born 1898; joined Dorset Regt. 1916; posted 1st Dorsets in India 1931; Regimental service in Bengal troubles, tour at Army HQ, then Brigade-Major Khyber; returned India 1943 Commanding 2nd Dorsets, then 25th Indian Div., Burma.

Mary WOOD, born Malaya 1904; married Capt. George Wood 1928; stations Dacca, Delhi, Simla; left India 1935.

Charles WRIGHT, born 1898; went out to India 1922 as private in the Black Watch; served in Allahabad, Multan, Meerut and Barrackpore; returned to England as CSM in 1935.

A SHORT GLOSSARY
OF 'ANGLO-INDIAN' WORDS,
PHRASES AND SLANG

In addition to those Indian or 'Anglo-Indian' words contained in the text I have included some of the more common 'Brindian' or Anglo-Indian expressions of the period. 'BOR' here refers to slang common among British Other Ranks, 'Indian Domestic' to words used by servants in British households and their mem-sahibs. The spelling of Indian words given here is basic rather than academic thus *ucha* rather than *achchha* [very well]. Readers familiar with Urdu or Hindustani will be aware of the difficulties of rendering English approximations where, for instance, a word like *derzi* [tailor] may equally be rendered *dirzi*, *darzi*, *durzi* or even *derzee*.

'Anglo-Indian' patois or hobson-jobson can be found in three basic forms. The first involved Urdu interspersed with English, thus (from 'Coping with Cook', verses from the *Onlooker* 1942):

Roz roz kitab getting higher;	The 'Daily Book' is getting higher;
Annas char for *ek papaya.*	four annas for one papaya fruit.
Kab the sahib *yeh chiz dekhenge,*	When the sahib is shown this,
Ekdam bahut cut *karenge.*	he will immediately make a big cut.

The second form involved Urdu words given a new meaning, thus a word like *koi-hai* [who's there] was also used to describe an 'old India hand'. The third and perhaps the most interesting use of Indian words involved their corruption or amalgamation with English, as in the well-known admonition said to have been delivered by an irate BOR to a native bystander: 'You *dekko*ed me *giro* in the *peenika pani* and you *cooch biwani*ed. You *soono*ed me *bolo. Iswasti* I'll *gurrum* your *peechi.*' [You saw me fall in the (drinking) water and you did nothing. You heard me speak. For this I'll warm your behind.]

Those seeking further enlightenment should consult 'Hobson-Jobson', the nineteenth-century glossary of 'Anglo-Indian' words and phrases.

A

abdar – head servant (at the club)

act – deputising, thus 'to do an act'

adha seer – one pound, derogatory, term for Anglo-Indians

admi – chap (lit. 'person')

AFI – Auxiliary Forces India, European or Anglo-Indian civilian 'Home Guard'

amir-parwa – defender of the rich

Anglo-Indian – originally British persons in India but later specifically those of mixed blood (v. 'Eurasian')

anna – one-sixteenth of a rupee (thus 'twelve annas to a rupee' to describe Eurasian)

apke-wasti – a toady (lit. 'at your honour's command')

ayah – native nurse; lady's maid

B

baba – baby (from English), thus *baba-log* – 'baby people' and 'missy *baba*' – 'little miss'

babu – native clerk (lit. honorific 'father' but also derogatory, thus '*babu* language', 'babuisms')

baht – language (thus '*bolo* the *baht* a *tora*' – speak the language a little', BOR)

'*Bajke bajao, khabadar*' – 'look out!' (rickshaw coolie's cry)

bandook – gun ('my old *bandook*', BOR)

banya – moneylender, thus '*banya ki raj*' – rule of the money-lender

base-*wallah* – brass hat; man who avoided front line (BOR)

bazaar – native market

bearer – house valet

'Beecham *Sahibki gooli*' – Beecham's pills (station vendor's cry, lit. 'Master Beecham's balls')

begum – princess

bhai – see 'boy'

bhai-bund – brotherhood (Indian Army)

bheesti – native water carrier

bibby – native woman (BOR) from *bibi* – 'high class woman', thus *bibi khana* – 'kept woman's quarters'

bint – native woman (BOR, Arabic deriv.)

bistra – bedding roll

'black velvet – native girl 'comfort'

Blighty – Britain (from *'billayat'* – kingdom) thus *'billayati pani'* – English water (soda water)

Blighty-ticket – service discharge; wound requiring repatriation (BOR)

blood-chit – written authorization (BOR)

bobajee – cook (from *'biwarchi'*) thus bobajee-*khana* – cookhouse

bobbery – angry (BOR – 'don't get bobbery'), (from *'bapre!'* – exclam. of surprise or danger), (lit. 'Oh father!'); also 'bobbery-bob' – from *'bapre-bap!'*

Bombay bowler – service issue pith helmet (BOR)

Bombay milk-cart – waste disposal wagon (BOR)

BOR – British Other Ranks, ie. NCOs and men

bowli-glass – finger bowl (domestic Indian)

boy – servant; call for servant (from *bhai* – lit. 'younger brother')

box-wallah – derogatory term for European businessman derived from Indian door-to-door salesmen

Brahmins – highest caste among Hindus

browned off – overcooked (BOR) thus 'fed-up'

buddli – temporary servant

buckshee – free (from *'baksheesh'* – alms)

bullumteer – volunteer (Indian Army)

Bunby – Bombay

bund – raised embankment

bundo – arrangement (from *'bundobust'* – tie up loose ends') thus 'let's make a bundo'

bungalow – country house (*'bungla'* – country)

bungy – sweeper (see also *'mehta'*)

Burma Road – rice pudding (BOR)

burra – great; big, thus *burra* bungalow – manager's bungalow; *burra-din* – big day, Christmas Day; *burra-khana* – big dinner, celebration; *burra-mem* – senior lady; *burra nam* – big name; *burra*-peg – double tot of whisky; *burra*-sahib – important man; senior sahib

bus! – enough!

bustee – native quarter, thus 'where's your *bustee*, Glasgow?' (BOR)

butcha – baby, thus *Tum soor ka butcha* – 'You son of a pig' (BOR)

C

Cages – Bombay red light district

cantonment – military area of station (pron. 'cantoonment')

chapattis – unleavened bread

chapplis – sandals

chaprassi – office servant; messenger (from *chapras* – brass buckle worn on belt)

cha – tea, thus '*cha* and a wad' and *char-wallah* – 'tea boy', also man who drinks a great deal of tea (BOR)

charpoy – wooden frame bed with webbing, thus *charpoy*-bashing – 'sleeping' and charp – bed (BOR)

chee-chee – derogatory term for Eurasians derived from their sing-song speech

chelo! – get a move on! (BOR lit. *chalo* – 'Come on')

cheroot – native cigar

chibberow! – be quiet (BOR, from *chup rao*)

chiko – child (BOR from 'chokra')

chit – letter; note (from '*chitti*') thus 'chit-up' – 'approach someone in authority' (thence, possibly, 'chat up')

chokidar – caretaker, night watchman (see *choky*)

chokker – fed-up (BOR, from '*chauki*') thus 'I'm a bit chokker'

chokra – native boy, also inexperienced young sahib

choky – lock-up (BOR from *chauki* – see *chokidar*)

cholera-belt – flannel girdle worn supposedly to prevent cholera until *c.* 1920

chota – small, thus *chota bungalow* – assistant's bungalow; *chota hazri* – early morning tea; *chota peg* – single tot of whisky; *chota* sahib – junior sahib; sahib's son

chuckeroo – youngster (BOR, see '*chokra*')

chukka – period of play in polo

chung – platform, thus *chung* bungalow – house on raised platform, found in East India

chummery – shared household, usually of bachelors

chup! – be quiet!

civil lines – area of station inhabited by British civilians civil list – Warrant or Order of Precedence, also known as the Green, Red or Blue Book

class regiment – Indian Army regiment drawn from one racial group, e.g. Gurkhas, Sikhs, as opposed to mixed regiments

Club – usually a private gymkhana or polo club owned by its members and restricted in membership

Collector – chief administrator of district, originally collector of revenue (see 'DO')

compound – enclosed area surrounding bungalow and servants' quarters

Congress – principal Indian national political party

conjie-house – gaol (BOR)

coolie – native porter; labourer, thus *coolie*-catcher – labour officer

Corporal Forbes – *cholera morbus* (BOR)

covenanted servants – those entered into formal contract with Secretary of State for India, specifically the ICS

CP – Central Provinces

crab – stomach pain (BOR, *khrab* – bad)

cummerbund – waistbelt (lit. loin-band)

country-born – European born in India

country-bred – European educated in India, used with derogatory overtones

'curry and rice' days – nineteenth c. from humorous book of this title

cushy – easy (BOR, from *khush* – pleasure)

custel brun – caramel custard (domestic Indian), traditionally served up at *dak* bungalows

D

dacoit – robber, thus 'dacoity' – robbery

dak – post, thus *dak-wallah* – postman and *dak-bungalow* – government staging house

dal – lentils

dandy – open litter, much used in the Himalayas, carried by four *dandy-wallahs*

Dashera – Major Hindu religious festival, celebrated in October

dastur – bribe or perk (lit. 'custom')

district – one of 250 units of administration in British India

D.O. – District Officer, executive head of district known as Collector, Deputy Commissioner or District Magistrate

dekshi – see 'dixie'

Delhi-Simla – Central Government axis based after 1912 in Delhi (cold weather) and Simla (hot weather and rains)

derzi – tailor

Dewali – Hindu festival of lights, celebrated in autumn

dewan – gatekeeper

dhobi – washerman, also 'flying dhobi' – 'express laundry'

dhobi-itch – skin irritation, usually ringworm, supposedly from excessive starch in laundered underwear (BOR)

dhol – drum

dhoti – loose loincloth worn by caste Hindus

dhurri – rough cotton rug

dikky – troublesome (BOR, from *dik* – trouble)

dixie – cooking pot (BOR, from *dekshi*)

doolally – mad (BOR), said to be derived from Deolaly, transit camp near Bombay (thus 'doolally *tap*' – fever) but probably from '*diwana*' – mad

dolly – tray of gifts, usually offered at Christmas (from *dali*)

dome – untouchable sweeper

doob – grass grown on Indian lawns

dooley – covered litter

double *terai* – double layered hat

double *khana* – dinner-party

double *roti* – English loaf of bread

dub-up – pay up (BOR)

dudh-wallah – milkman

dufta – office (BOR from '*daftur*')

dunpoke – baked dish (domestic Indian)

durbar – court; levee

E

ekdum – immediately, thus 'do it *ekdum*' (BOR, lit. 'one breath')

ekka – small two-wheeled pony cart

Eurasian – persons of mixed descent, with derogatory overtones. The term Anglo-Indian was officially adopted in 1900 but remained synonymous with 'British in India' for another forty years.

F

feriadi – humble petitioner

feringi – European (lit. foreigner)

FFI – army VD inspection (abbr. 'free from infection') also 'Inspection Short-Arm' (BOR)

first toast – starter at dinner

Fishing Fleet – girls who came out to India for the Cold Weather in search of husbands (See 'Returned Empties')

furlough – leave (home or local)

G

gharib-parwav – defender of the poor, honorific form of address

gai-wallah – milkman ('*gai*' – 'cow')

garrum – hot; also VD case

ghaskutta – grass-cutter for horses

ghari – cart; lorry, thus *ghora-ghari* – 'horse-cart'

godown – storeroom

goonda – bad character (hence 'goon', perhaps?)

goolmal – muddle, thus, 'to make a *goolmal*'

gonga – mad, 'up the gonga' (BOR from '*ganga*' – 'river') supposedly because lunatic asylums were up-river

grass *bidi* – casual country prostitute

grass widow – wife at hill-station temporarily separated from husband in the plains

Great Game – Anglo-Russian rivalry and counter espionage on the Northern Frontiers of India

Green Book – see civil list

grim – North-West Frontier 'on the grim' (BOR)

gup – gossip

gussal-khana – bathroom

gymkhana – sports ground; sports meeting

H

hamal – house servant (West India)

hath-butti – hurricane lamp

hazur – sir, honorific (lit. 'the presence')

heaven-born – honorific often used to denote the ICS

hill station – stations above 5,000 feet to which state and central governments transferred in the hot weather

'Hindu pani' – 'water for Hindus' (station vendor's cry)

Hindustani – simple form of Urdu

housey-housey – British Army numbers game, now known as bingo

Holi – Hindu fertility festival, celebrated in spring

howa-khana – a breather, 'let's take a *howa-khana*'

howdah – palanquin on elephant

hullaballoo – uproar (from *holo-bolo* – to make a noise)

hunting clan – married BORS (BOR)

I

ICS – Indian Civil Service

IFS – Indian Forestry Service

IMS – Indian Medical Service

IP – Indian Police

IPS – Indian Political Service

J

jemadar and *jemadar*-sahib – junior viceroy's Commissioned Officers, also ironical title given to low-caste water-carriers

jhampani – rickshaw coolie

jirga – tribal gathering (North-West Frontier)

John Company – Honourable East India Company, formed in 1599 and from 1833 to 1858 the recognized governing body of British India

jow! – go! (BOR, from *jao!*)

juldi – quickly, thus 'do a *juldi* move' (BOR)

jungli – wild, uncultivated, thus 'he's a bit *jungli*' and 'jungle-*wallah*' – forest officer

jungli-moorgi – wild fowl

K

K – knighthood, 'to get a K,' usually KCIE

Kadir Cup – annual pig-sticking meet held on alluvial plains near Meerut

kafilah – camel caravan (Arabic)

kala jugga – secluded corner off dance hall (lit. 'dark place')

Kali – malevolent black goddess requiring propitiation through sacrifice, much worshipped in Eastern India.

koel – cuckoo, often confused with the brain-fever bird (Common Hawk Cuckoo)

khana – meal, usually dinner, also place

khansama – cook

khas-khas tatti – screen made of grass matting and hung round doors in hot weather

khitmagar – butler; waiter (often referred to as *'khit'*)

khubber – news, thus 'what's the *khubber*?'

khud – steep hillside, thus *'khud*-racing'

khyfer – skirt, thus 'a bit of khyfer' (BOR)

koi-hai – used when calling servants; also 'character', or old India hand (lit. 'Is anyone there?')

krait – small but highly-venomous snake

kshatrias – warrior caste among Hindus

kutchahal – raw state of things

kulang – crane

kutcha – raw, incomplete, thus *'kutcha hal'* – uncooked truth

L

Lanes – high class brothel area of Calcutta

Lat Sahib – Lord Sahib (Governor or Governor General)

lines – usually housing quarters of troops

lingam – male fertility symbol

logh – people, thus 'sahib-*logh*' – Europeans

loose-*wallah* – thief (BOR)

loot – plunder (*'lut'*)

M

ma-bap – mother and father (*'ap mai ma-bap hai'* – 'you are my mother and father') honorific form of address

machan – shooting platform

maharanee – great queen

mahout – elephant driver

maidan – public land; parade ground

malum – understood? (BOR lit. 'knowledge')

mali – gardener

mamlet – marmalade (domestic Indian)

masalchee – scullion

matey – servant's assistant

maumlet – omlette (domestic Indian)

mehtar – term used ironically when addressing sweeper (lit. prince)

memsahib – lady, from 'madam-sahib'

meta-pani – soft drink (lit. 'sweet water')

mishast o barkhast – code of etiquette (poss. Persian deriv.)

mofussil – up-country; the provinces

mohur – Mogul gold coin, also 'mohur tree'

Mohurram – Mohammedan festival

molish – polish (Indian domestic)

moorghi – chicken

moorghi-khana – ladies' room in club (lit. 'hen room')

mottongost – mutton (domestic Indian, from '*gosh*'-meat)

'mozzinet' – mosquito-net (BOR)

mufti – civilian clothes; civvies (BOR)

mulaquati – visitors; petitioners (upper India)

mulligatawny – spicey soup, traditionally served on Sundays

munshi – interpreter; teacher of languages

musical chair – latrine (BOR)

'*Mussulman pani*' – 'water for Moslems' (station vendor's cry)

'*mut karo!*' – don't do that!

N

Nadge – Poona red light district

nazir – counsellor, subordinate official

nappy – barber (BOR, from '*napi*')

O

oolta-poolta – topsy-turvy

P

paddy – rice field ('*padi*')

pagoda tree – 'to shake the pagoda tree' (nineteenth century) to make a quick fortune

'*pahn-biri*' – 'cigarettes and pahn-leaf' (station vendor's cry)

balka-ghari – covered wagon for women in purdah

palmyra – palm tree

pani – water, thus *pani-wallah* – water-carrier; scullion, also
kala pani – ocean (lit. 'black water')

patwari – village official

pau-peg – quarter tot of whisky (*Pau* – *quarter*)

peenika-pani – drinking water

peenika cheez – drinks (lit. *'something* to drink')

peepul – Indian fig tree

peg – tot, see *'chota*-peg'

peon – messenger; orderly

phal-phul – flowers and fruit, the only gifts allowed to government officials

phut – useless (thus, 'to go phut')

pi dog – mongrel found all over India (abbrev. of pariah)

PIFFERS – Punjab Frontier Force

pith helmet – light topee made of vegetable fibre

planter's long-sleevers – chairs with arm and leg rests

poodle-faker – womanizer, especially in hill stations, hence
'poodle-faking'

P & O – The Peninsular and Oriental Steam Navigation Company, the largest and most popular shipping company for
those going out East

POSH – supposedly derived from 'Port Out, Starboard Home',
those being the coolest sides of the ship

puggaree – turban

pukka – proper, thus *'pukka* house' – brick as against mud and
thatch; *'pukka* major' – regimental major; *'pukka* sahib' – real
gentleman; *'pukka* road' – tarred road

pukkeroo – to go and grab (BOR, from *'pakrao'*)

punkah – fan, properly one suspended from ceiling and pulled
by a *'punkah-wallah'*

purdah – seclusion, expected of high-class Indian women (lit.
'curtain')

PWD – Public Works Department

Q

Quoi-Hai – see *Koi-Hai*

R

Rains – rainy season from June to August

raj – kingdom, used in twentieth century chiefly to denote British rule in India from 1858 to 1947, hence rajah – ruler; and maharajah – great ruler

Rajrifs – Rajputana Rifles

'Ram! Ram!' Hindu prayer intoning name of god

ranee – Queen

remount – horse (army)

'rice corps' – Royal Indian Army Service Corps

risaldar – Indian Cavalry equivalent of *subadar*

roll on – 'roll on that boat,' 'roll on the fours and sevens,' BOR referring to end of tours of Indian duty

Roorkee chair – camp chair with canvas base, presumably from Roorkee

rooty-gong – long service medal (BOR, from *'roti'* – bread)

rumble-tumble – scrambled eggs (domestic Indian)

rum-johnie – prostitute (BOR from *'ramjani'* – 'dancing girl')

rupee – standard coinage, worth about 1s 6d

S

sadar – headquarters

sadhu – holy man

sahib – sir; European, also affixed rank, thus 'Collector sahib'

sakht burra mem. – tough old memsahib (*sakht* – hard)

salaam – salutation (thus, 'Give my salaams to . . .'), also, salaam *wasti* – to pay respects

sambhur – large Indian deer

sammy – *swami* – holy man (BOR)

sari – Indian woman's costume

satyagraha – civil disobedience on Gandhian principles of non-violence

shabash – well done

shamiana – marquee

shauq – dominant interest, hobby

shikar – sport (shooting and hunting), thus *shikari* – native hunter; European sportsman

sircar – the Government

shite-hawk – kite; outsider; 4th Indian Division insignia (BOR)

shufti – look (Arabic) BOR 'to take a shufti'

sikkins – savouries (domestic Indian)

simkin – champagne (domestic Indian)

sirdar – local chieftain

sloth-belt – derogatory expression for South India

solar topee – heavy pith helmet

sowar – mounted Indian soldier or policeman

spatch-cock – grilled jungle fowl (domestic Indian)

spine-pad – felt pads worn by British troops supposedly to protect spine from sun. Abandoned c. 1920

Station – place where officials of district live

subadar – and *subadar-major* senior Viceroy's Commissioned (Indian) Officers (roughly equivalent to RSM)

submukin – 'the whole submukin lot' (BOR, *sub* – all)

surmai – drum

Swaraj – Home Rule

'sudden death' – *dak* bungalow chicken (seen alive and eaten shortly after)

sweeper – native of untouchable caste who cleans latrines

syce – groom

T

'*Tahsa char, garumi garum*' – 'fresh tea, hot, hot' (station vendor's cry)

tahsildar – local tax collector

talkies – audience with VIP at state functions

tamasha – spectacle, thus 'a great *tamasha*'

tank – artificial lake

tat – native pony

teapoy – small tripod table

teen pau – three-quarters, derog. term for Anglo-Indians

terai – plains country below Himalayas

tetul gat shakshi – 'tamarind tree witness' (Bengal); false witness

thunder box – earth closet

tiffin – luncheon

tikka-ghari – four-wheeled horse drawn carriage

tin-pot bird – Crimson Breasted Barbet

tonga – two-wheeled horse-drawn carriage, seats back to back

topee – cork helmet ('*topi*' – hat)

'tory peechy' – delayed repatriation, 'the good ship tory peechy' (BOR from *'tora peechee'* – a little later)

tree-rat – squirrel; also native prostitute (BOR)

tumlet – glass tumbler (domestic Indian)

tum-tum – dog-cart (corruption of 'tandem')

tunda – cold, thus 'I'll *tunda* you' – (cool you down); also Tunda Pani Chowkidars – Coldstream Guards (who never served in India)

tundice – ice bucket (used in train compartments prior to air conditioning)

twice born – honorific, based on Hindu caste, often used to describe ICS

U

undarzi – vague, thus 'he's a bit *undarzi*'

UP – United Provinces

up-country – the provinces; upper India (see *mofussil*)

Urdu – lingua franca of upper India (lit. 'language of the camp' see Hindustani

up the line – on active duty on the North-West Frontier (BOR)

V

Vaisyas – merchant caste among Hindus

Vakil – Indian attorney; court pleader

verandah – open gallery round bungalow

VCO – Viceroy's Commissioned Officer, formerly Native Officer

W

wallah – man

waler – horse imported from Australia (originally New South Wales)

Y

yogi – Hindu ascetic

Z

zan-zar-zamin – land, gold and women, traditional objects of crime in the Sind and North-West Frontier

zemindar – landowner, thus *zemindari* – landowner's estate

zenana – women's quarter of Indian house

zubberdust – tyrannical